Lenox in 1839.
[A reprint from Barber's "Hist. Coll. of Mass."]

Lenox

and the
Berkshire Highlands

R. DeWitt Mallary

Heritage Books
2024

HERITAGE BOOKS
AN IMPRINT OF HERITAGE BOOKS, INC.

Books, CDs, and more—Worldwide

For our listing of thousands of titles see our website
at
www.HeritageBooks.com

Published 2008 by
HERITAGE BOOKS, INC.
Publishing Division
100 Railroad Ave. #104
Westminster, Maryland 21157

Copyright © 1902 R. DeWitt Mallary

All rights reserved. No part of this book may be reproduced or transmitted in any form or by any means, electronic or mechanical, including photocopying, recording or by any information storage and retrieval system without written permission from the author, except for the inclusion of brief quotations in a review.

International Standard Book Numbers
Paperbound: 978-0-7884-2172-3
Clothbound: 978-0-7884-7617-4

TO THE MEMORY OF
RICHARD H. WALKER, Esq.
THE GRANDFATHER OF MY CHILDREN
AND
THE GRANDSON OF ONE OF THE EARLY
SETTLERS OF LENOX

PREFACE

THE author's desire in the publication of these essays and addresses, some of which have been read before various literary and historical societies, is to orient the stranger who is within the gates of the Berkshire country. Lenox has become so notably on the beaten path of travel as to demand, in convenient form, some handbook of information which shall play the part of guide. The aim of this book is not to write history but to tell enough of the story of the past to aid in making the region intelligible.

Great pains has been taken to insure historical accuracy, but inasmuch as authorities are not always in perfect agreement it is too much to be hoped that inerrancy has been secured in every instance. In order to compass the aim of absolute veracity, the author, after consulting the sources, whether in books, town and church records, or in the collections of historical societies, submitted the manuscript of this book to the perusal of a few townsmen. Kindly acknowledgments are herewith returned to my friends and college mates, Robert C. Rockwell, Esq., and Richard Goodman, Esq., both of Lenox, for valuable suggestions. I am also indebted to Miss Anna L. White, of the Lenox Library, for assistance in proof-reading.

R. DeW. Mallary.

"Springcroft,"
    Lenox, Mass.,
        January 16, 1902.

CONTENTS

CHAPTER	PAGE
I.—OLD-TIME LENOX	1
II.—LENOX AND ITS ENVIRONMENT, IN LITERATURE.	47
III.—CATHERINE MARIA SEDGWICK: HER MESSAGE AND HER WORK	108
IV.—WITH HAWTHORNE IN LENOX.	136
V.—MODERN LENOX	161
VI.—THE VICINAGE.	207
VII.—THE GENESIS OF VILLAGE IMPROVEMENT AND THE LAUREL HILL ASSOCIATION, STOCKBRIDGE, MASS.	275
VIII.—THE CHURCH OF BERKSHIRE UNTIL THE DISESTABLISHMENT IN 1834	294
IX.—EPITAPHS IN BERKSHIRE CHURCHYARDS	342
INDEX	357

ILLUSTRATIONS

	PAGE
Stockbridge Bowl or Lake Mahkeenac *Frontispiece*	

("Monument" and "The Dome" in the distance.)
This was the view Hawthorne's "little red house"
commanded. (See p. 144.)

Lenox in 1839 2

(A reprint from Barber's *Hist. Coll. of Mass.*)

The Council of Washington and his Generals
before Monmouth 8

(Bas-relief on monument at Freehold, N. J.)
The council is evenly divided. La Fayette is urging
the advance; Paterson is sitting at his right, in
front of Washington, and is in sympathy with
the speaker.

First County Court-House, erected 1792. Monument to Major-General John Paterson . 14

The old Lenox Academy, erected 1803 (now
used as High School) 20

Walker Street, Lenox 26

At the junction of Main and Cliffwood Streets,
Congregational Church in the distance . 36

Illustrations

	PAGE
Second County Court-House (erected 1816), now Sedgwick Hall	46
Fanny Kemble	74
Laurel Lake from "Walker's Hill"	84
Main Street, Lenox, looking down from the Church-on-the-Hill, "Rattlesnake" and "Monument" in the distance	102
Catherine Maria Sedgwick	128
(From the painting by Ingham.)	
The "little red house" where Hawthorne lived when he was in Lenox, 1850–1851. Here was written *The House of Seven Gables*	146
(Destroyed by fire June 22, 1890.)	
A vista, Lenox. Taghconics in the distance, Bald Head at the left	166
The view from the Aspinwall piazza	180
Rattlesnake Mt., Monument Mt., Stockbridge Bowl, Taghconics.	
Yokun Avenue, Lenox	188
Laurel Lake	194
Trinity Episcopal Church, Kemble Street	198
Greylock from Onota Lake, Pittsfield	210
The Haystack Monument at Williams College, marking the birthplace of American Foreign Missions, Williamstown, Mass.	214

Illustrations   xi

                                                                   PAGE

The home of Longfellow's wife, Pittsfield,
  where stood the "Old Clock on the Stairs,"
  the original of the well-known poem by
  that name   224
    " Somewhat back from the village street
    Stands the old-fashioned country-seat."

The home of Catherine Maria Sedgwick, Stockbridge   236

The house where William Cullen Bryant lived
  when he was a lawyer and town-clerk in
  Great Barrington, 1816–1822 . . . 252

The Indian Monument, Stockbridge, Mass. . 282

The Rev. Samuel Shepard, D.D. . . . 338
    Pastor Congregational Church, Lenox, Mass., 1795–
    1846.

The Church-on-the-Hill   352
    Lenox Congregational Church, dedicated January
    1, 1806. Monument with urn at the left marks
    Dr. Shepard's grave.

The design used on the cover of this volume
  was reproduced from the coat of arms of
  Lennox, Duke of Richmond, a picture of
  which is hanging in the Town Library,
  Lenox.

THE BERKSHIRE HILLS

Age-long, the joy of succeeding generations;
Rock-ribbed, an eternal parable of firmness;
Commanding visions that emancipate and calm,
    beauteous in the daily and seasonal changes;
Whose many villas, crowning graceful slopes, deck
    Nature's bosom with Art's most lavish adornments;
Whose fame in letters, joined with pastoral beauty,
    rightly names the region the "Lake Country of
    America."

Stockbridge Bowl or Lake Mahkeenac.

("Monument" and "The Dome" in the distance.)
This was the view Hawthorne's "little red house" commanded.

LENOX

I

OLD-TIME LENOX

MIDWAY between the mountain sentinels, "Greylock" and "The Dome," which stand guard one at either end of Berkshire, Lenox lifts its head among the many eminences which seem thrown in profusion by some Titanic hand throughout this westernmost county of Massachusetts. Inhabited since 1750 and incorporated in 1767, the village became twenty years later, with the settlement of the county northward, the shire-town, and thither the tribes went up, as to some Jerusalem of old, for the inspiration that affected their social, civil, and religious life. During the Revolutionary struggle it was the cradle of a genuine American patriotism, as was this whole region, and hardly had that appeal to arms been decided when Lenox entered upon its career as the county seat, a fount of judicial wisdom, scholastic learning, and social etiquette. Its first Court-house, erected in 1792, for many years occupied for town purposes and as the post-office; its second Court-house, a more pretentious structure, built in 1816 and said to have been surpassed in stateliness and elegance by few of its kind in all New England, now used by the Town Library Association and by others as a hive of professional offices; its Academy, constructed in 1803, where for threescore years and more was conducted one of the most famous preparatory schools of that period; its justly celebrated school for girls under the direction of Mrs. Sedgwick, who carried it on from 1828 until her death in 1864; its village church on the hilltop dedicated to the service of God the first day of the year 1806, were long the most noted material survivals of a former generation, and most of these, with now and then a house of hoary age, are still the vivid reminders of a notable period in the history of this ancient town, showing that Lenox, rearing her head into and above the clouds, viewing landscapes of unsurpassed

Old-Time Lenox

loveliness, and touched with the artistic adornment of many villas, is also crowned with an aureole of glory, a mystical coronet of literary, civil, moral, and social greatness whose lustre pales not before its later splendor.

Berkshire, which contains an area of 950 square miles and was separated from Hampshire in 1761, was not "discovered" until about a hundred years after the Pilgrim fathers set foot on Plymouth Rock. It was a trackless wilderness save as the war-path of the Mohican Indians could be traced here and there, these aborigines having settled along the Housatunnuk (Housatonic), at the "Great Wigwam" which was located near the site of the present Congregational church, Great Barrington. With the gradual settlement of the county, the settlers coming from over the Hoosac Mountains and more numerously from Connecticut, the redskins were in 1736 collected in one place, Stockbridge, where they remained until after the war of the Revolution. They were peaceable aborigines and have been lovingly and appropriately termed "the friends of our fathers." It was not, however, until the close of the second French and Indian war that the settlement of Berkshire proceeded at any pace. The district between the Housatonic and the

Hudson was equally claimed by both Massachusetts and New York; the boundary-line not having been fixed till constant reprisals and bloodshed between Puritan and Dutchman made it necessary toward the very end of the eighteenth century. Moreover it was a region in which there was certainly the fear of aboriginal invasions from savages who swooped down from Canada upon unsuspecting settlers in adjoining counties and left nothing but ashes and gore behind. One such incursion did actually take place in Berkshire. The earliest settler to drive a stake in Lenox came in 1750, but in 1755 he with others fled before the marauding redskins acting in unholy collusion with the French. What with the Dutchman and the Indian who would seek to dispossess, and the mountain barriers on all sides, Berkshire lay isolated, uninhabited for a century after the Pilgrim debarkation, fringed by life and activity, yet not participating in any of the movements of civilization; and even after it began to be known, a country that seemed like golden fleece to intending Argonauts because of the dragon guarding it.

Wolfe was the modern Jason who freed this country for the settler to come in, and that victory at Quebec, by ending French misrule, pushed back the tide of savagery far into the outposts. Berkshire was thenceforward greedily and rapidly invaded. Of the thirty-two towns at present existing in the county twenty were incorporated between the close of the French and Indian wars and the end of the Revolution, while only three were incorporated prior to 1760. For the first twenty-five years after Montcalm's forces were defeated and Frontenac and the old régime had passed from power, the rapidity of incorporation was at the rate of a town a year.

On June 2, 1762, a parcel of property comprising the territory included now in the townships of Richmond and Lenox was sold at auction in the city of Boston by order of the General Court in order to relieve the finances of the colony. An unwieldy township in physical and municipal conditions, it was inevitable that it should be divided. Crossed in the centre from north to south by a mountain ridge, the part lying west and known as Mount Ephraim was incorporated June 21, 1765, under the name of Richmond, while that section lying east, and previously known as Yokuntown, was set off by act of incorporation February 26, 1767, under the name of Lenox, respectively the titular and family names of the Duke of Richmond, one of the liberal nobles of England, known to be a friend of the colonies. Scarcely eight years old, the little hamlet of Lenox, keenly interested in the doings of the Continental Congress, though grappling with the problems of a new settlement, found itself face to face with great national issues. The local questions were largely ecclesiastical, having reference to the building of a new church, the provision for the support of a minister, the levying and collecting of the church tax; and the town records of the period are filled with the differences between the minister, the Rev. Samuel Monson, who had been settled in 1770, and his flock. It will be borne in mind that at that time the church was the town and the town the church; even so small a matter as the selling of a pew in the sanctuary being a subject for town action. Mr. Monson's salary was only a trifle, and was partly paid in "fier-wood," but there were constant arrearages and the usual barbed criticism flew back and forth between minister and those ministered to. The little church, in which there was not a single young person, omitted to celebrate the memorial supper for seven years.

Yet during these Revolutionary days, marred

by unseemly ecclesiastical strife, the element of patriotism burned with a brilliant and unquenchable ardor. As soon as the couriers from Lexington could reach this region of the State, Lenox leaped as an armed man into the fray, and at least one distinguished soldier, Major-General Paterson, whose life has just been written by his grandson, the late Professor Thomas Egleston, of Columbia University, was one of its mighty contributions to that memorable and epoch-making contest. The non-importation agreement which hangs framed on the walls of the Town Library, a precious relic of that heroic age, was another. Its appropriations of clothing and of ammunition, and its sacrifice of men whose names were on the military roster, were others. I find this entry on the town records as early as December 25, 1775: "Voted, no more warrants shall be issued in his majesty's name to warn town-meetings." On June 3, 1777, the town directed its representative at the General Court, Boston, to "use your [his] utmost abilities with the Assembly, and they theirs with the Continental Congress that if they think it safe to declare independent of Great Britain we will stand by you with our lives and fortunes." And Lenox was as good as its word.

To-day as oft as Memorial Day returns, the graves of the soldier-dead who participated in the battles of Bunker Hill, Bennington, Saratoga, and Princeton are decked, with others, in the ancient churchyard which adjoins the village church; a cemetery which commands one of the finest prospects in the world, and of which Fanny Kemble said: " I want to lie here when I die, that upon the Resurrection morning I may wake up with this scene before me." Here for more than a century the dead have been laid at rest, and amidst this bivouac of the dead, sleeping on their arms so to speak, are those who threw back the threatened invasion of red-coats and defied the trained battalions of the mother-nation.

Lenox was, indeed, the hot-bed of revolt. A mountain country breeds rebellion against established tyranny. Wide horizons, even like those which the burgomasters looked out upon from their dykes in ancient Flanders and like those which the Vaudois-Huguenots viewed from their crags and clefts, insensibly enter into national character to broaden and enrich it. The education of a far-reaching landscape undermines the sway of tyrants or bigots. Lenox, by its very altitude had to be in sympathy with the Revolution. As Channing

[Bas-relief on monument at Freehold, N. J.]

The Council of Washington and his Generals before Monmouth.

The council is evenly divided. La Fayette is urging the advance; Paterson is sitting at his right, in front of Washington, and is in sympathy with the speaker.

said in the last address he ever delivered,—
and one, too, which was given in Lenox, August 1, 1842, on the anniversary of emancipation in the British West Indies:

"Men of Berkshire! whose nerves and souls the mountain-air has braced, do not these forest-crowned heights impart something of their own power and loftiness to men's souls? Should our Commonwealth ever be invaded by victorious armies, freedom's last asylum would be here. Here may a free spirit, may a reverence for all human rights, may sympathy for all the oppressed, may a stern, solemn purpose to give no sanction to oppression, take stronger and stronger possession of men's minds, and from these mountains may generous impulses spread far and wide."

Lenox entered upon its career as the county seat in 1787, twenty years after its incorporation, owing to the rapid settlement of the county northward and the necessity of providing a capital nearer the geographical centre of Berkshire. Thence on the village seemed a place to which all roads led. The stage and the post-rider always had to include the county seat in the itinerary of their journeyings. From a copy of the *Berkshire Chronicle* published in Pittsfield during the closing years of the eighteenth century I take the following advertisement which appeared in the issue of October 9, 1788:

"Zebulun Herrick respectfully informs the public that he has engaged to ride as a post, from the Printing Office in Pittsfield to the Southern part of the county, through the towns of Lenox (East-Road) Lee, Tyringham, New Marlboro, Sheffield, Great Barrington, West-Stockbridge and Richmond. Those gentlemen desirous of furnishing themselves with the *Berkshire Chronicle* in those several towns may be supplied regularly and reasonably. Those gentlemen who shall please to entrust him with other business may depend on being served with fidelity and dispatch by their humble servant.   Z. HERRICK."

Zebulun, doubtless, thought not his advertisement would be perused by curious and interested eyes a hundred years later, or that a sympathetic generation in the twentieth century would bestow immortality upon his brief business announcement. It was his custom to take his pay from his patrons in articles of food or merchandise, which he announced he would receive in place of the coin of the realm. Pittsfield received the Boston papers of Monday on Wednesday evening in those days, by another post-route from Springfield; on Thursday the news from these metropolitan journals was republished in the *Berkshire Chronicle* and then with horse "swift of foot" the doughty Zebulun dashed southward through the county. Lenox eagerly awaited his arrival and took the deepest interest in the budget of news he brought. Zebulun was the one living bond which connected the region with the great, wide world. The country newspaper then was a purveyor of dignified, solid information, chronicling as it did events of world-wide importance, instead of the petty items of gossip from the villages of the vicinage.

Later, from 1828 to 1842, Lenox published its own paper, known by various names as it changed ownership, but the early pattern set by the *Berkshire Chronicle* was scarcely at all departed from. An examination of the files of the papers of the county for fifty years after the Declaration of Independence gives scanty material of local importance, whereas to-day the country newspaper has almost nothing of general interest. The era of daily metropolitan journals brought by the iron horse fresh from the presses had not yet come. The country newspaper therefore supplied this deficiency and the doings of national importance crowded into small space the happenings of town and county.

It was not until 1838 that the peaceful solitudes of the Housatonic Valley were invaded by the din of the locomotive pursuing its tortuous way around the spurs, or through the passes, of the mountains. The first railroad was known as the Hudson & Berkshire Railroad, opened for travel to West Stockbridge in 1838; and three years later to Pittsfield. Miss Catherine Sedgwick, the author of *Hope Leslie* and many other tales, describes a journey she took in 1835 from Lenox to Boston, going by stage to Worcester, where the cars were taken for Boston. Six years after this journey railroad connections were established between Boston and Albany. It was long before this, however, that railway facilities were enjoyed along the Hudson River, and as early as 1826 the question of a railroad from some point in Berkshire to the city of Hudson was mooted, the first Berkshire County railroad convention being held in Lenox, November 16, 1827. In 1838 came the railroad from Hudson to West Stockbridge as has been said; in 1842 the Housatonic Railroad was opened from Bridgeport to West Stockbridge via Van Deusenville, twelve miles south of Lenox; on December 21, 1841, the first train went through Pittsfield from Albany to Boston; but it was not until 1850 that a railroad actually passed through the eastern border of Lenox, the Pittsfield & Stockbridge Railroad, connecting with the Housatonic at Van Deusenville.

Lenox was not, however, by any means desitute of means of egress and ingress. Prior to, and even during, this railroad agitation the village enjoyed the most elaborate stage connections, and the papers of the period are filled with the advertisements of this and that line, written in the most approved, *fin de siècle* style. There was the "Hudson and Pittsfield" line which passed through Lenox every morning at ten o'clock, and by way of Stockbridge, Great Barrington, Egremont, and Hillsdale reached Hudson at 5 P. M., the fare being $1.75. Returning by the same route the stage left Hudson at 5 A. M. and reached Lenox at 1.30 P. M. This line of stages made connections at Hudson, both going and coming, with the New York boat. Miss Sedgwick notes, September 11, 1832, a wonderful quickness in the transmission of the mails. She writes her brother Robert, who lived in New York City, on that date: "I received your letter last night at eight o'clock, only thirteen hours (!) from New York. This is an annihilation of space of which our fathers never dreamed." This was doubtless by stage and railway connections.

Notice that at this time, and for almost ten years afterwards, it was thirty-one hours to Boston,— by stage to Springfield in one day, and from there on the next to Worcester, where the cars were taken,—a journey lasting as long as that nowadays from New York City to Saint Paul! The stage line from Albany to Boston passed through Stockbridge, six miles south of Lenox, and the Albany and Hartford line of stages passed through Great Barrington, fourteen miles south of Lenox, but with these lines of travel the stage route from Lenox to Hudson intersected, thus enabling the residents of Berkshire's capital to reach remote and widely separated places by transfers at the proper points. Northward there was a line of stages through to Bennington from Pittsfield. In 1835 there was still another stage route opened from Albany to New Haven, passing through Lenox and Winsted, Conn. These were the main trunk-lines, making our forefathers' entrances to and exits from Lenox not so difficult after all. The arrival and departure of the stages, as the driver with a crack of the whip brought his turnout up before the "Berkshire Coffee House" (now Curtis Hotel), describing what Miss Sedgwick happily terms "one of those professional whirl-rounds," always frightening, if not endangering the occupants of the coach, must have been one of the daily spectacles on which the villagers looked with the keenest interest.

First County Court-House, erected 1792. Monument to Major-General John Paterson.

Old-Time Lenox

From one of the newspapers published in Lenox (the *Massachusetts Eagle*, September 25, 1834), I take the following account of 'Lenox in Court Week," one of the few local allusions, but valuable as the report of an eye-witness :

"The goddess has occupied her throne here for more than a week past, and our village has abounded with judges and jurors, lawyers and litigants, prosecutors and prosecuted. To us who live in the country the occasion is quite imposing. It presents us with a vast variety of characters: young attorneys in the bustle of new-found business and the older ones assuming more and more the dignified gravity of the bench; waiting jurymen chatting in little clusters by the wayside; worrying clients complaining of sleepless nights; witnesses of all orders, sizes, sexes and ages; spectators trading horses in the street, and politicians smoking over government affairs in the bar-room. Our boarding-houses have long tables lined on both sides with earnest applicants, and all expect more business. Messages are sent and errands done between one end of the county and the other, business accounts are settled, plans laid; caucuses, conventions and singing-schools agreed upon; newspapers subscribed for, and distant matters in general arranged for the ensuing winter."

This is probably a correct picture of Lenox in court season at any time during the eighty-one years it was the county seat. Modified by the changing styles of dress from decade to decade we can almost see the picture as if painted on canvas.

It is small wonder that Pittsfield, the growing municipal neighbor of Lenox, hungered to possess all this excess of life and trade by becoming the county seat herself, a thing she strove mightily to do from 1816 until 1868, when she succeeded. It is little wonder that Lenox struggled to retain possession of the courts. A man with a half-dollar close up to his eye can completely shut out the landscape. Lenox failed to see its larger future because its eye was solely riveted on its smaller gains. It knew not that it was to relinquish its prominence in the county that it might step forth into larger renown. Steadily the battle waged between Lenox and Pittsfield, and when the new Court-house was built in 1816, and again when it was enlarged in 1855, it was thought Pittsfield would accept the inevitable and cease to try to rob Lenox of its prestige. Not so. Referendums were submitted to the county for its decision three times during the progress of the dispute, on the question: "Shall the courts be removed to Pittsfield," and every time the popular decision was in favor of their being retained in Lenox. The county was sown an inch deep with campaign literature on both sides of this controversy. It was urged that Lenox was difficult of access to towns on the south on account of the many ups and downs of the road leading into the village from that quarter. This is the road that now leads past the Lanier, Sloane, and Bishop places. Lenox remedied that difficulty immediately by putting another road of easy grade right through her training-ground, where now the Episcopal church stands, to meet the other hilly road at a point two miles distant from the village. This new highway was laid out just before the year 1850, and has been named 'Kemble Street" after the distinguished actress, Mrs. Fanny Kemble-Butler, who lived on it in the house named by her " The Perch," and still so-called. The creation of this new thoroughfare for travel had the effect of causing a lull in the agitation, but the discontent organized itself again when the question of enlarging the Court-house came up in 1855. The soberest and most judicious minds of the Berkshire capital were stirred to the depths by the renewal of hostilities, and Lenox made much of the argument that as it was already north of the geographical centre by some rods, Pittsfield, which was six miles farther north, was out of the question.

But there came a day at last when arguments were useless. It was becoming from year to year more and more apparent that the summer visitors who were annually being attracted to Lenox, the gem of the Berkshires, were quite ready that the courts should go and with them the clatter and chatter and barter on the streets, the tying of horses in the public squares, the jostlings on the sidewalks, in short, the general hubbub and confusion of a small village congested with life. And so the decree that the courts should be removed was procured in 1868 — not so many years ago but that memories of the distinguished bench and bar and of celebrated cases are still told and retold by those scarce out of middle life, to say nothing of the treasury of reminiscences possessed by the oldest inhabitant with reference to the proud dignity of the court-period in the history of the village. Many still remember the jail, that shadow which stalks in the wake of Justice, and the faces looking out from the windows behind the bars of their prison, which stood on the site of the present Schermerhorn cottages on Main Street. A still more sombre recollection, the executions on "Gallows Hill," near the site of the Robeson place, has faded out of the minds of all. As nothing

Old-Time Lenox

but the good has in it the power of perduring, the bad tending to its own decay and extinction, so the memory of this olden period has survived only, or mainly, in sacred reminiscences and holy traditions which every villager is proud to rehearse.

Closely allied with the early history of Lenox, after it became the county seat, are two events which had the most incalculable influence on the town : one, the installation of the Rev. Samuel Shepard over the village church in 1795, his signally effective pastorate lasting a half-century ; the other, the establishment, in 1803, of Lenox Academy, a far-famed institution of classical learning in its day. To Dr. Shepard and his work some allusion will be made later.

Lenox Academy was incorporated by an act of the Legislature, February 22, 1803, and was granted a township in Maine, which was afterwards sold, the proceeds being added to the funds of the institution. The building still stands with the date 1803 painted on its ancient belfry, a venerable, unpretentious structure full of impressive associations and used to-day as the village high-school. It is almost too hallowed to be used by the children of an iconoclastic generation, out of touch with the traditions of its pure classicism and simple life. Its surrounding and overarching elms have looked down on succeeding classes as they have gone forth to make names for themselves in the catalogue of the world's worthies, the Hon. David Davis, of Illinois, President Mark Hopkins, Dr. Henry M. Field, Alexander H. Stephens, Vice-President of the Confederacy, and Governor Yancy, of South Carolina, being among the number of those who have here been educated. I have seen many of the programmes of Commencement Day in that olden institution. It was an all-day affair with speakers from a convenient hour after breakfast until nearly sundown; a sort of literary set-to, or intellectual sweetness long drawn out. The Congregational church was always the scene of these commencement exercises, the building being packed to overflowing.

To be a graduate of Lenox Academy was not only a distinction, it was a passport to any college, and often to the sophomore class of a higher institution of learning. The papers of the day within a radius of a hundred miles refer to this preparatory school with glowing commendation. Its pupils came from widely separated portions of the country and the fame of its examinations, which were of unusual

The old Lenox Academy, erected 1803 (now used as High School).

rigidity, attracted visitors from long distances, who repaired to their homes to spread the report of them. The tuition was very moderate, —$7 a term of fourteen weeks; and board reached the not exorbitant sum of "$1.25 to $1.50 per week in good families." The tradition has survived that one pupil (long a distinguished educator and only lately deceased) "lived like a dandy because he had rooms at the hotel, for which he paid $2 per week." Lenox Academy flourished until 1866. The men whose names are identified with this institution by long service therein as instructors were Levi Glezen, a somewhat eccentric individual but a rare disciplinarian and fine teacher; John Hotchkin, long-time its widely celebrated principal and the founder of the Lenox Library; and Matthew Buckham, now the President of Vermont University. Among Miss Kemble's poems is one with the title "To the young gentlemen about to graduate from Lenox Academy," and from it I take the following lines :

> "Ye were ordained to do, not to enjoy,
> To suffer, which is nobler than to dare.
> A sacred burthen is this life ye bear,
> Look on it, lift it, bear it solemnly ;
> Stand up and walk beneath it steadfastly.

> Fail not for sorrow, falter not for sin,
> But onward, upward, till the goal ye win.
> God guard you, God guide you on your way,
> Young pilgrim warriors who set forth to-day."

But Lenox Academy was not the only school of classical learning within the township. Here was located also a school for girls, managed continuously during its existence from 1828 until 1864 by Mrs. Charles Sedgwick, the wife of the Clerk of the Courts, who was himself one of the most prominent and widely respected men of the region, and whose sister, the gifted novelist, Catherine Sedgwick, made her home for many years in her brother's family at Lenox. A rare home was this graced by the presence of Catherine, who, though often in New York, where she always moved in the most literary circles of the metropolis, spent her summers regularly with Charles, in whose house she had a wing somewhat apart by herself, yet ever accessible to all. In another building on the same property Mrs. Charles Sedgwick kept her famous school; she herself an authoress who had written several books for children. It is not difficult to imagine that such a home of culture and refinement, honored and enlivened as it was by the presence of Catherine, who wrought here at her literary tasks, and who was the correspondent of Sismondi, Miss Martineau, Bryant, Irving, and many others of the choicest intellects of this and foreign lands, would be a lodestone drawing with irresistible attraction the young women who sought the advantages of an education. Among the pupils of this school at one time Harriet Hosmer was enrolled.

Many are the references in the books of the day to this celebrated school for girls. William Cullen Bryant, who practised the profession of the law in Great Barrington from 1816 until 1825, and who doubtless often appeared in the Lenox courts, gives us a pen-picture of Miss Sedgwick at a later period of her life, when she, the distinguished author of *Hope Leslie* and *Redwood*, and he, the maker of poems which were already aflame with immortality, were closely associated in the literary companionships of New York City. There in the homes of her distinguished brothers, Robert and Henry, men of eminence in the legal profession, Catherine found such constant visitors as Fenimore Cooper, Sands, Eastburn, Hillhouse, Halleck, Bleeker, and Morse and Cole the artists. Bryant renewed and cemented in the metropolis the friendship begun in the Berkshires, and he describes her as "well-formed, with regular features, eyes beaming with benevolence, a pleasing smile, a soft voice, and gentle and captivating manners." Such a member of the Lenox home would be to the young ladies who were there pursuing their studies a source of unfailing interest, an object of devotion, an inspiration to high ideals. It is a pleasure to stand near the wing of this simple, old-fashioned dwelling, until recently used as the residence of descendants of the Sedgwick family, to look off upon the superb view it commands down the valley for miles, to feel one's self invested with and possessed by the memories of other days,—to see bright young faces here and there on porch and lawn, and now and then moving among them, with something of an air of mystery, the form of one who was a fine specimen of the New England gentlewoman.

Two institutions of learning in the town, the presence from time to time of the court, the residence of the county officials, the superior advantages of a county seat for great county gatherings, the publication of a weekly newspaper, a bookstore and a bindery, a real live authoress moving along the quiet village streets, a prevailing type of high intelligence in the village folk themselves—these made Lenox a town of superior intellectual attractions, as it was also of rare physical beauty. It was in the very nature of things impossible that such a mountain village could long remain undiscovered by men and women of letters seeking rest and inspiration in its picturesqueness, in the tonic of its fresh pure breezes, and in the quiet village life pervaded with so high an order of culture and refinement. Their writings show the impression that Lenox made upon them, and to these records, as well as to those of an older literature, we do not turn in vain for pictures of "old-time Lenox." Hither in 1798, and again in 1799, came President Dwight, of Yale College, on his way from New Haven to Niagara. I find this entry in the voluminous jottings of his travels:

"Sept. 21, 1798.

" Lenox is the shire town of the county, and is principally built on a single street, upon a ridge declining rather pleasantly to the East and to the West, but disagreeably interrupted by several valleys crossing it at right angles. The soil and buildings are good, and the town exhibits many proofs of prosperity. The public buildings consist of a church, a Court House, a school house, and a gaol."

Later, in 1819, Prof. Benjamin Silliman, the distinguished physicist, came to Lenox on a carriage drive from Hartford to Quebec. His picture of this village and the Berkshires is vivid. " Sept. 1819 :—It was quite dark before we arrived at Sandisfield, but our road was good and the welcome light of the inn at length caught our eyes. We slept in a great vacant ball-room." Sandisfield is a "deserted village" now, but then it was one of the chief towns of the county in size and thrift, rivalling Pittsfield. The next day the distinguished traveller reached Lenox, of which he writes as follows :

" Lenox, the capital of Berkshire County, is a town of uncommon beauty. It is built on a high hill on two streets intersecting each other nearly at right angles. It is composed of handsome houses which with the exception of a few of brick are painted a brilliant white ; it is ornamented with three neat houses of public worship, one of which is large and handsome and stands upon a hill higher than the town and a little remote from the centre [the present Congregational church]. Lenox has a jail, a woollen manufactory, an academy of considerable size, and a Court House of brick in fine style of architecture, fronted with pillars. Lenox has fine mountain air, and is surrounded by equally fine mountain scenery. It is a gem among the mountains."

Pressing on towards New Lebanon, at a point where the road steadily rises and then curves, Prof. Silliman pauses for a last look at Lenox before it is lost to view.

Walker Street, Lenox.

Old-Time Lenox

"What a fine retrospect we had," he continues, "mountains receding one behind another some of whose summits were struggling through clouds and mist and rain in obscure and gloomy grandeur. Beautifully contrasted with these was the bright cluster of buildings in Lenox, in which turrets and Gothic pinnacles and Grecian pillars were conspicuous and seemed like a string of pearls upon the brow and declivity of the hill now sunk to one of moderate elevation."

Upon Miss Sedgwick, who came here after the breaking up of her home in Stockbridge, Lenox made a disagreeable impression at first, but that may have been due to the intense regret she felt in leaving her native town. When the fog of homesickness cleared away she no longer saw things distorted. "It is a bare and ugly little village" she writes in 1821, "dismally bleak and uncouth, reached only after six miles of steep and rough driving"; but in 1824, November 1st, she thus soliloquizes :

"As I stand at the window and gaze on the hills that stretch before me in every variety of height and position, the sun sends his gleamy smiles along their summits pleasantly and the little lake that sparkles in the valley, now that its leafy veil has fallen, is plainly seen. I perceive many beauties that I have been before quite blind to."

Afterwards during the many years of her residence in Lenox the fondest attachment to the place possessed her, and when she was away from her home in the Berkshires, her mind continually reverts to the hill-country. "I long to have my eye rest upon those mountains," she writes to the dear ones in Lenox. It was she who attracted to this region those gifted Englishwomen, Miss Martineau, Mrs. Jameson, and Miss Kemble; and she it was, also, who lured hither William Ellery Channing, who spent the last summer of his life amid these picturesque heights. Who would not have prized the opportunity of seeing these literary yoke-fellows in their rambles and rides and drives together! Of that last summer of Channing's life among the hills, Miss Sedgwick has left us scant data in her correspondence, but enough to show how delightfully the days passed in the unconventionality and simplicity of country life, in the intercourse of lofty minds and gifted spirits, and in the responsiveness of nature to the varying moods of human thought. Writing to Dr. Dewey of the events in Channing's visit she says:

"He seemed to have thrown off every shackle, to be rid of his precision; he was affectionate and playful with the young people; he liked our anti-conventionalism, our free ways of going on; he enjoyed, as if he had come home to his father's house, the forever-changing beauty of our hills and valleys, and he went away with more than half a promise to return to us next summer."

Lenox was the summer home of Mrs. Fanny Kemble during the many years of her sojourn in America, and her books bear testimony to the place this mountain village held in her affections. It was with her, "love at first sight," and it did not wear off in after years. Coming to Lenox in 1836 she so identified herself with the town as to buy property in 1851, participating in village affairs, knowing, and known of, all. It cannot be said that Lenox received kindly at first the advent of an actress. One of the papers of the day, published in the village the first year of her stay here, was unkind enough to say: "Miss Kemble lost all delicacy of sex, strolling about the country." The mimic world before the footlights was too great a contrast to the stern realism of New England to make the entrance of an actress into the midst of it either comprehensible or enjoyable. Behind the mask of Comedy the plain people of that day saw only the features of "the great adversary." One can scarcely think of a greater contradiction in terms than the village pastor and the world-renowned actress meeting on the streets of the quiet, conservative town. The germ of an interesting romance lies enfolded here. But if Mrs. Kemble's calling surrounded her with an air of mystery in the estimation of the village folk, her phenomenal eccentricities of manner, dress, and speech only thickened the veil which screened her from any true view. Little did she care for these misunderstandings, for she revelled in the beautiful scenery which fed her soul and of which until her death only a few years ago she retained the most distinct and fond impressions.

"I have been spending a month with my friends in a beautiful hill-region of the State of Massachusetts," she writes October 5, 1836, "and I never looked abroad upon the woods and valleys and lakes and mountains without thinking how great a privilege it would be to live in the midst of such beautiful things." "Here I am," she writes again August 24, 1838, "on the top of a hill in the village of Lenox in what its inhabitants tautologically call Berkshire County, Massachusetts, with a view before my window which would not disgrace the Jura itself! Immediately sloping before me, the green hillside, on the summit of which stands the house I am inhabiting, sinks softly down to a small valley, filled with thick, rich wood, in the centre of which a little jewel-like lake lies gleaming. Beyond this valley the hills rise one above another to the horizon, where they scoop the sky with a broken, irregular outline that the eye dwells on with ever new delight, as its colors glow or vary with the ascending or descending sunlight, and all the shadowy procession of the clouds. Ever since early morning, troops of cloud and wandering showers of rain and the all-prevailing sunbeams have chased each other over the wooded slopes, and down into the dark hollow where the lake lies sleeping, making a pageant far finer than the one Prospero raised for Ferdinand and Miranda on his desert island."

This was the view which could then be obtained from the hotel where Mrs. Kemble stayed during the early days of her coming to Lenox; a view which now is shut out at that point by densely spreading foliage. We would not wish to intimate that the Lenox folk of the present are tree-worshippers, yet some of the beautiful streets in the village once commanding vast prospects have been transformed into mere umbrageous corridors, lanes between trees two and three rows deep. It was not so in Mrs. Kemble's time, and here she thoroughly yielded herself up to the abandon of unconventional, recreative life. Every day she rode ten or twelve miles before breakfast, her horse being brought to the door of the "Red Inn," as she calls it, at seven o'clock. To Mrs. Jameson she writes of her manner of life as follows: " We laugh, we sing, we talk, we play, we discuss, we dance, we ride, drive, walk, run, scramble, and saunter, and amuse ourselves extremely; and we enjoy every day delightful intercourse with the Sedgwicks." Yet was it not all an idle holiday. Mrs. Kemble gave Shakespearian readings in the public hall for charitable objects, and often in private at Mrs. Sedgwick's before very select and critical audiences. Mrs. Kemble's residence in Lenox is vividly remembered by many, and the memory of it has been perpetuated by naming a street in her honor.

In the spring of the year preceding that in which Fanny Kemble bought property in Lenox, the author of *The Scarlet Letter* — a book which had just come out and was making a great stir — came to this hill-country and took a house on Stockbridge Bowl, a beautiful sheet of water lying less than two miles to the west of Lenox village. The house, a little frame cottage, was standing until within a few years. Its loss by fire ten years since was a distinct loss among the many objects of interest in this region, but the site is still hallowed, and although just over the line in the township of Stockbridge, Hawthorne and all those who have subsequently built elegant villas in this part of

he town have been solely identified with
Lenox life. Hawthorne's cottage commanded one of the most picturesque prospects
n all this country of charming views and
vistas. The little red house was the scene of
Titanic labors. Here were written *The House
f the Seven Gables, Wonder Book*, and the
lot of *The Blithedale Romance*, besides many
f the jottings for his *American Notes*, and
he fascinating letters which have been com-
iled by his distinguished children in separate
olumes.

" It was the period," says Julian Hawthorne,
of my father's greatest literary activity." *The
Touse of the Seven Gables* was written in five
onths of unremitting toil, and then Haw-
orne, to use Julian's words, "allowed himself
 vacation of about four months," during which
e devoted himself to the entertainment of his
ildren and the enjoyment of the region,
aking that summer of 1851 memorable ever
ter in the experiences of his little family.
harming is Julian's picture of those Lenox
ays:

" He made us boats to sail on the lake, and kites to fly
the air; he took us fishing and flower-gathering, and
ed to teach us swimming. In the autumn we would
nutting with my father and he would climb to the

3

topmost branches, swaying and soaring high aloft, a delightful mystery and miracle. It was all a splendid holiday, and I cannot remember when our father was not our playmate or when we ever desired any other playmate than he."

This section of the town is, indeed, alive with the memory of Hawthorne. Here one seeks to reproduce all this, to fancy the rather delicate-looking man of hollow eye and thoughtful mien, to the ordinary villager somewhat unsociable, as he trudged to and from the village, where in the post-office he received and corrected his proofs; to imagine him, in a picture of his own creating, sauntering out of the little cottage down the road, a child on each side, now going for flowers, and now to a neighboring farmhouse for milk, along a path which he facetiously styled "the milky way."

To that cosy home by the lake, bright with pictures, pervaded with the warmth and gladness of Hawthorne's personality, inspirited from without by the fascinating scenery, Oliver Wendell Holmes came now and then, riding down from Pittsfield, also James T. Fields, who drove up from Stockbridge. Hither came other friends quite as distinguished,— James Russell Lowell, E. P. Whipple, G. P. R. James, and many more of the literati of the day. One knows not whether to look within the home or without it, for the more engaging and enrapturing beauty. Which glows the more warmly, the loveliness of landscape or the group of masterful intellects there collected? We may say, *en passant*, that it was in the little red house, during this sojourn of her father, that Rose (Mrs. Lathrop) was born. In her *Memories of Hawthorne* Mrs. Lathrop has added not a little to our knowledge of the details of her father's stay in the Berkshires. To the gate of the little red house, which stood very near the road, Fanny Kemble would ride up, grab the little Julian, put him astride the pommel, and canter off furiously, and after a mad gallop down the road a piece would return, depositing the youngster at the gate again, saying "Take your boy, Julian the Apostate!" Mrs. Hawthorne writes thus to her mother, September, 1851: "It is very singular how much more we are in the midst of society in Lenox than we were in Salem, and all literary persons seem settling around us." G. P. R. James was in Stockbridge and Herman Melville was in Pittsfield. The Hawthorne home was a centre of life, light, and gladness. For nearly two years, winter and summer alike, it formed a marked addition to the daily life of Lenox and was only broken up by the rigorous severities of the colder seasons in these mountain altitudes — too rigorous, indeed, for such a frail constitution as that possessed by Nathaniel Hawthorne.

Not far from Hawthorne's cottage was the house where for many years Charlotte Cushman resided, and far on the other side of the town was the property bought by Henry Ward Beecher in 1853, now crowned with a magnificent villa and still known as "Beecher Hill." One has but to catch up *Star Papers* to perceive the undisguised joy, the exuberant ecstasy with which Lenox filled the soul of the great preacher. His house, a simple farm-dwelling, stood far over in the eastern part of the town, where a vast prospect is obtained up as well as down the Housatonic Valley. As Mr. Beecher said: "By a mere roll of the eyeball I can look from Greylock on the north to the dome of the Taghconic Mountains on the south, a range of sixty miles from peak to peak." Greylock is the highest mountain in the State, rising to the height of 3500 feet, and at its base is Williamstown, where Williams College is located; and the "Dome," sometimes called Mt. Everett, is 2800 feet high, its summit being the home of the Goodale sisters, much of

At the junction of Main and Cliffwood Streets, Congregational Church in the distance.

whose verse has been produced here on what they aptly term "Sky Farm." Mr. Beecher revelled in this extended view day by day. He freely confesses that he bought his property in Lenox, not to work as a farm,—though such it was,—but to "lie down upon." He always carried a book in his hand, "not to read, but to muse over," he said, as he sallied forth over his farm, finding here and there convenient places to sit or "lie down" and dream. The presence in town of so great a preacher was not permitted to pass by unimproved, and sometimes his voice was heard in the village church. It was he who said, standing in the porch of the church-on-the-hill, and surveying the beautiful prospect which might then be obtained from that ancient doorway, but which now has unfortunately been shut out by a luxuriant forest-growth : " I had rather be a doorkeeper in *his* house of my God, than to dwell in the tents of wickedness."

Like modest strawberries hidden in the tall grass, many other allusions to Lenox may be found in the varied literature of America, all the way from the *Travels* of the first President Dwight to the romances of Mrs. Burton Harrison, who has passed many summers in the town, but these will be the theme of a separate chapter. We have simply selected some references which came within the scope of our subject, "Old-time Lenox," and these allusions serve the double purpose of enabling us to see an earlier Lenox through the eyes of those who have been "strangers within the gates," as well as to see the distinguished visitors themselves who from time to time have formed a part of the very life of the town itself.

Perhaps this is as good a place as any to refer to the village church, and the exceptionally protracted pastorate of its second minister, the Rev. Samuel Shepard, D.D., who was its minister from 1795 until 1846. Church and State were welded into one throughout Massachusetts until 1834 and therefore the parish was the town. Other churches there were in Lenox from an early period, but the Congregational being a part of the State régime was *the* church, as was the case throughout all New England. It was indissolubly intertwined with the life and thought of the people. Democratic in spirit and polity, it was decidedly autocratic within its own province. Samuel Shepard was called to the pastorate of the village Congregational church when a mere boy just out of Yale College, where he graduated in 1793. He died with the harness on, having ministered continuously in the same place for fifty years and a few months. He was installed at an open-air service just outside the church door; his grave is near the identical spot of ground where that service was held, and is surmounted with a monument on which is this appropriate verse: "Remember the words which I spake unto you while I was yet with you."

The village is filled with the story of this man, who lived to baptize the great-grandchildren of his first converts, and who saw the promise of the Lord to "his children, and their seed and their seed's seed" fulfilled. Before me lie the installation sermon preached by Rev. Cyprian Strong when Samuel Shepard was "ordained to the pastoral office over the church in Lenox," April 30, 1795, and the semi-centennial sermon of Dr. Shepard himself, preached April 30, 1845, summarizing the fifty years of his labors in the parish. The whole number of persons received into the church during his ministry up to that time was 815. He officiated at 969 baptisms, and 953 funerals, within the limits of the town. He witnessed ten "special manifestations of the divine influence, or revivals," during which scores and even hundreds were gathered into the church. He was a man of cheerful, sunny temperament and social qualifications, somewhat different from the prevailing type of the clergy of the period. An earnest preacher with a peculiarly deep, sonorous voice, his sermons were listened to with more than formal attention. He prayed always with his eyes wide open, and some good stories have survived concerning this peculiarity of the beloved pastor. Once, it is said, while engaged in prayer, his eye caught an amusing spectacle in the gallery. It was the sight of a naughty youth having a sly bit of fun all by himself. The day being a cold one outside, and the church being insufficiently heated, this youth was holding up his hands near the red hair of the person seated immediately in front, as if before a fire, and rubbing his fingers into a glow! It is said that the praying pastor could not repress a smile. Dr. Shepard was a prominent man in the county, being one of the trustees of Williams College, and his services in public movements throughout the State were sought. He lives imperishably in the hearts of the people of Lenox, as do two other pastors of the same church in later years: the Rev. E. K. Alden, D.D., long-time the Secretary of the American Board of Missions; and the Rev. C. H. Parkhurst, D.D., now and for the last twenty-two years the distinguished pastor of Madison Square Presbyterian Church, New York City.

There is no time to speak of the great county gatherings which were wont to be held in Lenox because it was the county seat. Time and space would fail me to relate the tithe-part of the mass-meetings held here in the interest of temperance, music, literary culture, Bible-distribution, matters of public import affecting the western part of the commonwealth, politics, and the like. Lenox as the shire-town felt a natural right of priority in the matter of these colossal conventions, and most incalculable must have been their effect. The great temperance revival which swept the country in the thirties found in Berkshire a hearty response. Mass-meetings of citizens from all parts of the county, of physicians and hotel-keepers, were here attended, having to do with this subject alone. Berkshire physicians here adopted the following resolution: "We shall hereafter not consider it a mark of civility or hospitality to partake of this insidious and baneful poison; but will say when exhausted with fatigue and watching, 'Give us food and simple drinks such as nature craves.'"

It would seem from a careful examination of the county papers that the chief subjects of thought for ten years were temperance and sacred music. Great was the day when Lowell Mason appeared in Lenox to hold a musical convention. The spacious court-room was crowded to overflowing. Second to none in the place it held in shaping town-thought was the village lyceum which met for a great many years from week to week and was addressed by local professional men and by distinguished visitors on all conceivable sorts of subjects, the address being followed by open parliament or debate. The Fourth of July was observed in those early and simple years on a scale of surpassing patriotic grandeur, with firing of cannon, procession to the village church, speeches, toasts, and the like, and sometimes these patriotic occurrences were combined with special Sunday-school celebrations from surrounding towns. In this earlier history of the town were laid the foundations of the Town Library, which began to be in 1793. This early collection of books, with the library in use in the Academy, formed the nucleus of the present Town Library, which was organized in 1856, and which now contains nearly 14,000 volumes. John Fiske says that the town-meeting has been the making of the New England people, but this, great as its influence has always been in Lenox, could be said with equal aptness of other towns. In other respects it has been exceptional, and in nothing more so than in its hotel, whose owners, going back from Curtis to Wilson, to Platner and to Cook, and back to Williams and Whitlock, have maintained (on almost identically the same spot) for a hundred and twenty-five years a hostelry. The predecessor of the present house was built in 1829: the predecessor of that in 1797, and that replaced an older tavern kept on substantially the same site in 1773. It has been, indeed, a succession of inns whose reputations for hospitality, for bountiful store, and for upright management have added not a little to the fame and the attractiveness of the town. As a business centre Lenox has vied in other days with brisk Berkshire towns, having sustained large glass-works, an iron-foundry, two tanneries, a factory which turned out tin and willow ware, and it also operated a considerable iron-mine. These industries have ceased altogether. A specimen of plate glass produced here may still be found in the Patent Office at Washington, D. C. A word might be in order about the curious customs of a past age, but I fancy Lenox was not peculiar in this respect. The board where the banns of marriage used to be published still hangs on one side of the door as one enters the village church; queer and quaint epitaphs greet the eye in the churchyard, but all these could be paralleled in many another New England town.

Let us close this chapter by a reference to the great transformation by which the quiet village has become the famous resort. Inasmuch as the beginnings of modern Lenox have already been seen in the progress of the story of other days, it may be interesting to note simply the process of change. We have seen that Mrs. Kemble made the acquaintance of Lenox in 1836, and that thence on for twenty years she was a regular visitor in the summer seasons, excepting a few spent abroad. As early as September 3, 1838, I find the following entry in her journal:

"The village hostelry was never so graced before; it is having a blossoming time with sweet young faces shining about it in every direction. The Misses Appleton [one of whom afterward married the poet Longfellow] are here for a week, and there is a pretty daughter of Mr. Dewey's staying in the house besides with a pretty cousin."

We thus see that Lenox was a resort in a small way sixty years ago. October 21, 1849, Miss Sedgwick records the following in a letter: " The summer visitors are all gone"; but even before this, as early, indeed, as 1846, the creation of great estates here had begun. This is the beginning of the change by which Lenox has become a town of magnificent estates and mansions, the account of which belongs to a later period and will be told by itself in a separate chapter in this volume. Prior to 1868 when the courts were removed a number of these beautiful " places" had been created by people of large means and they dotted the landscape at considerable distances apart. Now more thickly sown, and even more pretentiously constructed, they crown every eminence, and peep out from their leafy coverts on every projecting spur of the mountains, surveying a picturesque expanse of landscape and admired by every beholder for their lavish profusion of art and beauty.

It would be difficult to estimate the immeasurable benefit which the coming of an affluent class has conferred upon Lenox, but one, only one, of its benefactions shall be chronicled here, because it belongs to the period I have been attempting to describe. I refer to the gift of the Court-house to the town by Mrs. Adeline E. Schermerhorn, who in 1853 purchased property in Lenox for a country-place. After the removal of the courts the question of the proper disposition of the property took shape through the county. Mrs. Schermerhorn at once intervened and with rare munificence and thoughtfulness prevented the removal of the ancient landmark. Purchasing the building, and the plot of ground on which it stood, from the county, she donated it to the town, designating, in her deed of gift, that the structure should be used for a library, and at the same time giving the Lenox Library Association a permanent and gratuitous lease of the necessary rooms. And so the venerable pile, invested with associations which are eloquent with the story of the dignity, glory, and former greatness of Lenox, links the town with its earlier history, which, amid the blaze of its later splendor, can never be forgotten.

Second County Court-House (erected 1816), now Sedgwick Hall.

II

LENOX AND ITS ENVIRONMENT, IN LITERATURE

IT is not difficult to understand how some regions, beautiful by reason of their scenic loveliness, should be stamped with a sort of predestination to a high place in literature. A natural beauty in the landscape does something more than attract the tourist; it appeals to those instincts which fashion the poet or the artist. It is also true that the literary traditions and artistic surroundings of any locality prepare a soil out of which spring the very conditions favorable to the maintenance of its prestige. By the river Arno, in the "lake region" of Cumberland and Westmoreland, or in the placid river which flows through the Concord meadows what congestion of literary associations! Like the instinct of the bee which, separated by great distances from the hive, possesses the infallible sense of direction for its return, so too the lovely " nooks and corners " on the earth's surface are irresistibly and unerringly attracting choice spirits, which some way are sure to find them out and pre-empt them in the interests of their craft or clan. Berkshire is no exception to this, and at one time Lenox was fairly entitled to the name it received, "a jungle of literary lions." It shall be our task in this chapter to present a few of the many pages where Lenox and the Berkshires have been the inspiring themes of graceful and distinguished writers ; to trace the literary thread in the story of the village and the region.

Just a little foreword, then, supplementing rather than repeating what was said in the previous chapter. It will be remembered that Berkshire lay practically undiscovered until 1724, when the first settlers obtained from the Mohican Indians, for the consideration of " £460, three barrels of cider, and thirty quarts of rum," that portion of land comprised in the present townships of Sheffield, Great Barrington, Mount Washington, Egremont, Alford, and some part of Stockbridge, West Stockbridge, and Lee. This is that section of the county which extends on the west side of the Housatonic River from the Taghconic

Lenox in Literature 49

Dome to Monument Mountain. In 1736, the General Court ordered to be laid out on the east side of same river four towns which became known as Tyringham, New Marlborough, Sandisfield, and Becket, but which were called at first simply and respectively townships 1, 2, 3, and 4; and in the same year the colonial legislature granted the Indians a township, or reservation, immediately north of, and contiguous to, the first-named section. This reservation was an exact square six miles, on each side, and embraced the land occupied by the present townships of Stockbridge and West Stockbridge. It was called by the Indians Wnoghque-too-koke, and here they were collected for missionary instruction under Sergeant. It would take us too far afield to recite here the order and extent of grants by the General Court to individuals in this part of Western Massachusetts, then, and until 1761, included in Hampshire County. Suffice it to say that it was not until 1750 that the first settler drove a stake in Lenox, although there had previously been two large land grants in the region, one in 1738 to the heirs of Judge Edmund Quincy in the northeast, and another, the same year, to some ministers in the south, of what is now Lenox township. The " Quincy

4

grant" contained a thousand acres, and its southern boundary was not far from the northern line of the present estate of Mrs. R. T. Auchmuty. The grant was in recognition of the eminent services of Judge Quincy to the State, he having been selected by the General Court to lay the matter of the disputed boundary between Massachusetts and New Hampshire before the home government, and dying soon after his arrival in London with smallpox contracted by inoculation. The "Ministers' grant," so-called, was a tract of four thousand acres, and comprised that tongue of land, in the southern part of the town, whose tip wedges in between Stockbridge and Lee, and, including what is now known as Laurel Lake, this grant extended northward considerably beyond the high ground on which Lenox village is situated.

It is in connection with this "Ministers' grant" that, I venture to say, the first association of Lenox with literature is traced, though more accurately it might be said with a name great in the sacred literature of the world — Jonathan Edwards. This extensive grant was divided among the seven grantees in parcels or strips from east to west, of 480 acres each, with one or two exceptions, and

Lenox in Literature

one fell to Jonathan Edwards, who at that time was minister to the church at Northampton. It is on that Edwards section that the village of Lenox, along one of its principal streets, Walker Street, stands. It is more customary to associate Edwards with Stockbridge, where until within a year the house in which he wrote *The Freedom of the Will* was still standing, but the distinguished theologian had a property interest in what was to be the future town of Lenox. It must have been that many times during the years of his Stockbridge pastorate, 1751–58, he would ride up the hills towards his real-estate holdings while he thought out some deep problem in metaphysics, or meditated some adroit manœuvre to circumvent those who constantly harassed the missionary interests and fleeced the Indians. It is at least pleasant to connect Lenox with the name of Edwards, to whose short ministry in Stockbridge, if not to the longer one "in the solitudes of the Northampton woods," Whittier refers in his poem, *The Preacher*:

"In the church of the wilderness Edwards wrought,
 Shaping his creed at the forge of thought;
 And with Thor's own hammer welded and bent
 The iron links of his argument,

> Which strove to grasp in its mighty span
> The purpose of God and the fate of man!"

Lenox during the first decade of its history, from 1750 until 1760, was such an unfavorable place for residence, owing to the fear of incursions of marauding bands of Indians, that its growth was much impeded, and, in common with all other parts of the county, it was not till the French power was crippled at Quebec in 1759, and thus the Indian incursions confined to the remoter territory at the north beyond the St. Lawrence, that the settlement of Berkshire could proceed. There was growth in the southern part of the county, but the middle and northern portions were unsafe prior to the year 1760. Hardly had peace been declared between Great Britain and France when settlers poured into Berkshire. So far as Lenox is concerned events proceed rapidly. The county of Berkshire was set off by the General Court in May, 1761, its northern boundary New Hampshire and its western boundary the somewhat indeterminate and disputed line between Massachusetts and New York, a line which was not accurately and satisfactorily run until the summer of 1787. On June 2, 1762, the General Court ordered ten townships to be sold in the western part

Lenox in Literature 53

of the State, and "Lot No. 8," comprising the present towns of Lenox and Richmond, was knocked down to the highest bidder, Josiah Dean, for £2550, but owing to some claims of the Indians, and a prior claim of one Samuel Brown, and others who had bought the land covered in the sale to Dean by purchase from the Indians for £1700, the grant was finally confirmed by the State to Brown, he paying Dean £650. This purchase did not of course, invalidate previous grants in the same district, and the whole, which had been named for the chiefs of whom the land had been bought, was incorporated under the name Richmond in 1765, until 1767, when that portion of the township which had gone by the name of Yokuntown was called Lenox, by act of incorporation.

It is a fitting place, then, to stop, and take a little measure of Lennox, Duke of Richmond, inasmuch as Governor Bernard (Francis Bernard, Governor of Massachusetts, 1760-69) bestowed the titular and family names of this eminent nobleman and statesman upon what were Mount Ephraim and Yokuntown. Charles Lennox, Duke of Richmond, and Baron Methuen in the peerage of Scotland, was born in London, February 22, 1734-35. Choosing the army for his profession he became attached to the court, and by rapid promotions was successively Lord of the Bedchamber (1760), Major-General (1761), Lord Lieutenant of Sussex (1763), and Secretary of State (1766). When the town of Lenox was named for him he was Minister Plenipotentiary of the Most Christian King. The Duke of Richmond played a very important part in the counsels of state incident to the troublous questions connected with the breaking out of the American Revolution and was a member of various ministries during and after the unsuccessful attempt of Great Britain to subdue her colonies. He was an earnest Whig, decidedly radical in his views and a vigorous exponent of democracy. On the pages of, Lecky's *History of England in the Eighteenth Century* he is conspicuous among the *dramatis personæ* of the time, and throughout the polished letters of that court-gossip, Horace Walpole, there are many very interesting references to the high social prominence of his Grace, the Duke of Richmond. He carried the sceptre with the dove at the coronation of George III. He opposed the war with America and was for surrendering the English dominion over the colonies, declaring this view as early as 1776, as he wished to make America England's ally in case of future wars with France, and as he feared a victory of England over America would give the Tory element at home a long lease of power, and would be fatal to English liberty. America had to be free, in other words, that England might be free.

It is not difficult to imagine that the Duke's radical views made him a little out of joint with the times, and as he took a rather gloomy view of England's cause and condition at the outbreak of the American Revolution, he abstained several years from the court of George III., being recalled to the service of the state and serving in the ministries of Rockingham and Pitt when the war was over. He was, however, always an interested participant in all national affairs; and favored universal suffrage, though Burke opposed it. He was a man, says Lecky, "of great influence and ability." He really was one of the founders of the Liberal party which began to be in those corrupt days preceding the Stamp Act, and which was fostered by some young men of high nobility, "high in rank," says Trevelyan, "with rare exceptions, and most of them too rich, and all too manly, to be purchased," whose creed was summed up by one of their own number, Edmund Burke, as "the principles of morality enlarged." There were many stormy scenes in Parliament where the Duke of Richmond was a centre of interest and dramatic action; once when he opposed a motion to clear the galleries, and thereby precipitated an uproar in the House of Lords, in the midst of which the Duke of Richmond himself walked out followed by a very large train of peers, protesting thus energetically against any Star-Chamber proceedings; and again when he moved in the Lords on the 7th of April, 1778, that the war with America be stopped, upon the best terms obtainable for England, to which resolution Chatham replied in an impassioned speech which caused him to sink in an apoplectic fit from which he did not recover. The Duke of Richmond became very unpopular on account of his radical political morality and intensely democratic spirit.

The family name Lennox was spelled with two *n*'s, though on the tomb of the Duke of Richmond it appears with only one; and the ancestor of the Duke for whom Lenox is named affixed his signature to the original grant by Charles I. to the Plymouth Colony as " Lenox." The omission of one *n* in the name of the town is ascribed to accident occa-

Lenox in Literature 57

tioned by the difference in writing double letters, which were written formerly as one letter through which passed a dash, indicating that the letter was to be repeated. It is thought the dash came to be omitted by inadvertence, and so the present spelling with one *n* adopted.

The literary traditions of Lenox and of the region could not be written without some reference to the "Stockbridge Indians," so-called, an extended reference to whom will be deferred until later. Suffice it to say that traces of aboriginal occupancy still survive, though somewhat faintly in connection with the names of mountain, lake, stream, and street, and though appearing as a palimpsest under other and less romantic names, yet the Indian nomenclature of nature's points of interest is not entirely obliterated. Afar off to the north rises Greylock thirty-five hundred feet, called Saddleback by the early settlers, but I cannot find that it ever had an Indian name. The Berkshire Mountains were the hunting-grounds for the "River Indians," living along the Mahecannituck (Hudson), and the little lake lying just north of Pittsfield has received the name Pontoosuck ("Field of the Winter Deer"), which was the original name of what is now the city of Pittsfield, although the lake itself was called by the Indians Skoon-keek-moon-keek. But if Greylock seems to have had no distinctive Indian name, the beauty which its name suggests has been repeatedly celebrated by the masters of poetry and prose. From Lenox it stands out an isolated saddle high up on the northern sky and fitted only for a Titan's frame. It is the highest mountain in the State, and its appearance in the form of a saddle is really formed by two summits, one rising a little behind and at the side of the other. Turning the eyes in the opposite direction from Greylock as one stands on the high elevation in Lenox just north of the village known as " Church Hill," and looking off to the south, it is not difficult to reclothe with their olden Mohican appellations the prominent features in the charming landscape stretching away from the beholder. Far away, twenty miles as the crow flies, rises the solitary Tagh-kan-nuc (" Forest "), or as it is called, and as it indeed appears in the central part of Berkshire, the " Dome of the Taghconics," and between it and the height from which we are looking rose to the redskin the tops of Maus-wa-see-khi (" Fisher's Nest "), now called Monument Mountain, and Deowkook, or " Hill of the Wolves," now

Rattlesnake, though another name by which the latter is said to have been known to the Indians is Mau-sku-fee-haunk. It is an enchanting prospect, one vast intervale walled in by the Hoosacs on the east and the Taghcones on the west, Deowkook, Maus-wa-see-khi, and Tagh-kan-nuc rising successively higher and higher into the far distance, while near us, nestling under the heights of Deowkook on the right is the placid and beautiful Mah-keenac, and on the hither side Per-quan-a-pa-qua ("Lake of the Still Water"), on whose surfaces are mirrored the surrounding hills.

If now we see the view before us at a higher altitude, as some eagle that only touches foot on the peaks to rest must see it in its flight through the upper airs, the mountains would be stunted, but running through the heart of the vale would be seen the extremely tortuous twistings and windings of the Hoo-es-ten-nuc (Housatonic), "Over the Mountain," as it makes its way from its sources by its west branch in Skoon-keek-moon-keek and Onota, near Pontoosuck (Pittsfield), onwards to the sea. At Wnogh-que-too-koke (Stockbridge), which lies there just beyond Mahkeenac, and on this side of Maus-wa-see-khi, we should see the Hoo-es-ten-nuc receiving the waters of the Konkapot brook, so named after the chief who lived beside it, then we should see the main stream of the valley cutting a way for itself through the gorge just below, called by the Indians " Pack-wa-ke " (a term signifying bend or elbow by which the aborigines designated the sharp turn in the Housatonic at Glendale), and becoming a little farther down " Sagistonac " (meaning " Water Splashing over the Rocks,") or falls, near which place the Waumpa-nick-se-poot or Green River, having itself just been swollen by the Seekonk (" Wild Goose "), joins the larger and main river of the valley. This place where the Hoo-es-ten-nuc and Waumpa-nick-se-poot unite was a " Skatekook," or " a place where a small stream enters into a large one, and corn-lands adjoin," and this name Skatekook was applied to the primitive and aboriginal settlement of what subsequently became Sheffield, the earliest town to be settled and incorporated in Berkshire. Almost all of this Indian nomenclature has disappeared from practical use, but a great many legends of the aborigines survive in various sections of Berkshire, and are told in Skinner's *Myths and Legends of Our Own Land.* Far off " Taghconic," called simply " The Dome," was christened "Mount Everett" by Dr. Hitchcock, State eologist, in 1839, in honor of Edward Everett, the Governor of the commonwealth, and though bitterly protested against the name has found its way into current use, particularly in the southern portion of the county, where its appearance as a dome is less marked. One of the most earnest opponents of the change of name was Miss Catherine Sedgwick, but she is the reputed originator of the name "Stockridge Bowl," which has entirely supplanted " Lake Mahkeenac " for which it was substituted.

It would take us too far afield to point out all the literary associations connected with the points of interest, as our eye sweeps the horizon and the magnificent prospect before us. Far off in the north on the farther slopes of Greylock, yet within the limits of the Berkshire country, Williams College has quietly pursued its academic ideals for a hundred years, and there the deep impress of Mark Hopkins's broad and classic spirit is still felt; nearer, and skirting the east of Pittsfield, is the region which is still redolent with the memory of Oliver Wendell Holmes, who spent seven summers, 1849–56, on a part of the old farm belonging originally to his great-grandfather, Jacob Wendell (three of Dr. Holmes's children having been born there during this Pittsfield sojourn), and we learn from the poet that "all of the present town of Pittsfield, except one thousand acres, was the property of my great-grandfather, who owned a section six miles square bought of the Province." There to the south are the steepling crags of Monument, which Bryant has immortalized, and near it the Green River, by whose banks he roamed when town clerk in the little village of Great Barrington, on the other side of Mauswaseekhi.

There are other literary names written across the picture, great names and small, and Lenox itself is resplendent in the galaxy of letters with many stars of the first magnitude. If you care to know, there on those hillside meadows yonder looking down on Skoon-keek-moon-keek, now called Pontoosuck Lake, "Josh Billings" was born, and you may see any day his huge granite sarcophagus, bearing his grotesque *nom de plume* in large letters, in the village cemetery near by. Nearer, and hard by the Pittsfield village of fifty years ago, dwelt Herman Melville, who appears often in the Hawthorne correspondence, and who was the author of *Typee*, *Omoo*, *Mardi*, *Redburn*, and other sea-tales, popular in their day, winning for their author two columns in Allibone, and still

Lenox in Literature

very much appreciated as first-rank stories of their kind. In the same place (Pittsfield) dwells to-day a much-talked of writer, William Stearns Davis, whose promising career opens brilliantly. Look off to the south and on the summit of the far-away "Dome" is "Sky Farm" where the Goodale sisters (Dora and Elaine) wrote of "Apple Blossoms," and girded themselves with the vigor of their rugged clime for the more serious duties of life; while off here to the west nestles a little lake, Queechy, just outside the county limits, where Susan Warner, the author of *The Wide, Wide World* and *Queechy*, lived and wrought in such a way as to make a very large public wait eagerly for her message.

Look up and down the county and mark the oft-frequency of those places where once flourished famous schools,—the Berkshire Medical College at Pittsfield, and the Maplewood Young Ladies' Institute in the same place, the Greylock Institute at South Williamstown, the Lenox Academy and Mrs. Charles Sedgwick's school for girls in Lenox, the Reid and Hoffman school in Stockbridge, and the South Berkshire Institute at New Marlborough, all of which institutions have quietly passed out of existence with no obsequies to commemorate their once efficient and famous services.

I cannot give the names of all those ministers of Berkshire who have become well known in the field of sacred literature from Samuel Hopkins and Jonathan Edwards, of whom something will be said hereafter, to Washington Gladden and Theodore T. Munger, who preached in the thriving city under the shadow of Greylock, and on to Charles H. Parkhurst, who scintillated both light and heat on this very mount before he was called to New York. I cannot dwell upon the representatives of art, from George Church to Barnard and French, the last named just now engaged in building a studio and mansion there by Pack-wa-ke, to all of whom Berkshire has furnished inspiration. I cannot tell the long but interesting story of distinguished visitors within the county come to add their literary prestige to this and that section in the enchanted realm of Berkshire, from abroad Mrs. Jameson, Miss Martineau, Dean Stanley, Lord Chief Justice Coleridge, and Matthew Arnold, and from our own catalogue of worthies more names than there is space to write. It is all one charming story of literary interest, aside from scenic charm or the thrilling march

Lenox in Literature

of historic events, and many are the books the scenes of whose plots are laid in Berkshire, or in which scattered notices of the region appear. It is to be our task in this chapter to reproduce some of those passages.

And first let us get the view from distant "Taghconic Dome" as President Timothy Dwight of Yale College saw it one hundred and twenty years ago. Dr. Dwight was a great traveller and a voluminous writer, returning like Herodotus to recount tale after tale of his journeyings.

"In the year 1781," he says, "I ascended the loftiest summit of this mountain [the Dome], and found a most extensive and splendid prospect spread around me. On the north rose Saddle mountain, at the head of the Hooestennuc Valley at the distance of forty miles. At the same distance the Catskill mountains formed on the west the boundary of the vast valley of the Hudson; and in the southwest the most northern summit of the Highlands. The chain of the Green Mountains on the east stretched its long succession of summits from north to south a prodigious length, while over them at a distance rose the single, solitary point of Mount Tom, and farther still at the termination of fifty or sixty miles, ascended successively various eminences. Monadnock at the distance of seventy miles on the northeast is distinctly discernible in a clear day."

Dr. Dwight in 1798 revisited the region, and journeying northward through Great

Barrington he substantiates what we know from the *Memoirs* of Hopkins about the notorious irreligion then prevailing in that village, —horse racing the chief business, houses decayed, unthrift on all sides, the church in ruins and a shelter for sheep, having had no pastor for over thirty years, during and after the troublous Revolutionary times. Yet here was where the great Hopkins labored, being dismissed, after a twenty-five years' pastorate, in 1769. Dr. Dwight continues his journey over Monument Mountain so called because here was buried one of the aborigines, a girl, who, disappointed in love, had killed herself by leaping off a precipice on the west side, and each Indian who passed her grave threw a stone upon the place of sepulture, by which custom, practised many years, the heap had come to assume the proportions of a *monument* to the dead. This distinguished traveller calls attention to the "Eastern front of 'Monument,' a magnificent and awful precipice, formed by ragged perpendicular cliffs of white quartz and rising immediately west of the road between five and six hundred feet"; and he notices, also, *en passant*, the tremendous geologic convulsion known as "Ice Glen," described so weirdly and vividly by Miss Sedgwick in *A*

Lenox in Literature 67

New England Tale (1822) and visited annually by scores of people.

Proceeding on his journey President Dwight, after a short stay in Stockbridge (the Indians had been gone then twelve years), comes to Lenox, which he describes as given in the chapter on the earlier history of the town.

A monument was unveiled recently on the grounds of Yale College to Benjamin Silliman, physicist, the distinguished professor of chemistry in that institution from 1802 until 1853. Dr. Silliman, following the example of President Dwight, made a journey in 1819 through New England and reported what he had seen in a volume entitled, *Silliman's Tour to Quebec*. Dwight rode; Silliman's was a carriage journey, and I find in the record of his travels quite an extended reference to Lenox. This has already been given on page 26, and is only referred to again to call attention to the little bit of local color. Lenox at that time was in the beginning of its prolonged and friendly contest with Pittsfield for the primacy among the towns of the county, and it was thought the matter had been settled by the erection three years before (1816) of the new county Court-house, now, and since 1874, the Public Library building, and known as Sedgwick Hall.

This is the edifice Silliman describes, and I append here the rest of the reference which the distinguished traveller makes to the town.

"I did not count the houses," he says, "but I should think there might be one hundred houses and stores. Its population is one thousand, three hundred and ten. White marble is often the material of their steps, foundations and pavements. Our treatment and dinner at the inn were such as a reasonable traveller would have been very well satisfied with, at a country tavern in England. Still probably no small town in England is so beautiful as Lenox."

Professor Silliman is rapturously enthusiastic over the scenery of this Berkshire region, even if, in the rather turgid style of Xenophon, he measures off the "parasangs" from town to town; and so he passes on his way, seeing "the lofty Hoosac with its double summit" (Greylock) "on our right." It will be seen from the reference to the "inn" of that day, which stood upon the same site as the present substantial and commodious "Curtis Hotel," that this corner in the village has enjoyed for nearly if not quite a century a prestige for hospitality and the entertainment of distinguished travellers. The present hotel, entirely reconstructed within recent years, had for its predecessor on the same site a brick structure built in 1829 and called "The Berkshire Coffee-House," and it is specifically that house which has the literary associations of great names. Mrs. Kemble, even so far back as 1839, speaks of it as the "Old Red Inn"; and Mrs. Jameson, the English author and the intimate friend of Miss Catherine Sedgwick, refers, in a letter to the latter, August 20, 1838, to "the little view of the hills from the window of the inn at Lenox where we used to sit."

It would be far from the purpose of this chapter to make a complete list of those books of description containing scattered references to Lenox, or its environment; yet it would be a very grave omission not to see this region through the eyes of some of the English visitors who have from time to time come hither; one of whom, Mrs. Kemble, to whom reference has been made, became so enamored with Berkshire as to make her residence in Lenox for years. The Lenox during the period of Mrs. Kemble's sojourn, 1836–53, is the subject of many references on the pages of her *Records of Later Life*. Mr. Samuel G. Ward, American representative of the Baring

Brothers, London, had purchased in 1846 some farms near Stockbridge Bowl, thus pioneering the way for the creation of vast estates here by the lavish and artistic hand of Wealth. Other notable purchases followed right away. Miss Catherine Sedgwick was toiling at her voluminous task, always the centre of a literary coterie attracted to her side, whether in New York or here in Lenox, where her home was a veritable salon, though perfectly simple and informal, graced by the presence of Channing, Sumner, Mrs. Kemble, distinguished and exiled Italian patriots of 1848, and many others. Lenox was being "discovered." Charles Sumner writes Dr. Howe, September 13, 1844, from Lenox, where he is staying with his friend Ward: "Last evening at the Sedgwicks' I heard Fanny Kemble read the First Act of *Macbeth*, and sing a ballad." Oliver Wendell Holmes writes his mother from Pittsfield, August 17, 1849: "To-day I rode my little horse to Lenox. Mr. ——'s place is one of the most beautiful spots I ever saw anywhere; perfect almost to a miracle." Before Mrs. Kemble left the creation of beautiful estates had begun; the "inn" was always filled to overflowing; the waning star of Miss Sedgwick's literary greatness had commenced

Lenox in Literature 71

to set; Hawthorne and Beecher were here; and with the dignity of court-life at the stated periods, the bustle and stir of the county business when the courts were in session, the appearance of a student-corps in attendance upon the famous classical schools located here, Lenox was an altogether different place from what it is to-day.

Some additional references to the Lenox of Mrs. Kemble's day are here presented from her own writings. In her *Records of Later Life* she says:

> "Being asked by my friends in Lenox to give a public reading, it became a question to what purpose the proceeds of the entertainment could best be applied. I suggested 'the poor of the village,' but 'We have no poor' was the reply, and the sum produced by the reading was added to a fund which established an excellent public library, for though Lenox had no paupers, it had numerous intelligent readers among its population."

It may be that the chief reason there were no paupers then was that there was no pauper spirit! Mrs. Kemble also relates how her

> 'most admirable friend, Mr. Charles Sedgwick, seriously expostulated with me" (her), because she sent some beer out to some laborers in the hay-lot " as introducing among the laborers of Lenox a mischievous need and deleterious habit till then utterly unknown there; in short my

poor barrel of beer was an offence to the manners and morals of the community I lived in, and my meadow was mowed upon cold water from the well."

In all the journeyings of this famous actress her heart turns back to the Berkshire town, and its mountain environment, "a district," she says, "chiefly inhabited by Sedgwicks and their belongings," and one wonders which delighted her innermost soul the more, the scenery or the mental companionship of Catherine Sedgwick. The most enthusiastic descriptions of the loveliness of the region are only rivalled in rapture by her oft-allusions to the American woman of letters who was her guide to Channing and who was her country-woman's (Mrs. Jameson's) friend, as this little bit from a letter of Anna Jameson to Catherine Sedgwick (August 20, 1838) shows: "I have known you only to feel how hard it is to be without you, dear sunshiny Kate."

As early as 1843 (October 3d), Mrs. Kemble longs for a residence in the Berkshires:

"You do not know," she writes, "how earnestly I desire to live up there. I do believe mountains and hills are kindred of mine,— larger and smaller relations, taller and shorter cousins, for my heart expands and rejoices and beats more freely among them, and doubtless, in the days which 'I can hardly remem-

Lenox in Literature 73

ber' I was a bear, or a wolf, or at the very least a wildcat, with unlimited range of forest and mountain. . . . That cottage by the lake-side haunts me, and to be able to realize that day-dream is now certainly as near an approach to happiness as I can ever contemplate."

In London, December 9, 1845, the Berkshire picture is before her:

" My little sketch of Lenox lake lies always open before me, and I look at it very often with yearning eyes, for the splendid rosy sunsets over the dark-blue mountain tops, and for the clear and lovely expanse of pure waters reflecting both, above all for the white-footed streams that come leaping down the steep stairways of the hills. I believe I do like places better than people."

In Rome, May 20, 1846, she remembers Lenox :

" The beautiful aspect of this enchanting region recalls the hill country in America that I am so fond of. The district of country round Lenox rejoices in a number of small lakes (from one hillside one sees five) of a few miles in circumference, which, lying in the laps of the hills, with fine wooded slopes sweeping down to their bright basins, give a peculiar charm to the scenery."

In another place she writes, " It is the most picturesque scenery I have ever seen," and after describing the beauties of landscape about Stockbridge and Lenox, lavishes unstinted praise upon the scenic charm " in the neighborhood of a small town called Salisbury, thirty miles from Lenox. This," she continues, "is situated in a plain surrounded by mountains, and upon the same level lie four beautiful small lakes; close above this valley rises Mount Washington, or as some Swiss charcoal-burners, who have emigrated hither, have christened it, Mount Righi." The mountain referred to here is "The Dome," which stands like a sentinel at the southern end of the Berkshire country.

Mrs. Kemble revelled in all the prodigality of rich landscape here, a rare lover of nature, oblivious to criticisms upon her singularity as she strolled or rode here and there. Charles Sumner, who spent some weeks in Pittsfield recuperating from a severe illness, writes his friend Howe, September 11, 1844:

"To-morrow I move to Lenox where I sojourn with Ward and count much upon the readings of Shakespeare, the conversation and society of Fanny Kemble, who has promised to ride with me and introduce me to the beautiful lanes and wild paths of these mountains. She seems a noble woman, peculiar, bold, masculine, and unaccommodating, but with a burning sympathy with all that is high, true, and humane."

At another time he speaks of riding in Mrs. Butler's (Fanny Kemble's) company, who "proposed to accompany me back to Pitts-

Fanny Kemble.

Lenox in Literature

field. We rode the longest way and I enjoyed my companion very much"; and at another he and his friend, Mr. Ward, " looked on while, in a field not far off, the girls and others engaged in the sport of archery. Mrs. Butler hit the target in the golden middle." Hawthorne, who spent the busiest eighteen months of his life in a literary way in Lenox, from the spring of 1850 until the autumn of 1851, was thrown into the society of Mrs. Butler (so far as he, the unsocial man, could be thrown into any society), and as we see her dash up on easy and familiar terms before the " little old red house," reining in her fiery steed,—which there is a tradition, here in Lenox, she rode *à la chevalier*,—we may wonder if either understood the other, so unlike were they in many ways.

Hawthorne would jump over the fence to avoid meeting strangers; Mrs. Kemble was excessively social. Hawthorne tired of the scenery; it grew upon her the more she saw it. Julian Hawthorne, writing of the Lenox period in his father's life, says she " often rode up to the door on her strong black horse, and conversed, in heroic phrases, with the inmates of the red house." She was a strong personality, full of kindliness and an " enthusiasm of humanity," not in love with her profession, a deep thinker on religious questions, raptly in love with nature, and a writer of most interesting and readable letters. Her love for the Berkshires took the form of the creation of a "place" called "The Perch," and since her removal, though before her death, the town named the street on which her place was located in her honor. Toward the close of her long life she brought out a book, *Far Away and Long Ago*, showing that in the English home where she passed the evening of her days, the memories of a far-off hill-country were uppermost. She published in 1858 a volume of poems, some of which were inspired by her Lenox residence. We recognize the influence of the *locale* in

> "Greylock, cloud-girdled, from his purple throne
>   A shout of gladness sends,
> And up soft meadow slopes, a warbling tone
>   The Housatonic blends."

Of other English visitors who have written about Berkshire we shall not speak so much at length. Miss Harriet Martineau made a somewhat protracted stay of two years in America (1834-36), a small portion of the time being spent in the Berkshires, visiting

Miss Catherine Sedgwick at Stockbridge, where the house is still standing in which Catherine was born in 1789. It was here Miss Martineau was entertained in November, 1834.

"We have been exquisitely happy in Stockbridge with the Sedgwicks. Miss Sedgwick is all I heard of her, which is saying everything. . . . Such a country of mountain and lake and towering wood! I was 'Lafayetted' as they say to great advantage. All business was suspended and almost the whole population was busy in giving me pleasure and information. We were carried to Pittsfield to an annual agricultural assemblage where I learned much of the people. Oh! the bliss of not seeing a single beggar. . . . I have learned more than I well know how to stow, at Stockbridge, the unrivalled village where the best refinements of the town are mingled with the wildest pleasures of the country. I never saw so beautiful a company of children as were always offering me roses. Miss Sedgwick is the beloved and gentle queen of the little community."

Miss Martineau's tour through America was at a critical time so far as politics were concerned, owing to the divisive and persistent question of slavery, and her "impressions" of the United States were given to the public in a book entitled *Society in America*, published after her return to England and bringing down upon its author's head a storm of abuse from the press on this side of the Atlantic;

but we are grateful for its descriptions of the prominent people of the day, and notably of Miss Catherine Sedgwick.

"I remember Miss Sedgwick," writes Harriet Martineau, "starting back in the path, one day when she and I were walking beside the sweet Housatonic, and snatching her arm from mine when I said, in answer to her inquiry what I thought the issue of the controversy must be, 'The dissolution of the Union!' she cried, 'The Union is sacred, and must be preserved at all cost.'"

There are many interesting references to Miss Sedgwick in Miss Martineau's *Autobiography*, and to Harriet Martineau in Catherine Sedgwick's *Life and Letters*. Harriet and Catherine were respectively thirty-three and forty-six when they had their "drives together or strolled along the sweet Housatonic" in 1835, but they were too utterly dissimilar in many ways to cement an unbroken friendship. Catherine's affectionate tenderness was misinterpreted for flattery by Harriet, and naturally when the younger told the older that she "dreaded to receive her letters because instead of what I wished to hear, I found praise of myself," their correspondence ceased. Miss Martineau, however, had "a great admiration for Miss Sedgwick's character," and reviewed the American novelist's works in the *Westminster Review* of October, 1837, particularly praising as "wonderfully beautiful" the smaller tales such as *Home* and *Live and Let Live*.

It is a more congenial and inspiring friendship which greets one in the long comradeship between Mrs. Jameson and Miss Sedgwick, but its value for us here is in its bearing upon the subject of this chapter. Catherine Sedgwick returned, in 1839, the visit which Anna Jameson made in America in 1837, and among the friendships of literary women there are few more intense or mutually stimulating. They were nearly of the same age, and their correspondence continuing through the last twenty years of Mrs. Jameson's life is a mirror of the literary activity of the period. In her London home Mrs. Jameson keeps prominently before her "the house where Catherine Sedgwick was born, and, also, the little view of the hills from the window of the inn at Lenox," as she writes August 20, 1838.

Indeed, with the names of Harriet Martineau, Anna Jameson, Fanny Kemble, Harriet Beecher Stowe, Frederika Bremer, Harriet Hosmer, Mary Dewey, and Catherine Sedgwick at one and another time not very far apart written into the Berkshire story, it will be seen how much woman has contributed to enhance the literary prestige of the region. Miss Bremer was attracted to the Berkshire country through her long friendship with Miss Sedgwick, and Harriet Hosmer was a pupil in the "Young Ladies School" conducted for many years in Lenox by Mrs. Charles Sedgwick and famous in its day. Mary Dewey, the daughter of a distinguished Unitarian clergyman, Rev. Orville Dewey, D.D., was, like her father, whose *Life* she wrote, born in Sheffield, the earliest settlement in Berkshire County, and was, owing to theological and literary affinities, thrown much into the society of the Lenox coterie. Mrs. Stowe, both through her distinguished brother, Henry Ward Beecher, who acquired property in Lenox in 1853, and through her son-in-law, Mr. Allen, the rector at one time of the Episcopal church in Stockbridge, was an oft-visitor in the region, and an amusing *rencontre* between Fanny Kemble and her is told by Mrs. Kemble-Butler in her *Records*. Mrs. Stowe was expressing to Fanny Kemble, in a call made by herself and daughter upon the actress in Lenox, her belief in Planchette, and the undoubted conviction she entertained that it was immediately inspired by Satanic influences on account of the "language it uses." "Really," said Mrs. Kemble with ill-suppressed laughter; "may I inquire what language it does use?" "Why," returned Mrs. Stowe, with evident reluctance to utter the words that followed, "it told us the last time we consulted it that we were all a pack of d——d fools, and we must certainly give up having anything to do with it." Mrs. Kemble was now convulsed with laughter and exclaimed: "Oh! I believe in Planchette! I believe in Planchette," but seeing that Mrs. Stowe was offended and shocked by her levity, changed her tone to seriousness and asked her if she really believed the devil had anything to do with it. Upon the reiteration of Mrs. Stowe's conviction Mrs. Kemble "turned," to use her own language, "in boundless amazement to the younger lady, whose mischievous countenance, with a broad grin upon it, at once settled all my doubts as to the devilish influence under which Planchette had spoken such home truths to her family circle!"

It would be interesting to pursue this digression upon the literary women whose names are part of the Berkshire story, to associate still further with the loveliness of the region hereabouts many others, like Rose Hawthorne Lathrop, author of *Memories of Hawthorne*

(1897), who was born in the "little red house" her father occupied in 1850–51 ; Mrs. Sigourney, whose poem on "Stockbridge Bowl" is worth preserving, and Mrs. Charles Sedgwick whose husband was Catherine's brother, and whose *Talks with My Pupils*, published in 1862, was the outcome of her tender and advisory relations with the young ladies who resorted for thirty years to her school here in Lenox from all parts of the country. Mrs. Sedgwick christened her school a "character-factory" and such she assiduously strove to make it. Her book is really a collection of most stimulating "heart-talks" which I am sure any young lady of the present would find extremely profitable and fascinating reading. I cannot forbear giving one reference from this book to the religious character of Mrs. Kemble-Butler, and any one who has read her *Records of Later Life* will have received the same profound impression concerning this actress, showing that histrionism and moral earnestness are not necessarily antagonistic.

"Mrs. Kemble, the great revealer of Shakespeare," writes Mrs. Sedgwick, "once said to me, that it was with Shakespeare as with the Bible, she never opened it without finding something new. And, in illustration, she quoted a line in *Romeo and Juliet,* which had that day particularly attracted her attention, in which Juliet calls

Romeo 'lover, husband, friend,' making the last epithet the culmination of all the rest. . . . That word FRIEND is a glorious old Saxon word. Do all you can to illustrate its meaning."

The name of another great actress, Charlotte Cushman, belongs to the Lenox story. In the year 1875, after her life work on the stage had been completed, Miss Cushman came, in rather enfeebled health, to this mountain village, where she had purchased a little cottage with the intention of making it her summer home. She was not permitted to enjoy it, however, more than one summer, as she died February 18, 1876, yet the house she occupied is still known as the "Charlotte Cushman cottage."

I am sure this reference to the women who have entwined Lenox with the literary world would be very incomplete if no mention were made of Mrs. Burton Harrison, who for many years has been a summer resident in this mountain village and who makes frequent allusions in her books to Lenox, as a resort, and to the enchanting scenic beauty of the region. Lately another woman distinguished in letters, Mrs. Edith Wharton, has become enamored of the Berkshire country, and after a few years' residence in Lenox is erecting here a country-seat, beautifully located near Laurel Lake, and looking off upon the Hoosacs and the Tyringham Pass. Indeed, it may be said incidentally, this section of the town is full of literary associations. North of Mrs. Wharton's on the high ground rising towards Lenox village stood the home of Fanny Kemble, called by her "The Perch," and still so called; farther round to the east, overlooking the same lake and on the crest of a hill, was the Henry Ward Beecher place, where by a turn of the eyeball that noted preacher said he could command Greylock and the Dome; adjoining the old Beecher place is "Coldbrooke," the summer residence of James Barnes, the war-correspondent and writer; coming nearer the lake is the country-place of the late John O. Sargent, the distinguished Horatian scholar and brother of Epes Sargent, both of whom enjoyed friendships in the innermost circles of American letters; and across the lake five miles distant in the ancient town of Tyringham is Richard Watson Gilder's side-hill farm, where the poet looks northward to the Lenox church over a pleasing prospect, and westward upon "The Shadow Bridge," which each afternoon spans the intervale between him and Bear Mountain opposite.

Laurel Lake from "Walker's Hill."

Lenox in Literature

Returning then from this digression concerning the literary women whose names are associated with Lenox and its environment, we recur once more to what other English travellers have said concerning Berkshire. Charles Kingsley was here in 1874 and compared its forests and streams to "the best parts of the Eifel and Black Forest." Dean Stanley was for some time the guest of Cyrus W. Field, Esq., in Stockbridge, during the autumn of 1878, and he writes to friends in England:

> "I am extremely glad I did not lose this place. It is a village buried among the Berkshire hills, the scene of the first Indian missions, the burial-place of the Indians of this part of America, the residence of the great Calvinist, Jonathan Edwards, the birth, and the burial-place of this family of the Fields."

And we might add that no account of the literary traditions of Berkshire could be written without assigning a large place to this very distinguished family. In the village church at Stockbridge Dean Stanley preached a sermon in which with utter nobility of soul and largeness of vision he recognized the good there was in Edwards's "hard system." "Even in the most unlovely of theologians," the generous-minded Dean of Westminster Abbey said in the sermon referred to, "whether in Geneva or Massachusetts, there is still something to invigorate and to stimulate, when we reflect that they were trying to fortify the eternal principles of truth and righteousness against the temptations which beset us all."

Edwards's *Freedom of the Will*, which Professor Allen says was "one of the literary sensations of the eighteenth century," was written in Stockbridge and published in 1754 and is admittedly one of the mightiest products of the American intellect. The house where it was composed should have been a literary shrine always, no matter to what extent theology may have reacted from the older type. Few towns in America can boast two such Meccas for all literary pilgrims as the house where Hawthorne wrote his *House of the Seven Gables* in 1851, and the house where Jonathan Edwards wrote the *Freedom of the Will* a hundred years earlier—yet the former was burned down, and the latter torn down. It is certainly to be hoped that both these sites will be fittingly marked. Such a monument as that to the Indians, for example, in Stockbridge, a simple column of field-stone, derives new sacredness and charm from the fact that here Dean Stanley stood reverently, remarking to one near, "The grave of the Stockbridge

Indians, the friends of our fathers, places me on the boundary of those days when the savage and the civilized man still met, like Goth and Roman, in the varied vicissitudes of peace and war."

We must pass over with the merest mention the names of other illustrious English travellers who have at various times been guests in Lenox, or the vicinity, and who by their presence here have added to the prestige of the *locale*,—Lord Chief Justice Coleridge, the guest of John E. Parsons of Lenox, Lord Kelvin, the guest of George Westinghouse, Esq., of Lenox, " Ian Maclaren," and Samuel Chisholm, Lord Provost of Glasgow University, the guests of John Sloane, Esq., of Lenox, the Princess Augusta and her husband, a distinguished educator of Germany, guests of Dr. and Mrs. F. P. Kinnicutt. Our purpose is a simple one, to gather together the recorded descriptions of the region on the pages of literature, and so we will offer a few references to the hill-country of Western Massachusetts from the *Letters of Matthew Arnold*. Here is a letter dated Stockbridge, Mass., July 8, 1886 :

" This is a pretty place with many hills of 2000 feet, and one of 3500. There are a great many people in the neighborhood, some of them nice. The country is pleasing but not to be compared to Westmoreland. It is wider and opener, and neither hills nor lakes are so effective. The villas are very pretty. The American wooden villa with its great piazza where the family live in hot weather, is the prettiest villa in the world. And the trees are everywhere; indeed they cover the hills too much, to the exclusion of the truly mountainous effects which we get from the not higher mountains of Langdale."

Again in a letter to Mr. Grant Duff, dated Stockbridge, Mass., July 29, 1886, Matthew Arnold says:

"This Berkshire county in Massachusetts where I now am, which the Americans extol, is not to be compared to the Lakes of Scotland. The heat is great in summer, and in winter the cold is excessive. But the flowers and trees are delightfully interesting";

and after enumerating the varieties of wild flowers he had found in strolls and drives, all of which he calls by their botanical names, he continues:

"What would I give to go in your company for even one mile on any of the roads out of Stockbridge! The trees too delight me. I had no notion what maples were, thinking only of our pretty hedgerow shrub at home, but they are as, of course, you know, trees of the family of our sycamore but more imposing than our sycamore. The American elm I cannot prefer to the English, but still I admire it extremely."

As autumn approaches our distinguished critic becomes rather more reconciled to the climate, which had rather accentuated the heart-trouble from which he suffered. August 24th he writes:

"This place [Stockbridge] has become very enjoyable. I see at last what an American autumn which they so praise is and it deserves the praise given it. I wish you could have been with us yesterday, that is, if you are not nervous in a carriage, for the roads look impossible in places and the hills are awful. We went to a lake called Long Lake near which we could see to the south a wide valley with the Dome and the other Taconic Mountains in the sunset at the end of it. We were perpetually stopping the carriage in the woods through which we drove, the flowers were so attractive. You have no notion how beautiful the asters are till you see them."

Three days later (August 27th) he writes Charles Eliot Norton:

"I like Berkshire more and more. The Dome is a really imposing and beautiful mass; I have seen it now from many points and in many lights, and with ever increasing admiration. I was shown the Green River yesterday, the river immortalized by the American Wordsworth, *i. e.*, Bryant. But the Dome, at any rate, will live in my admiring memory."

On Matthew Arnold's return to England he writes to his daughter in America:

"You cannot think how often Stockbridge and its landscape come into my mind. None of the cities could attach me, not even Boston; but I could get fond of Stockbridge."

But if Arnold could not forgive Berkshire its climate for the sake of its scenery, it is at least admissible and not at all retaliatory to entertain the thought that an Englishman's meteorological tastes may be perverted. Mrs. Kemble-Butler became so converted to Berkshire weather as to taunt her English friends with their leaden skies and ceaseless drizzles, and she chuckles as she writes from Lenox to some one in England: "What a good place you are in to wear out umbrellas!" Indeed, Mrs Jameson when she reaches England is facetious enough to write as follows to Catherine Sedgwick:

"We are having real 'English weather,' leaden sky, fog and a drizzling rain. It reminds me of one of Marryat's stories of an old quartermaster who, returning from a three years' voyage to the East Indies, and approaching the English shore in weather such as this, looked up into the dull sky and hazy atmosphere, and sniffing up the damp air and buttoning his pea-jacket over his chest, exclaimed with exultation, 'Ay, this is something like,—none of your d——d blue skies here!'"

It is not my purpose to collect every " scrap and scription " of what has been written about

Lenox, or its environment, in literature, yet we may turn now from this incomplete presentation of the region as seen through other eyes to a close-range view of this state, rather than county, of Berkshire, for walled in on every side its very isolation has intensified a feeling of unity. Berkshire is an entity by itself rather than a part of something else. It emits like the diamond from its many facets an interior brilliancy no matter on which side you study it. What has Berkshire not given to the literatures of patriotism, religion, education, romance, and poetry! What untold and incalculable literary inspirations has not the Berkshire college in Williamstown, which celebrated eight years ago its centennial, created and fostered! What a student-corps, destined to play a leading part in statesmanship, religion, education, and literature, has had its spirit baptized with the stimulating beauties and glories of a Berkshire environment! If we turn the pages of the educational literature of the nineteenth century in America a distinctively Berkshire name stands out luminously and conspicuously,—Mark Hopkins, President of Williams College, and connected with the institution for almost sixty years, a Thomas Arnold among teachers. If we turn the pages of our early patriotic literature, you cannot read far before you come upon another Berkshire name, Major-General John Paterson of Lenox, the friend, counsellor, and comrade of General Washington throughout that long Revolutionary struggle. There are many references to Lenox in the *Life of General Paterson* by the late Professor Egleston. The literature of American patriotism has no brighter or more thrilling pages than the story of Bennington and the Berkshire troops, with "Parson" Allen of the First Church, Pittsfield, filled with both the ministering and militant spirit; the story of the non-importation compacts, one of which, the original, yellowed with age and bearing the signatures of many yeomen, hangs as we have said, on the walls of the Lenox Library, a thing of pride and inspiration to their descendants; the march and countermarch, campaigns and sufferings of the Berkshire regiment, many of whom were Lenox men inspired by General Paterson's enthusiasm, as told in Field and Holland and the biographies of distinguished soldiers in all the American wars from Paterson to Bartlett. If we turn to the literature of religion we are confronted at once with some of the most massive works on theology the American intellect has yet produced, —a *System of Divinity*, written by Samuel Hopkins, who was for twenty-five years the pastor of the church down yonder in Great Barrington, and who in this theological work, published after leaving Berkshire, moulds New England thought for nearly four generations. To Jonathan Edwards's celebrated treatise on the Will we have referred. Those seven years of Edwards's life in Stockbridge were busier and more productive in a literary way than any other heptade in his life. Other theological works by West, Catlin, and others show the temper and calibre of that olden ministry. It would weary the patience of the reader to recount here all the contributions to religious literature by the Berkshire pulpit. In West's *Life of Samuel Hopkins*, and in Hyde's *Life of Stephen West*, as in all the "Lives" of Edwards, the story between the lines which interests us here is that of the region. A complete bibliographical list of all the theological works, biographies, sermons, and addresses, by those who have at one time and another had a more or less prolonged connection with the Berkshire pulpit, from Edwards and Hopkins to Munger and Gladden and Parkhurst, would include many noteworthy

contributions to American religious literature.
I have re-examined much of this material for
the Berkshire story, and much of it has been
interwoven, or will be, in the progress of these
chapters. One very rare book, *Memoirs of
Housatunnuk Indians*, by Samuel Hopkins (of
Springfield), I have only found copies of in
Boston and Springfield, and it brings one in the
most realistic way face to face with Indian life,
beliefs, and customs in Stockbridge one hundred
and sixty-seven years ago in its truly aboriginal
cast. Here we see the primitive settlements,
with Captain Konkapot at Wnahktukook
(Stockbridge), and Lieutenant Umpachene at
Skatekook (Sheffield), farther down the river,
and now and then Yokun appears on the
scene; we see great meetings between the
Indians and the State Commissioners taking
place with the giving of belts of wampum; we
see Sergeant moving about in the picture, now
preaching in their own tongue to the blank-
eted redskins, now going with them on their
protracted expeditions into the sugar-bush,
where they seem to have been the first to
have discovered the art of making maple-
sugar, and now busy with the scheme that
rested on his heart, the industrial education
of the Indian, thus anticipating by a century

and a half Hampton, Carlisle, and Tuskegee. We read on the pages of this old chronicler the rather astonishing information that "Sergeant was taken with the intermitting [*sic*] fever the common distemper of all new-comers to Housatunnuk"; certainly hygienic conditions are better now and no country is more noted for its salubrity. We also read in this ancient memoir that

"the large heap of stones, I suppose ten cartloads, on the way to Wnahktukook (Stockbridge) have been thrown together by Indians in passing without knowing the end of it, only they (the Indians) say their fathers used to do so and they do it because it was the custom of their fathers."

I cannot believe that Dr. Hopkins understood correctly in this visit of 1734 what later and uniformly has been given as the reason for this collection of stones, viz., to mark a grave, —hence "Monument" Mountain.

But let us come to some of the other great names in American literature which are associated with the Berkshire picture. Miss Catherine Sedgwick and Nathaniel Hawthorne will be noticed in separate chapters. Their names are written imperishably into the region. We have already seen in this chapter the brilliant coterie of women whom Miss

Sedgwick attracted to the Berkshires; and in Hawthorne's *Note-books* the records of the visits of eminent literati are faithfully kept. Oliver Wendell Holmes is a frequent caller; also Herman Melville. Here are other entries: "E. P. Whipple called"; "J. T. Headley called"; "J. R. Lowell called in the evening"; "Walked to Scott's pond [Laurel Lake] with Ellery Channing." Indeed, with Hawthorne's *American Note-books* in hand the Berkshire landscape not only possesses the charm of reflecting from all its varied points and angles his descriptions but is peopled with congenial literary spirits. It is enough to say, in reply to the oft-assertion that Hawthorne's house was in Stockbridge, that while technically that is true the novelist could flip a stone over the line into Lenox, wrote "Lenox" in his note-books, went to the Lenox post-office daily for his mail, and was identified in every way with Lenox.

Stand with me a moment, then, on the site of the "little red house," and let me call up some other sacred literary associations of the region, as our eyes rest here and there on the varied points of interest. Remember that the spot where we are standing is itself redolent with the inspirations of Hawthorne's

Lenox in Literature 97

genius and impregnated with the memories of his great literary achievements. " Stockbridge Bowl" lies down at our feet, beyond are the mountains, and behind us to the right rises Bald Head," while to the left, also in the rear, the ground continually ascending is crowned at its summit by the ancient town of Lenox, with its many villas peeping out from their eminences and over all the gilded belfry-tower of the village church looming up behind. It is a spectacle of rare beauty profaned only by eyes that cannot see its loveliness. "Monument" in front has its separate delight as in the *Note-book*, changing from green to red and from red to white to suit the seasons, now " enveloped in mist," now " enwreathed with cloud," now a "headless sphinx wrapped in a Persian shawl." Clad in the investiture of Hawthorne's poetic conceptions, it greets with reflected glare from its " beetling cliffs " the first pencillings of dawn, and " floats in a sea of chrysolite and opal " at close of day.

Hawthorne's genius, however, is not the only one which comes back to us from its rugged dales and yonder picturesque and entrancing landscape. William Cullen Bryant, who was born in Cummington, in the neighboring county of Hampshire, November 3, 1794, came to Great Barrington in 1816, and opening there a law-office passed the ensuing six years in the Berkshire village. Here he was "town clerk," here married. Though his earliest consciousness of poetic power had been awakened before coming hither, yet its acknowledgment by the world was delayed through his own modesty in making public the productions of his genius. Anticipating his friend Catherine Sedgwick in the neighboring village of Stockbridge, who in 1822 literally "awoke one morning and found herself famous" through the appearance of her first novel, *A New England Tale*, Bryant by the publication of *Thanatopsis* in 1817 and *Lines to a Waterfowl* in 1818 evoked instant recognition. It was impossible for Great Barrington to keep him from the larger field his talents demanded, and the poet removed to New York. But his poems *Green River* and *Monument Mountain* are inseparably and imperishably associated with his Berkshire residence; the former the Waumpa-nick-se-poot of the Housatonic Indians, and the latter their Maus-wa-see-khi. *Green River* reflects, as the tranquil waters the sylvan or pastoral scenes along its banks, the inner questionings of the poet

"... forced to drudge for the dregs of men
And scrawl strange words with the barbarous pen,"

who was beginning to find the prosaic duties of town clerk irksome.

"Yet fair as thou art, thou shun'st to glide
Beautiful stream! by the village side;
But windest away from haunts of men,
To quiet valley and shaded glen,—
And forest, and meadow, and slope of hill
Around thee, are lonely, lovely, and still.
Lonely—save when, by thy rippling tides,
From thicket to thicket the angler glides;
Or the simpler comes with basket and book
For herbs of power on thy banks to look;
Or haply, some idle dreamer, like me
To wander, and muse, and gaze on thee

. . . . . .

But I wish that fate had left me free
To wander these quiet haunts with thee
Till the eating cares of earth should depart
And the peace of the scene pass into my heart."

Monument Mountain is the exquisitely beautiful recital of the Indian legend of a maiden who, crossed in love, because she could not marry her cousin, madly and fatally threw herself from its "hanging crags" and "bare old cliffs"—

' Hugh pillars that in middle heaven upbear
Their weather-beaten capitals, here dark
With the thick moss of centuries, and there

Of chalky-whiteness where the thunderbolt
Has splintered them."

Look again from the "boudoir-window of the red house" at the "round head of the dome of Taconic" in the far distance, generally, says Hawthorne, "a dark blue unvaried mountain-top." Then follow around to the right the miles of "intervening hill-country" until the eye rests on "Bald Head" rising directly back of us, and then read those descriptive preludes in *The Wonder Book for Children.* It is a region which gives back to us the greatest American novelist, Nathaniel Hawthorne, and as we stand looking down at "Stockbridge Bowl," a burnished mirror at our feet, how thronging the literary associations! — the change of its name from old Mahkeenac to "Stockbridge Bowl" by Catherine Sedgwick; the poem of which it is the subject, "high set among the breezy hills, a classic vase," by Mrs. Sigourney; and finally the walks of Hawthorne with his children across its "adamantine surface" in the winter season. At the foot of "Monument" as the eye turns to the left is "Ice Glen" where Crazy Bet in *A New England Tale* finds in its wildness congenial society for her disordered intellect, and whence she roams to the "very top of

Taghcounick." Farther around but hidden by the near shoulder of "Rattlesnake" is the Tyringham valley, where last summer (1901) an ex-President of the United States had his country-seat, adjoining that of his friend, the poet, Richard Watson Gilder, whose *Rhyme of Tyringham* and *Evening in Tyringham Valley* are in rhythm, description, and depth of feeling in Mr. Gilder's best vein. I may say, in passing, that this very spot where we are standing, the site of Hawthorne's "little red house," Mr. Gilder thinks should be appropriately marked, and in a letter to the author expressed his preference that the memorial should take the form of an exedra. It is a focal spot where Holmes and Lowell and Hawthorne stood and joined hands with Bryant across the little lake, while lesser workmen in the guild of letters oft-visitors hither range themselves around, and up from the village-on-the-plain just over the brow of yonder knoll come the memories of one of the most illustrious families in this country of ours, the distinguished family of the Rev. David Dudley Field, pastor of the Stockbridge church (1819–37), one of whom, a well-known and voluminous contributor to the literature of travel, the Rev. Henry M. Field, D.D., is now enjoying his respite after a busy "day's work" in his loved Berkshire village.

My effort to trace the literary thread in the Berkshire story, so imperfectly done, is nearly finished. William Ellery Channing spent several weeks in Lenox, a guest at the Berkshire Coffee-House (now Curtis Hotel), though most of the time in the company of the Sedgwicks, during the summer of 1842, his last summer on earth, and the last public address he ever gave was delivered August 1st in the village church on the hill. This period of his *Memoirs* abounds in the most extravagant praise of the Berkshire environment, the charming informality and sweet dignity of the life at the Sedgwicks', the "fine sights" and "pleasant excursions," and above all the liberty-loving spirit which a mountain-country created. He calls it all "truly Elysian" and says again and again it was the "happiest summer of his life." The occasion of the address from which we have taken a local reference (see p. 9) was the anniversary of emancipation in the West Indies and of Channing at the time of its delivery there are many beautiful memorabilia in the *Memoirs of Channing*, and in Catherine Sedgwick's *Life and Letters*. Mrs. Charles Sedgwick says: "I shall never

Main Street, Lenox, looking down from the Church-on-the-Hill, Rattlesnake and Monument Mountains in the distance.

forget Dr. Channing's appearance in the pulpit that day. His countenance was full of spiritual beauty and he looked like one inspired."

Another distinguished preacher whose memory is imperishably intertwined with the literary traditions of Lenox is Henry Ward Beecher, and one of his best-known books, *Star Papers*, is a Berkshire nature-study. Mr. Beecher acquired property in Lenox in 1853, and thence on for a few summers took his vacations in these tip-top eyries of the Berkshire hills. Previous to his Berkshire sojourn he had been taking his annual outing at Salisbury, on the south side of Taghconic Dome, but in the summer of 1853 he goes prospecting into the hill-country for a summer home. As he passes through Great Barrington he feels that " it is one of those places which one never enters without wishing never to leave ; it is a place to be desired as a summer residence," but on reaching Stockbridge he writes :

"I came near purchasing the old house of Dr. West for a summer-home; it is located on the northern ridge where one sees the Housatonic winding, in great circuits, through the valley and the horizon piled and terraced with mountains."

Mr. Beecher adds, as he passes through Stockbridge, " an excellent hotel is kept and is usually well filled in summer with refugees from the arid city." Lenox, however, lured the rider on, rising every now and then to "overlook the bold prospect," and here he confesses himself captivated by the "singular purity and exhilarating effects of its air and by the beauty of its mountain scenery. One would hardly seek another home in summer, if he should spend July or October in Lenox." I am not going to weary the reader with the vivid descriptions of Berkshire scenery or spread out the pastoral idylls in prose which everywhere abound throughout the *Star Papers*, showing how thoroughly Mr. Beecher's poetic temperament, which he says he received from his mother, was *en rapport* with the region.

I have not tried to make a list of distinguished literati who have from time to time sojourned for a longer or a shorter period in Lenox. Such a list would include nearly every one of prominence in American letters. It is quite enough to add, in conclusion, that Lenox and its environment are becoming known through specific books on the Berkshire country. Catherine Sedgwick wove the scenes and the people of her native region into some of her stories, and we have already al-

Lenox in Literature

luded to the part Berkshire plays in Hawthorne's *Wonder Book for Children*. Very lately two books have appeared, John Coleman Adams's *Nature Studies in Berkshire*, a charming prose-poem devoted exclusively to the natural beauty of the region, and Edward Bellamy's *Duke of Stockbridge*. Mrs. Burton Harrison in *Leaves from the Diary of Ruth Marchmont, Spinster*, deals rather with social Lenox, yet she makes her "spinster" ardent in praise of the scenic beauty.

"Some of the views from the verandas of this house where I am staying," writes Ruth, "are like Turner's best canvases in point of rich, soft, luminous color. I do not wonder that wealthy, leisurely folk come here to linger away from New York and Boston until nearly Christmas-time. The air of the place, the houses and the entertainments are more quiet and mellow than anything in Newport or Bar Harbor. The inevitable dinners and luncheons go on just as in the other resorts named, but one comes in to dress for them after rides and drives into the very fastnesses of Nature, through shady, moss-carpeted woods amid a rain of tinted leaves, or upon good roads high among the hills looking over miles of peaceful rural country. . . . There is more land enclosed here, for purposes of pleasure, around the houses, than in most places of resort I know; and I dare say that, after all, is what gives Lenox its air of undeniable good-breeding and reserve."

It fits into this reference to country-houses in

the Berkshire resort to give a description of one from another author, Charles Dudley Warner, who has brought Lenox into his story, *A Little Journey around the World.*

"The Arbuser cottage at Lenox was really a magnificent villa. Richardson had built it. At a distance it had the appearance of a mediæval structure with its low doorways, picturesque gables, and steep roofs, and in its situation on a gentle swell of green turf backed by native forest-trees it imparted to the landscape an ancestral tone which is much valued in these days. But near to, it was seen to be mediævalism adapted to the sunny hospitality of our climate, with generous verandas and projecting balconies shaded by gay awnings, and within spacious, open to the breezes, and from its broad windows offering views of lawns and flower-beds and ornamental trees, of a great sweep of pastures, and forests and miniature lakes, with graceful and reposeful hills on the horizon."

There are other references in Mr. Warner's book to Lenox — mostly to social Lenox, a theme which appears and reappears in Robert Grant's *Face to Face;* and there are other books, of lesser worth, where we thread our way through familiar Berkshire scenes.

Is it any wonder then that a Berkshire man finds it impossible to speak of his country in anything else than the language of exaggeration? It certainly is not the least charm about

Lenox, and its environment in the Berkshire hills, that the whole country hereabouts is associated with some of the mightiest intellects and most graceful writers America has produced.

III

CATHERINE MARIA SEDGWICK: HER MESSAGE AND HER WORK

THE fate of the popular novelist is pathetic: like some rare flower, radiant and redolent, yet after it is "pressed," its beauty faded, its fragrance departed, its distorted form brittle and ready to drop to pieces,—a breath almost, and it is gone. Thousands and hundreds of thousands of readers in our own and other lands literally hung on Miss Sedgwick's pen during the long period of her literary creativeness, lasting about thirty-six years, and waited eagerly for her books to appear; now she is scarcely read, and only faintly known, more's the pity! A pioneer in American literature, a voluminous writer of novels, perhaps a score in all, and short tales, the intimate friend of the leading thinkers in many countries besides her own, a moralist who never loses sight of the highest ideals, a keen observer of life and of the manners and customs of her own times, a passionate lover of nature and thoroughly *en rapport* with the scenic fascinations of her native Berkshire, Miss Catherine Sedgwick needs to make no apology to the present age for that very natural liking we all have to be remembered, but deserves, on the contrary, to be perpetually enshrined in her appropriate niche in the world's great Temple of Literature.

Edmund Gosse has perhaps rightly said of eighteenth-century English novelists that the names of three only stand in the front rank: Richardson, Fielding, and Smollett; but who ever reads their works to-day outside of the class-room? Defoe's *Robinson Crusoe* (1719), Swift's *Gulliver's Travels* (1726), and Goldsmith's *Vicar of Wakefield* (1766), and one or two other tales by English writers of that century may be found in the book-stalls to-day. Smollett's *Peregrine Pickle* (1751), Fielding's *Tom Jones* (1749), Johnson's *Rasselas* (1759), Sterne's *Tristram Shandy* (1761) and *Sentimental Journey* (1768), complete the list of English works of fiction which may with any fairness be said to have retained their hold on the reading-public, albeit a very faint and possibly weakening one. Literary immortality is not easily won. Catherine Sedgwick belongs to another century,— the nineteenth; and one would not be justified in placing her with the great immortals, but certainly she takes a foremost place among the women who have during these last hundred years wrought at the "forge of thought,"—Miss Edgeworth, Jane Austen, Miss Mitford, Miss Craik-Mulock, Miss Martineau, Mrs. Jameson, Miss Strickland, Mrs. Sigourney, Miss Mühlbach, Miss Kirkland, Mrs. Harriet Beecher Stowe, Miss Marian Evans (Geo. Eliot), Mme. Dudevant (Geo. Sand), Margaret Fuller Ossoli, Mrs. Oliphant, Mrs. Prentiss, Mrs. Alcott, Amelia E. Barr, *et multæ aliæ*. Possibly I have mentioned some names in this list of female writers, once splendid and potent, names to conjure by, now dimmed and forgotten; yet what of that? They rendered a real service in their day. Have they no claims on us for that?

Catherine Maria Sedgwick shares with Cooper and Irving the place of pioneers in American fiction, Irving finding his materials in the Dutch region along the Hudson; Cooper his in the red man's wigwam and war-path; and Miss Sedgwick hers in the simple, rustic scenes of New England life. Each was original in the field chosen, and the first to enter it; therefore a sort of prototype of all the rest who have gleaned after them, as Mrs. Stowe later was the first to enter our great Southern section and portray its life. These foundation writers deserve to be recalled for what they did. Irving's grave at Sleepy Hollow is the shrine of literary pilgrims, as the vandal-hands of those who have chipped its slab attest; Cooper's overlooking Glimmerglass and hard by the church where he worshipped is another; but someway I greatly fear Catherine Sedgwick's at Stockbridge misses this grateful incense of the remembrance of her countrymen. And yet her novels, a score or more, served in their way as distinct a purpose as either of those "immortals," were quite as popular in England as they were in America, passed through edition after edition and into translations in French, Italian, German, and Spanish, and were reviewed by such magazines here as the *North American,* and on the other side as the *London Quarterly,* *Athenæum,* and *Westminster.* The distinguished Miss Mitford writes Miss Sedgwick from England (September 6, 1830), when our American novelist was still in the beginning of her literary career, this very graceful tribute:

"I want to express my strong feelings of obligation for *Redwood* and *A New England Tale*. . . ." "Cooper," Miss Mitford continues, "is certainly, next to Scott, the most popular novel-writer of the age. Washington Irving enjoys a high and fast reputation; the eloquence of Dr. Channing if less widely is perhaps more deeply felt; and *a lady whom I need not name* takes her place amongst these great men as Miss Edgeworth does among our Scotts and Chalmerses"; and Miss Mitford adds, "your novels and those of Cooper will make American literature known and valued in England."

Let us try then to gain a nearer view of this first female novelist of America,—first certainly in the order of time, and yielding only the first place in the matter of contemporaneous popularity to Harriet Beecher Stowe of all the women writers America has yet produced.

Catherine Sedgwick is a distinctive Berkshire product. A physical environment of mountains, if one lends himself to their influence, their ruggedness and beauty, the lovely views and vistas they command, the breadth and sweep of vision from their summits, the lights and shades and hues of their slopes,—the green of summer, the fire-red tints of autumn, the hoary-heads of winter, the cloud-shadows always playing up and down their sides; a physical environment of this sort, I say, must produce, has always produced, a distinct race of men. But Nature never reveals her secrets to those who only get out of her the streams which turn their mills, or the ore which fills their coffers, or the building-sites which put a fancy value on their farms. Our gods and shrines give to us only what we bring to them. Catherine Sedgwick responded to the entrancing picturesqueness of the region with rare loveliness of character and to the far-off reach of vision the mountains afforded with a breadth of intellectual vision which made her seventy years ahead of her time. We have only now just begun, so to speak, to come around to her views, and her first novel, *A New England Tale*, which in my judgment she never surpassed, was written seventy-eight years ago. What a beautiful tribute to that loveliness of character so conspicuous in Miss Catherine Sedgwick is this from her intimate friend, Mrs. Anna Jameson, the distinguished author, who, about to leave America, writes (December 23, 1837) to her American craftswoman :

"I never think of you without being glad and grateful have known you, to have you to think of and talk of; farewell, and God bless you; keep me a little wee corner in that good heart"; and later (February, 1838), when actually sailing away from these shores, writes Miss

8

Sedgwick thus: "About four in the afternoon I was told we were just losing sight of land, so I crawled up and took one last look as the shores of America faded away under the western sun and in my heart I stretched out my arms to you for a last embrace and blessed that land because it was *your* land."

But with this attractive and winning character, which all who knew her felt the spell of, went great independence, liberty, breadth of thought, and freedom of utterance to the last degree. She was heretic, moralist, Christian all in one. As she herself says in her autobiography, and as her novels and tales everywhere attest, " Love of freedom and a habit of doing our own thinking has always characterized our clan." The dominant theology of her time, whose tyranny was the blight upon all spiritual life, was mercilessly exposed and rendered *hors de combat* at the point of her pen.

Yes, mountain scenery has a way of beautifying and broadening, inspiring, strengthening, and enriching character, so that what Miss Sedgwick became she owed in some degree to her environment, but birth and training were even far more creative influences. Born in 1789 in Stockbridge, she was reared amid plenty, culture, and refinement, and the society of kinsfolk who, with her, had in their veins the very best blood in Berkshire. She lived to be seventy-eight years old, dying in 1867, and roughly it may be said that the first half of her life was spent in Stockbridge and the latter half in Lenox, though both periods were much diversified by regular and prolonged stays in New York, at the homes of her brothers, themselves men of the highest legal and social standing in that city. Catherine Sedgwick came of distinguished parentage; her father eminent throughout the commonwealth and country for his public services as a soldier of the Revolution, Congressman, United States Senator, and Judge of the Supreme Court, and enjoying the rare honor of Washington's friendship and confidence; her mother a Dwight, connected by birth with the Williams, the Hopkins, and the Sargents, "river-gods," as they were called, of the valleys to the east. Catherine's girlhood was just one of those ordinary girlhoods which belong to any one of good family; and especially to one whose father served in the highest public station, only at home for brief intervals. At eleven years of age, in the year 1800, she visits New York and attends dancing-school; at thirteen we find her at Payne's school at Boston; and during the years immediately following at school in Vermont and in Albany; and many visits to New York City were also recorded. To one who reflects on the means of getting about in those early days, and on the very brilliant intellectual company into which she was constantly thrown, it will not seem strange that Catherine was early broadened and matured beyond the maidens of her native village, or moulded by influences which ripened and deepened her mental and spiritual life. In 1807 her mother died, Catherine then being eighteen, but while a loss it was in one sense a relief, as the mother had been a chronic nervous invalid, whose rest came only in the mercifulness of death itself. In the six years following, her father marrying again after, as Miss Sedgwick says, the traditional "year and a day," the New York visits are many and frequent; and we are to think of the New York of that period as an altogether different affair from the modern, enormous city. The future novelist was there gathering all unknown to herself the materials for some of her best stories—*The Linwoods*, *Live and Let Live*, *Married or Single* for example, which give us a very valuable picture of early New York. In 1813 we find Catherine in Boston with her father, whom she accompanies in his invalid condition for treatment, and there at her aged parent's deathbed the services of a minister, William Ellery Channing, are procured and there begins the deep and abiding friendship of Miss Sedgwick and Dr. Channing, which lasted until the death of that illustrious teacher; a friendship which doubtless went far to lead Miss Sedgwick, eight years after her father's death, out of the orthodox pale into the Unitarian Church and thus into the extremely effective service she rendered the cause of truth by subjecting the sterile orthodoxy of her day to the sting of her satire and the powerfulness of her rebukes, so justly deserved.

I pass over the years of Miss Sedgwick's life immediately after her father's death, when she was twenty-four years of age, and was duly installed housekeeper by the return of her step-mother to her own people. In *Married or Single* Miss Sedgwick makes one of her characters say, "My father married for his second wife the *tenth dilution* of a woman"; and I have wondered if the novelist had not in mind her own step-mother, to whom she refers in her biography in the not very complimentary way,—as having "left us without inspiring either respect or affection." From 1813, then, Catherine was housekeeper in the old Stockbridge home for her brothers, during a period of ten years or so, with visits thrown in here and there, to Boston, New York, Philadelphia, Baltimore, and Washington. The "War of 1812" came and went, and during one of the winters of that war some "French officers in the British service were quartered at Stockbridge as prisoners," affording Catherine many agreeable diversions. The country was developing a national character; the "era of good feeling" was approaching; the democracy of Jefferson, Madison, and Monroe was steadily tending towards a more conservative ideal; the great Erie Canal was being built; already great inventions were startling the world; and in New York City where Catherine passed so much of her time De Witt Clinton was the stuff mayors were made of. There was, however, no fictitious literature, or what there was, was so under the ban that to read novels was to court the wrath of God and invite the disfavor of the Church. New England was being torn and rent by the coming of the Unitarian schism, and in 1819, only two years before Miss Sedgwick withdrew from orthodoxy, the Unitarian Church was formally launched. The very next year after her change of faith appeared her first novel

(1822), and what she calls a "little tract" ran through several editions here and abroad; surely a phenomenal thing. There had been no literary antecedents; Miss Sedgwick was a woman of thirty-three years when she became an author, and had never written before. Scott had begun eight years before his Waverley novels; Irving was just beginning to be known; Cooper had answered two years earlier the British taunt, "Who ever reads an American book?" by commencing his Leather-stocking Series; Hawthorne was but eighteen and Bulwer but seventeen; Thackeray was eleven, and Dickens and Harriet Beecher Stowe but ten; and Marian Evans was toddling, a girl of two. And here was a woman of thirty-three, who had never shown literary workmanship, at a time when the novel was tabooed, achieving instant and world-wide fame! And achieving it, too, by a brilliant but fearless arraignment of the orthodox faith of New England. She literally "awoke to find herself famous"; and not only famous, but the target of many unkind reproaches. Her first book, *A New England Tale*, had accomplished its purpose; and her polished quiver had winged its way straight to the vulnerable part of New England theology. Dogma was shown up, with no unsparing hand, associated with sterile and unlovely spiritual life; the scene of her first story is laid in her native town of Stockbridge. Usually literary promise precedes great workmanship in letters; there are hints that a star is on the eve of being discovered; but in this case it bursts full-orbed upon the world without a warning.

Everybody was surprised, including the author. She writes soon after the appearance of her book:

"I protest against being supposed to make any pretension as an author: my production is a very small affair anyway. . . . I hardly know any treasure I would not exchange to be where I was before my crow-tracks passed into the hands of printer's devils. I began that little story as a tract and because I wanted some pursuit, and felt spiritless and sad, and thought I might perhaps lend a helping hand to some of the humbler virtues."

Thence on the life-story of Catherine Maria Sedgwick is simply the story of her books and in her books, one following another in rapid succession for thirty-six years, interrupted only in 1839 by a trip to England and Europe, where she already had made hosts of friends by her romances. Two years after *A New England Tale* followed *Red-*

vood (1824), and immediately ran through several editions, appearing abroad in English French, German, Italian, and Spanish reprints: a book of which G. P. R. James says: "No home ought to be without a copy for study and amusement." Her brother writes her from New York: "The book-sellers are all teasing me to know when another work will come from the author of *Redwood*. They say it will go as well or better than one from Cooper or Irving." *The Travellers* followed in the next year (1825); and two years later (1827), her most celebrated work, *Hope Leslie*, a tale of the early colonists, of which Donald G. Mitchell says in his recent *American Lands and Letters:*

"I can recall even now with vividness the great relish with which — more than sixty years ago — a company of school-boys in the middle of New England devoured its pages and lavished their noisy sympathies upon the perils of 'Everell' or the daring of the generous 'Maganisca.'"

With the publication of *Clarence* (1830), *The Linwoods* (1835), and *Tales and Sketches* (1835), Miss Sedgwick's literary fame was secure; the only difficulty was to keep up with the demand. It was not far from this time that Catherine removed to Lenox for her summer home, making her abode with her brother Charles, who was for nearly forty years the Clerk of the Courts in that mountain town, then the county seat of Berkshire, a dignity it maintained for eighty-one years. Now a fashionable resort, and bereft of its character as a seat of learning, culture, and great social distinction, save as it shines by the reflected light of the great wealth and refinement of those who have pre-empted its heights for magnificent and costly villas, Lenox was then in the zenith of its glory as the shire-town. It is with this town, then, that Miss Sedgwick's later life is to be identified; and it is no wonder that subsequently with Hawthorne, Fanny Kemble, John O. Sargent, Henry Ward Beecher, and Miss Sedgwick living in the immediate neighborhood, and such persons as Lowell, Holmes, Fields, Sumner, and Channing to be seen in their fellowship, Lenox should have been fairly entitled to its high literary renown.

We purposely turned from the story of Miss Sedgwick's books to the town where she cast in the lot of her later years, though with regular winter sojourns in New York City, in order that in returning to the record

of her works we may notice the distinct change
in her literary purpose and achievement.
Fourteen years of elaborate story-writing are
followed by fourteen years of tales for children: *Home* (1836); *The Poor Rich Man and
the Rich Poor Man* (1836); *Live and Let
Live* (1837); *Love-token for Children* (1838);
Means and Ends (1838); *Stories for Young
Persons* (1840); *Wilton Harvey;* *Morals and
Manners* (1846); *Facts and Fancies for School
Days; Mount Righi Boy* (1848); *City Clerk
and his Porter* (1850); and *The Irish Girl*
(1850). Many of these passed through several
editions; and the first five named I would
earnestly commend to all. All these short
stories for juvenile readers have the ideal
home as the refrain and underlying thought
of their simple tales. *Live and Let Live* ought
to be bound up with the Bible and called the
"Epistle to the Americans," by Saint Catherine; and then every housewife should read it
at least once a year. It tells the story of the
daughter of a gentlewoman going out to
service, and the whole domestic economy of
homes is shown up truthfully. It abounds in
practical common-sense. It might be criticised as too Utopian for this work-a-day world,
but that's what we are always saying about

ideals that seem too high. *Home* is another one of these short stories whose purpose is sufficiently told in its title, but the story itself is without action,—a fault that could in a general way be urged against all Miss Sedgwick's larger works. Plot and counter-plot, uncertainty as to the way the story will end, and the ability to manage dramatic situations without, so to speak, lugging them in — all these Miss Sedgwick's books are sadly deficient in and that is one reason why she is no longer read. But the question will arise, What do we read novels for? For their story merely? Or for their philosophy of life, their description of manners and customs, their literary workmanship, and a host of other things more important? Miss Sedgwick was essentially the moralist, more than the story-teller; and in these short stories written by the mature woman in the prime of her vigor she reaches her high-water mark. They reached multitudes, passed through several editions, were universally commended, and to this day and for this day might be read with unspeakable profit. The discipline of home, the courtesy and sacrifice and refinement that should obtain in the family, the development of the child by emphasizing self-

Catherine Maria Sedgwick

ontrol rather than mere parental control, he treatment of domestic help, the care of he children's reading, the earnest and contant commendation of the spiritual life, the ιatred of shams, the unwisdom of the acumulation of large fortunes for children, the pirit of democracy, the cultivation of the menities of life, conversation at table, habits of politeness and reverence, the true manιood and womanhood—all these make a message for *to-day;* I have felt my own heart noved and stirred by listening to the sublime :thical philosophy of these short stories; and feel ready to endorse what Harriet Martineau aid of them : " Wonderfully beautiful."

When Miss Sedgwick had fulfilled her purose of speaking to the young people of the vorld in these short ethical tractates, she laid ιside her pen for awhile. She was then sixtyιne years old; Mitchell calls her " the fine old ady of the Berkshire highlands." With a are record of achievement, with the rarest riendships at home and abroad, it might have ;eemed natural to lay down the pen forever, ιarticularly as Dickens, Thackeray, Lytton, Reade were splendid luminaries, and new starςeniuses, Marian Evans and Mrs. Stowe were ιlready rising, while Catherine Sedgwick's star was westering. But the old spell was upon her; one more message must be said, and at sixty-eight she brings out her last great work, *Married or Single* (1857). I have omitted from the record of her books two biographies which she wrote, one on *Miss Lucretia Davidson, a Poet*, and one on *Joseph Curtis, a Model Man;* also a book of travels recounting her stay in England and Europe, *Letters from Abroad to Kindred at Home* (1841). Any such toiler as this woman could rightly have pleaded at sixty-eight — only two years from the three-score-and-ten mark — exemption from further service, but it is a great tribute, I think, to her force as a writer that this last novel, *Married or Single*, was one of her very best. Doctor A. P. Peabody pronounced it "*the best* of the series which she wrote." It has more action than her other stories; more literary workmanship; is full of bits of wisdom on the married state; and was written to combat the idea that an unmarried woman must necessarily view her life as useless. Miss Sedgwick was a believer in marriage; but she did not believe that a single life need make any one unhappy or useless as a member of society. The scenes of the story are laid in New York City for the most part, and portray ocial customs. The preparation of the book ras slow and laborious at her age, and accompanied by an extremely lonely feeling that her ld readers had passed away; yet she persevered and accomplished the work she had in and. The pen was then put away, and her iission done. Ten years followed, during /hich her life was a sweet benediction in and ut of the family circle, a period of pleasant nemories and tender ministries, of rich friendhips and correspondence; the slow sinking of er sun beneath the western horizon, a mild ight of peace and restfulness suffusing all, and he hush of evening's silent tread stealing upon ife's long and busy day. Catherine Sedgwick lied in 1867, at the age of seventy-eight, and s buried in the Stockbridge Cemetery surounded by the dust of many generations of er kinsfolk.

If there were space it would be a tribute vorth the while to record the intimate friendhips of this woman with the great of her own and, and of the various countries of Europe. \ few only must suffice. *Friendships* they vere, real, intense, and abiding. Sismondi, Miss Frederika Bremer, Mrs. Jameson, William Cullen Bryant, and Dr. Channing, with Fanny Kemble, who was lured to the Berkshires by

Miss Sedgwick's influence, and afterwards spent many years in Lenox as her constant and intimate friend, have left beautiful tributes to her.

"It is long since I have written you dearest Catherine," writes Mrs. Jameson; "long since I have heard from you. One might as well have friends in heaven as across the Atlantic" — that was sixty years ago when mail delivery across the ocean was not as now a matter of five or six days — "but your kind affectionate face is before me and I feel that I cannot afford to be forgotten by you, my good and dear friend."

Miss Kemble writes, "Catherine Sedgwick is my best friend in this country," and those who know the story of the intellectual company in the Lenox Sedgwick home, graced so often by Miss Kemble's appearance, and honored by her Shakspearian readings, at which many literary people were present, can well believe that theirs was no common friendship.

Dr. Channing spent his last summer on earth in Lenox, and thus writes June 12, 1842:

"This summer I have determined to try inland air, and am in the mountainous district of Massachusetts. . . . One of my great pleasures is that my friend Miss Sedgwick lives a door or two from me. I wish

Catherine Maria Sedgwick.

[*From the painting by Ingham.*]

you could see her in her family almost worshipped not for her genius, but for her loveliness of character and the shedding of blessed influences."

William Cullen Bryant, who was her very warm and true friend throughout a half-century and whose genius was in a way discovered by the Sedgwicks, who urged him to leave Great Barrington, where he was a young lawyer and the town clerk, and come to New York, has left a picture of her as she was when Ingham painted his fine portrait of her (1820): " Well-formed, slightly inclining to plumpness, with regular features, eyes beaming with benevolence, a pleasing smile, a soft voice, and gentle and captivating manners." Bryant's tribute to her character at her death is exquisite, but is too long to be reproduced here.

And these were only a few of her friends. She knew Longfellow, and Dana, and Haleck, and Cooper, and Willis, and Hawhorne, and Irving, and Fields, and Sumner, and Curtis, and Mrs. Stowe, and Mrs. Howe, and Bayard Taylor, and on the other side she made the acquaintance of Hallam and Macaulay and Carlyle. And yet she shines not by their reflected light; rather do they themselves borrow something from her, though they give more.

Of the memories of Miss Sedgwick in Lenox and Stockbridge, of the many references to her loved Berkshire in her works, and of the services she rendered the cause of liberal theology much could be written, but I pass on to speak in closing of her place in literature.

It is evident when Cooper's and Irving's works are still read, and Miss Sedgwick, their contemporary, is only dimly remembered, if at all, that her works are not of the first order in a literary point of view. They lack action, and they lack style, or rather because the "style is the man," they lack style because the woman herself was perfectly modest and transparent. Still there are quotable bits, and the characters are many of them vividly drawn; and the philosophy of the whole is sunny, profound, truthful, liberal, and deeply religious. Miss Mitford is, as she says in writing to a friend, "surprised at the freedom from cant in Miss Sedgwick's works, considering the do-me-good nature of her books." They are moral tales pre-eminently, with the ever-accompanying thread of love,—a string on which she ties her pearls of wisdom and ethical philosophy; but they are no ordinary pearls,—the superficial advice, the homely counsel, the preaching of pious exhortations,—rather are they the choicest possible truths, the union of the liberal and the deeply spiritual spirit, the deepest and sanest counsels, living inspirations and impulses of power, seed-truths which must fructify once planted in the soil of the heart. Miss Sedgwick's books are studies in ethics. Take Bryant's summing up of her character: "*an unerring sense of rectitude, a love of truth, a ready sympathy, an active and cheerful beneficence, winning and gracious manners,*" and add anything if you can. He knew her; and tell me if a character such as that would not be sane and deep in its ethical teaching. Her books are not "goody-goody," yet she never wrote one without a purpose. She portrayed sin but always to make one loathe it; never, as so many of our present-day novelists do, to make it attractive. To give to prurient scenes realism in the name of art, to array moral rot in a shining verbal vesture and so degrade literary workmanship, as do some whose books make our libraries a doubtful blessing, was far, very far from her. On the contrary, to preach and rant and exhort and nag, she was equally far from. She taught by examples not maxims. Daniel Prime in *Tales and Sketches*, a typical avaricious fiend, whose palm so itches for gold that he slays his own daughter, in whose favor the will of her grandfather was drawn, and by the murder of whom, being a minor, the father hoped to get her fortune, is a sermon in himself without a moral being drawn. Dame Wilson in *A New England Tale*, a cruel, grasping, selfish, and unlovely creature of most faultless orthodoxy, tells in clarion tones though altogether by inference the perfectly sterile living which may go with mere intellectual acceptance of a creed. Miss Sedgwick was versed in the theology of the day, and the vigorous raps she gives it are severe, and ingenious, and bitter. It is no wonder, as her brother wrote her, "the Calvinists are miffed"—but that was her mission to get people to live right. It was life, not belief, she was after; and she valorously, fearlessly went at it. She was radical, but constructive; liberal but spiritual; independent, but modest and sweet; religious, but no canting fanatic with a hobby; literary, but not a juggler with words, nor would she degrade her art by a flesh-tinted realism; ethical, but not hortatory; and truthful, but not dogmatic. As Horace Mann once said of Miss Sedgwick: "She is, indeed, a noble woman. Humanity exhales from her whole being. Her benevo-

Catherine Maria Sedgwick

lence, conscientiousness, and reverence express themselves in all her novels." It is impossible to fix her exact place in the literature of America. She was a pioneer in American letters. She made American books respected abroad. She was perfectly fearless, as is shown by using the novel to convey truth, and by her sharp arraignment of New England theology. She taught high and sane ethics. She was a keen observer and the manners and life of her age are there photographed on her page. She loved Berkshire and many are the allusions to it in her works. She had intimate friends among the great everywhere. She possessed a beautiful character. She wrought diligently and well, producing many books. She is second only to Mrs. Stowe among American women of letters.

I will close with just one paragraph from *A New England Tale*, her first and to me her best book. It is a passage which more than any other shows what she was after; her mission to get people to see what was the real heart of religion, a life of obedience, of service, and sacrifice, and sympathy, and courtesy, and not psalm-singing, church-going, prayers, and Bible-reading; love, righteousness, truth, not mere piety and creed.

Dame Wilson had been all her long life a strict orthodox believer, but had never done any one a kindness; was the very innermost soul of hard-hearted, close-fisted, harsh-tongued repulsiveness, though outwardly respectable. Her ward and niece, Jane Elton, was her pet victim; and Mr. Lloyd who loved Jane was a Quaker, and deeply in sympathy with Jane's wrongs from this " religious " woman, who had family prayers, went to church, and believed all the Calvinistic dogmas, but was selfish and cruel and unfeeling, with harsh judgments, a tight purse, and a heart of stone. And now she was dead, and the funeral had taken place, and Jane and Mr. Lloyd are talking over her life.

"'Then you believe,' replied Jane, 'that my aunt deceived herself by her clamorous profession?'

"'Undoubtedly,' said Mr. Lloyd. 'Ought we wonder that she deceived herself since we have heard in her funeral sermon her experiences detailed as the triumphs of a saint; her attendance upon ordinances commended as if they were the end and not the means of the religious life; since we (who cannot remember a single gracious act of humility in her whole life) have been told as a proof of her gracious state that the last rational words she pronounced were that she was of sinners the chief.' . . . '*Professions and declarations have crept in among the Protestants to take the place of the mortifications and penances of the ancient church; so prone are men to find some easier way to heaven than the toilsome path of obedience.'"*

Is there not need of Miss Sedgwick's message to-day?

IV

WITH HAWTHORNE IN LENOX

THE advent of General Zachary Taylor to the Presidency, in 1849, caused one Nathaniel Hawthorne, Democrat, to be removed from his office in the Salem custom-house. The Whigs had professed, with the usual hollowness of party platforms, to be opposed to the doctrine "To the victors belong the spoils," but their wolfish hunger by long abstention could hardly conceal itself 'neath the fleecy clothing of their political shibboleths. Hawthorne received word, within three months after the coming into power of the new régime, that he was turned out of office, and the axes of Taylor's headsmen chopped merrily, outrivalling the busy work of Jackson's spoliators, twenty years before.

The Salem custom-house officer took his dismissal philosophically, and the good wife at home said to him bravely: "Now you will have time to write your book." The next spring that book appeared,— *The Scarlet Letter*, written within the six months which followed his dismissal, with nothing to live upon but the savings which his wife had managed to lay up out of his meagre salary. It was the merest chance that prevented that book from being written in Lenox, for just prior to his removal from office, the Berkshire capital is talked about as a place to spend the summer, and after the dismissal, the Hawthornes regret they had not "taken the Lenox cottage." Without office, it was all the more the purpose of Hawthorne to get away into the Berkshires, where he could write his book. August 8th, he writes his brother-in-law, Horace Mann:

"My surveyorship is lost and I have no expectation, nor any desire, of regaining it. . . . I mean, as soon as possible;— that is to say, as soon as I can find a cheap, pleasant and healthy residence,— to remove into the country and bid farewell forever to this abominable city";

and as early as September 2d, Mrs. Hawthorne writes her mother, "the prospect of mountainous air already vivifies the blood." What this means is explained in a letter she herself receives September 10, 1849, from a friend who says: "I am glad you are going to Lenox because it is such a beautiful place and you have so many friends there." It was here, then, where Hawthorne was to have written the famous romance which caused his genius to be universally recognized. The reason why he deferred his coming to Berkshire for six months, and so caused his first great novel to see the light in Salem instead, is not given. His own mother's illness and death that summer broke up his plans for an early getting away, and the fall of the year seems inopportune to go into the country; particularly into the Berkshires.

With the early spring of the following year, 1850, the book is published; and in May Hawthorne, worn out with the experiences of the twelvemonth,— discharge from office, and the consequent worry as to the support of his family on the haphazard means at his command, the death of his mother, and the languor of body and mind due to the labor of creating his first romance,— repairs to Lenox, the pure air of whose hills he inhales at the same time as there wafts toward him the fragrant incense of praise from all parts of the world. What a contrast this affords!

from the "abominable city" with its hated wharves and dingy warehouses, to the heights of Lenox with the most entrancing of landscapes to look out upon! from being as he styled himself "the obscurest man in American letters," although he had published four years before *The Mosses from an old Manse* (1846) and nine years before that *Twice-Told Tales* (1837), to the pinnacle of fame, and comparisons between himself and Shakespeare! from the disappointment and anxiety due to removal from office, to the elation and security of an assured literary career! from a life of daily drudgery with weights and measures, to the vocation of his life—to write;—a prisoner dragging his chain and ball transformed into a freeman, whose name in tones of worshipful admiration and respect was upon every tongue! Let us bless the axe of the Whig headsman after all, and love it for the gory stains it bears of a certain custom-house officer's scalp! The kick became a boost. In the light of what happened, therefore, it is a pleasure to read Mrs. Hawthorne's words, on the very day that Hawthorne was deposed from office (June 8, 1849):

"Mr. Hawthorne never liked the office at all and is rather relieved than otherwise that it is taken out of his hands, and has an inward confidence that something better and more suitable for him will turn up. As for me, you know I am composed of Faith and Hope, and while I have my husband and children I feel as if Montezuma's diamonds and emeralds were spiritually in my possession."

Hawthorne, then, came to Lenox in the first flush of the dawn of his literary reputation, May, 1850, almost forty-six years of age. He was twenty-five years out of Bowdoin, had written a good deal of the type of the magazine article, and published in addition to his great romance two books of short stories, and at thirty-eight years, rather late in life, had married Miss Sophie Peabody, an invalid whom he loved enough to ask only the privilege of ministering to, as Browning to Elizabeth Barrett, but to whom as not to Mrs. Browning came health in the marriage relation. It was with wife and two children that Hawthorne came to the Berkshires, and it was here in the little house they occupied that a third child, Rose, came to bless and grace the home circle. Lenox was at that time the shire-town and the centre as well of great literary prestige. Miss Catherine Sedgwick was nearing the end of her literary labors and her creative energy was almost a spent force, and Mrs. Fanny Kemble-Butler was still in her heyday of vigor; both women residents of Lenox, and attracting here wits and statesmen, authors and divines to their brilliant society and the hilltop breezes and landscapes. In Stockbridge were staying temporarily such men as Lowell, Whipple, and G. P R. James, while in Pittsfield lived Dr. Holmes and Herman Melville. At or about this time the memories of the visits of Channing, Miss Martineau, Mrs. Jameson, Curtis, Longfellow, Sumner, and Miss Frederika Bremer were fresh in the minds of all. Indeed, Berkshire has not inaptly been called the "lake-country" of America because its cluster of literary brilliants was set in the midst of great picturesque beauty.

But we must remember that Hawthorne in coming to Berkshire left behind him companionships with men of letters who paled to a degree the brilliancy of his newer fellow-craftsmen. His Concord days were not to be reproduced: days when he had the rarest intimacy with the choice spirits and minds of the greatest in American letters,— tramping with Emerson, dining again and again with Longfellow, his classmate, at Parker's or the Tremont, boating with Ellery Channing up and down the river that flowed through the old Concord battle-field, entertaining Thoreau at the Old Manse, strolling with Lowell in familiar chat and giving him advice and encouragement as his elder by fifteen years, and keyed up to the highest intellectual tension by the society of the brilliant Margaret Fuller Ossoli; for these were the creators and prophets who discovered Hawthorne's genius long, long before the publication of his first romance. Hawthorne came to Lenox obscure in a way, only just beginning to be known, it is true, but it seems to me a somewhat colossal joke to claim that Herman Melville, by his notice of *The Scarlet Letter* in the columns of a literary journal, "discovered" him! It was natural that Hawthorne, who wrote of his days with Emerson at Concord, "It was impossible to dwell in his vicinity without inhaling more or less the mountain atmosphere of his lofty thought," should write to Longfellow after a year at Lenox: "Here I feel remote and quite beyond companionship." And not only had the great of America's best minds recognized Hawthorne's genius and taken him into their innermost fellowship long before *The Scarlet Letter*, and long before any such person as Melville was known, ut across the water his power was felt. Dickens," says Forster, "put into my hands *Mosses from an Old Manse*, with injunctions to read it"; and Miss Marian Evans confesses about this time: "Hawthorne is a grand favorite of mine."

The light of an author's success reveals usually his earlier works, which before that had failed to make themselves known. The *Mosses* are as beautiful as anything Hawthorne ever wrote, and the "Old Manse" seems to have walked out of a picture-frame so real is its quiet, classic beauty, with the historic river and battle-field hard by. Yet not until Hester and Dimmesdale became living realities on the canvas of human thought did the world see the creative energy of a new artist and turn to look at the character of his earlier productions.

It is here, then, in Lenox that we find Hawthorne in the spring of 1850, resting after the mighty creation which had placed forever, in the galaxy of letters, a new star. It was a tiny house, that "little red house" he occupied, set upon the hillside and overlooking a bit of landscape whose charm, whose lights and shadows, and whose tints gave to the lake and mountains beyond a meaning and an inspiration which were constant sources of blessing, restfulness, and invigoration. Indeed, the fascination of the scenery was so alluring that he said, " I cannot write in the presence of that view." On all these points about us the eye of Hawthorne rested in mute and lavish admiration, though it was a view of which he tired to some extent, as he wearied of the climate so trying in mountainous altitudes. Dr. Holmes rides down from Pittsfield to visit the Hawthornes, the second year of their stay, and Hawthorne insists upon holding Dr. Holmes's horse while its rider dismounts to step inside to get the view through the boudoir-window. On coming out the genial doctor said, " Is there another man in all America who ever had so great an honor as to have the author of *The Scarlet Letter* hold his horse?" Let us get this view in Hawthorne's own language:

"The house stands on a gently sloping eminence, a short distance away in the lap of the valley a beautiful lake, reflecting a perfect image of its own wooded banks, and of the summits of the more distant hills, as it gleamed in glassy tranquillity without the trace of a winged breeze on any part of its bosom. There is a glen between this house and the lake, through which winds a little brook with pools and tiny waterfalls over the great roots of trees. The glen is deep and narrow and filled with trees, so that it is all a dense shadow of bscurity. Beyond the lake is Monument Mountain looking like a headless sphinx wrapped in a Persian shawl, when clad in the rich and diversified autumnal foliage of its woods; and beyond Monument the dome of Taconic whose round head is more distinct than ever in winter when its snow-patches are visible but which generally is a dark blue unvaried mountain-top. There are many nearer hills which border the valley and all this intervening hill-country is rugged. The sunsets of winter are incomparably splendid, and when the ground is covered with snow no brilliancy of tint expressible by words can come within an infinite distance of the effect. Our southern view at that time, with the clouds and atmospherical hues, can neither be described, nor imagined, and the various distances of the hills which lie between us and the remote dome of Taconic are brought out with accuracy. And yet the face of nature can never look more beautiful than in May when Monument and its brethren are green; and the lightness of the tint takes away something from their massiveness and ponderosity, and they respond with livelier effect to the shine and shade of the sky. Each tree then stands out in its own individuality of hue."

It must be added, in the interest of historical veracity, that there is a passage in the Introduction to *Tanglewood Tales*, written within two years after the Hawthornes left Lenox, showing that the novelist grew rather a-weary with the sameness of the entrancing landscape just described. Hawthorne is back now (1853) in Concord, and writes:

"It was idle to imagine that an airy guest from Monument Mountain, Bald-Summit, and old Greylock, shaggy with primeval forests, could see anything to admire in my broad meadows and gentle eminences. Yet to me there is a peculiar quiet charm about them. They are better than mountains, because they do not stamp and stereotype themselves into the brain, and thus grow wearisome with the same strong impression, repeated day after day. A few summer weeks among mountains, a lifetime among green meadows and placid slopes, with outlines forever new because continually fading out of the memory,— such would be my sober choice."

Beautiful as was the exterior view greeting the occupants of "Tanglewood," Mrs. Hawthorne describes the interior in a way which shows that the inner beauty of the "little red house" was in keeping with the outer charm, with engravings, rugs, ottomans, quaint old furniture, and a rare delicacy of taste in all the simple appointments. Soon the household economy was in smooth running order, after the break-up at Salem, and the family settle down to the enjoyment of their new surroundings before other literary work is begun. Four months pass this way, and in the end of August Hawthorne begins to write his next great romance, *The House of the Seven Gables*, that grim treatise on the Second Commandment, or the children's suffering for the father's sins. The

The "little red house" where Hawthorne lived when he was in Lenox, 1850–1851. Here was written "The House of Seven Gables."

[Destroyed by fire June 22, 1890.]

life in "Tanglewood" is now a methodical affair: the literary creator busy mornings with his Maules and Pyncheons, with Hepzibah and Clifford, their mimic experiences the shadows of great realities; the daily walk to the post-office in Lenox, the walk with the children to a farmhouse half a mile distant for milk along a road the gentle father styled to their ears "the milky way," the play-hour with Una and Julian, who averred there never was "such a playmate" as their father, and the evening readings with and to the good wife who was raptly devoted to the brilliant man who loved her with a perfect love, to which she responded as the imaged sky in the lake's glassy surface to the blue vault above, each perfectly matching the other.

Hawthorne in the *Mosses* had said during the first years of their married life in the beautiful Concord days, "Here I recline upon the unwithered grass and whisper to myself O perfect day! O beautiful world! O beneficent God!'" and from Lenox he writes Longfellow: "I am as happy as mortal can be." It was an idyllic life: scenery that entranced, a growing fame filling the world, a home where love reigned; work which called out his soul's best strength, and an abandon to sport in the play-hour with the children, flying kites, or "coasting," or walking on the "marble pavement" of the frozen lake in the season, making a palace of snow with ice-windows, nutting with them and climbing into the tip-top of the trees, lying on the lake-shore while the children covered him with leaves,—a perfect companion whose presence was enjoyed by the children as that of no other, and who told them in simple phrase classic stories as they walked by his side, and listened, rapt auditors. Both agreed that he had the sweetest smile, that "tall, broad-shouldered, handsome man with the low voice and shy, gentle ways," as Whipple has described him, " with a dash of gray in his hair, and a grave but kindly face, and with the most wonderful eyes in the world, searching as lightning and unfathomable as night: the most gentle, genial, and humane of men." He had no ear for music and declared that he could not distinguish between *Hail Columbia* and *Yankee Doodle*, but Lowell pronounced him "the greatest poet, though he wrote in prose, that America has given to the world." Abnormally shy and retiring before strangers, so modest that it is said he once leaped a wall in Lenox to avoid some pedestrians coming up the road, his presence was the life of the home; and yet the majority of people who knew Hawthorne in Lenox fifty years ago set down his quiet modesty for moroseness, a quality which I believe has been attributed to him more from the sad vein that runs through all his books than from the fact that he was melancholy, or morbid. Standing on Bald Head he calls himself to his children in *The Wonder Book* the "*silent man.*" Yet 'quiet, sensitive, and shy" as he was, the whole region is eloquent with his presence, and as at Cooperstown one inbreathes the memory of the first writer of American fiction, so at Lenox the presence of Hawthorne is stamped on lake and dell, on peak and crag, on highway and meadow, forming part of the charm of the landscape itself as we reflect that he viewed it and loved it.

The Lenox chapter in Hawthorne's life was, however, one of busy toil. The workman was ' shaping at the forge of thought " his mighty conceptions. Let it be remembered that when he came to the Berkshires he had just finished his first romance. Four months of rest ensued, and then in the end of August he begins *The House of the Seven Gables*, which was finished January 26th, 1851. The first proofs came in the middle of February, and the book was out in March in response to large advance orders. In the estimate of its author it was a better book, in some respects, than his earlier and more celebrated novel; "more characteristic of me," he says, "and more natural for me to write"; and Lowell writes him: "It is a great triumph, and will build you a monument." The style is as pellucid as the waters of the lake he looked out upon when he wrote it, for Hawthorne was a consummate master of clear diction and literary art. The story is in the line of that "anatomy of melancholy" in which Hawthorne revelled, but it has what Mrs. Hawthorne styled "flowers of Paradise scattered all over its dark places."

A few months only elapsed between *The House of the Seven Gables* and his next book, *A Wonder Book for Boys and Girls*, begun in June and finished in a month and a half. This is practically a retelling of the classic stories of mythology for children; and the Eustace Bright who relates them, a college boy home on a vacation, to children who go by the names of Primrose, Sweet Fern, Blue-eye, Clover, Cowslip, and so on, is none other than Hawthorne himself, relating talks with his own children, Una and Julian, as he had played, and coasted, and tramped, and climbed with them in the neighborhood of "Tanglewood." This is the Berkshire book, describing "Tanglewood," Shadow Brook, and Bald Head, where the stories are told. It was read in manuscript to his children, and their rapt delight was as satisfactory to its author as his wife's painful interest in the reading from manuscript of *The House of the Seven Gables* had been, for she sometimes begged him to stop as she could hear no more. *The Wonder Book* was finished July 15th, and was published soon after. Almost as soon as the summer was over, Hawthorne was at work over a new collection of "Twice-Told Tales" entitled *The Snow Image and Other Tales*, which had been written, many of them, in earlier days, but were now brought together in one volume, whose "preface" bears date "Lenox, Nov. 1, 1851."

This was the last literary work Hawthorne did in Lenox, which he left November 21st, but we must not forget the Diary which he so faithfully kept all his life — "seventeen quartos," Lowell says, almost as voluminous as John Quincy Adams's daily chronicles. From this Diary came the posthumous *American Notes*, where the daily happenings at "Tanglewood" are recorded. And we must also not forget that *The Blithedale Romance*, with its "Brook Farm" reminiscences, written the winter after Hawthorne left Lenox, was here conceived, and to a great extent shaped, for Hawthorne only could write when he had distinctly conceived. He did not develop as he wrote, but conceived and then wrote; although he had the faculty of, and great facility in, improvisation, he did not so write his great works. In July, just after finishing *The Wonder Book*, he writes his friend Pike that he has in mind another romance embodying " my experiences and observations at Brook Farm." In Dr. Hale's recent book, *James Russell Lowell and His Friends*, there is a hint of the laborious scholarship down at the bottom of Hawthorne's romances in a reference to a remark of Lowell, who was always using superlatives to describe Hawthorne's genius. "Hawthorne," he said, "proved that our own past was an ample storehouse for the brightest works of imagination or fancy." All that last summer Hawthorne spent in Berkshire he was reading or thinking along the line of the coming *Blithedale Romance*.

This, then, is the sum of the literary activity of Hawthorne in Lenox, where he resided a year and a half so pleasantly, and all the more delightfully because at work,—"happy," as he himself said, "as mortal can be." And why not, pray?—when Mr. Fields writes him, "Your books are printed in Paris, as much as in England"; and Browning says, "Hawthorne is the greatest genius who has appeared in English literature for many years"; and when the choice minds of Germany were already buried deep and absorbingly in his pages, Amelie Bötta writing him: "We know *The House of the Seven Gables*, which is a lesson to family pride. You write as if you wrote for Germany." These testimonies came just a few weeks after leaving Lenox, but they have to do with the Lenox work.

Yet Hawthorne has met an enemy in the Berkshire climate with its sudden changes and longs to get away. He does not actually bid farewell to Berkshire until late November, 1851, but there are hints six months before of the coming departure. In May he writes Longfellow: "My soul gets troublous with too much peace and rest. . . . I need to smell sea-breezes and dock mud and to tread pavements." But in July it seems as if his plans to leave Lenox might be indefinitely postponed.

"We intend to take Mrs. Kemble's house in October

or the beginning of November," he writes his friend Bridge, July 22d. "We shall lose a beautiful prospect and gain a much more convenient and comfortable house. . . . I mean to buy a house before a great while, but it shall not be in Berkshire. I prefer the sea-coast."

Two days later he writes another friend:

"I do not feel at home among these hills and should not like to consider myself permanently settled here. I am continually catching cold and am none so vigorous as I used to be on the sea-coast. The same is the case with my wife."

Seven days later, Hawthorne, who is staying with Julian alone in the "Red Shanty," or "La Maison Rouge," as he styles it interchangeably, while Mrs. Hawthorne is away for a few weeks with Una, has the following entry in the daily journal:

"This is a horrible, horrible, most hor-ri-ble climate, one knows not for ten minutes together, whether he is too cool or too warm, but he is always one or the other, and the constant result is a miserable disturbance of the system. I detest it! I detest it!! I detest it!!! I hate Berkshire with my whole soul and would joyfully see its mountains laid flat."

A few weeks later Mrs. Hawthorne writes her mother, September 7th:

"It is very singular how much more we are in the centre of society in Lenox than we were in Salem, and all literary persons seem settling around us. But when they get established here, I dare say *we shall take flight.*"

The next month the plan of taking the Kemble place was given up, and by October 11th, the plan for leaving Berkshire had matured, for on that date Hawthorne writes Bridge: "We shall leave here, with much joy, on the first day of December." And indeed, their departure was a little sooner than the date set, for on November 21, 1851, appears this entry in the Diary: "We left Lenox in a storm of snow and sleet." Julian remembers that five house cats, pets of the family, followed them down the road a piece, as they rumbled off with their trunks in a farmer's wagon. It was a dreary leave-taking of Berkshire and its charming scenic beauty, blurred in the November storm; but the Lenox residence of Nathaniel Hawthorne had given to the region some of its most cherished memories and traditions, as it had given to him some of his grandest inspirations.

Lenox preserved the memory of the Hawthorne visit by repeated pilgrimages out to the border of the town where the "little red house" stood, and many were the strolls and drives hither to this literary shrine during those days the house was standing. Its owner, who is possessed of many gentlemanly and scholarly qualities,—"a horn of benefits," Mrs. Hawthorne called him,—took pleasure in keeping the house as its distinguished occupant left it. Sad was the day, twelve years ago, when the house went up in smoke, but the site forever remains, though the view from it is greatly marred by the growth of trees. An effort has been made to mark the site with an appropriate memorial; one very distinguished gentleman in the field of letters suggesting to me an exedra, a sort of wayside shrine with seat, where one may vividly call up the memory of the great novelist in the presence of the inspiring view he loved. The street leading out to this site has already been renamed in honor of Hawthorne. The village library has a table which once was his, though the one on which he wrote *The House of the Seven Gables* is in the Athenæum, Pittsfield. Various charred relics of the "old red house" are preserved in the region round about.

Few other material reminders of the presence of this mighty workman are left. The village retains the tradition that he was morose, because he was "silent." "Speech," said Ellis, "was travail to Hawthorne"; and with this accords Emerson's testimony: "It was easy to talk to Hawthorne, only he said so little that I talked too much." Mrs. Browning, who met him at Rome, said of him: "It is not his way to converse." It is easy to see, then, how the impression got abroad in Lenox that he was morose; and this impression was strengthened by what Longfellow calls "the same old dull pain that runs through all his writings." He was not melancholy, as wife and children and friends attest, as passages of sublime optimism everywhere in his writings, a continual play of humor, and a steadfast application to toil prove. He diagnosed sin to heal, not to expose. He made sin sinful and repellent, not attractive. His books were all of them written with a purpose, and therefore they all have a message. The Puritan survived under his graceful, transparent diction. He was "gray and grand," says Longfellow writing of him in 1863, "but there was something very pathetic about him"; and Motley four years earlier writes: "Hawthorne is the most bashful man, I believe, that ever lived, certainly the most bashful American . . . but he is a very sincere, unsophisticated, kind person and looks the man of genius he undoubtedly is." It is so easy to mistake silence for moodiness, bashfulness for sullenness, a disposition to avoid men for an inclination to dislike them, quiet for morbidness, that it is small wonder those outside the charmed circle of friendship misjudged him.

We are not concerned here with the subsequent story of Hawthorne's career. Books followed and a Liverpool consulate with long residence abroad and a return to America in the most critical of the ante-bellum days, just before the outbreak of the Civil War, when he wrote one of his greatest romances, *The Marble Faun.* A Democrat, and the intimate friend of Franklin Pierce, "the Northern man with Southern sentiments," Hawthorne met rebuff and stigma in his old haunts. Whittier and the whole abolitionist school had little patience with slavery apologists and allowed only short shrift to those who went not to their lengths. But a passage in Hawthorne's Diary, "I am an abolitionist in feelings, if not in principle," goes far to redeem him in the minds of those who felt the passion of the slavery reform like a consuming fire within their breasts. He died during the progress of the war and towards its close, brokenhearted because brothers were in conflict. He was laid to rest under the pines in his loved Concord, on a matchless day in late May, the orchards and meadows clad in bloom and filled with song,—

> "Though all its splendor could not chase away
> The omnipresent pain,"—

and his burial was attended by his devoted friends, Longfellow, Emerson, Agassiz, Lowell, Holmes, Whipple, and Pierce, who mourned sincerely, not the quenching of his productive genius only, but the going away of a congenial spirit, who had graced and refined and blessed and hallowed their fellowship.

> "There in seclusion and remote from men
> The wizard hand lies cold
> Which at its topmost speed let fall the pen
> And left the tale half told."

It is not for me here to attempt an estimate of Hawthorne as a writer. Emerson says: "I never read his books with pleasure; they are too young"; and he frankly confessed he never could read one through. Moreover he advised the young not to read Hawthorne. Lowell, on the contrary, pronounces Hawthorne "the rarest creative imagination of the century, the rarest in some ideal respects since Shakespeare; the most original mind America has given to the world." Estimates will in between these extremes, but, unless I mistake, the world agrees with Lowell, rather than with Emerson. Anyway, proud was the day for Berkshire which added the name of Nathaniel Hawthorne to the roll of those who have caused the lustre of their achievements to shine resplendently upon the county they honored, and proud will be the day when the hallowed site of the red house by the lake where Hawthorne wrought some of his mightiest creations shall be appropriately marked with some memorial to this master-workman: Nathaniel Hawthorne, who, though he wrote not in verse, possessed the soul of the poetic spirit, insight, and grace, and, though he was a stranger to the laws of musical numbers, sang his stern messages into the ear of the world with infinitely melodious rhythm and cadence.

V

MODERN LENOX

NATURE'S inspiring canvas in a frame of Art,— this is the Lenox of to-day. More than half of the area of the township has passed into the possession of those who, with large means, have touched the olden picture of scenic charm only to adorn it. An urban class seeking rural retreats has added to the charm of the region by the creation of beautiful estates, and one is diverted for the moment from the scenery to the elegance of these extensive properties, whose villas have been built, in recent years, upon an increasing scale of magnificence. The village itself has been transformed, its roads improved, trimmed, and kept free from dust, thus imparting a park-like appearance to the town; and often during the "season," when handsome equipages are rolling along on every highway and the exploring tourist on foot or wheel is abroad in the land (for the town is now on the beaten path of summer travel), one hears this question asked: "What is the effect of the incoming of wealth upon Lenox?"

The most immediate and perceptible effect of all this change in outward conditions has been a complete change in the internal life of the village. The removal of the courts in 1869 took out of Lenox the very core of its culture, and this was followed in the next twenty years by such a rush for building sites that landholders disposed of property and migrated. Farms that were worth $50 an acre for potatoes sold for $1000 per acre for building purposes. Ten years before the courts were removed the village property of Judge Pierpont — sometime Minister to England — was sold for $5600. Another village property, hardly more than a stone's throw off, with a finer view, but containing only two acres and a third, sold scarcely more than ten years after the removal of the courts for $35,000 to the family of a member of President Arthur's cabinet. The land on which the present Episcopal church, rectory, and parish-house now stand — a triangular tongue of about half an acre — cost the society $19,000. This scale of prices was established proportionately throughout the township as soon as the lightning of public favor struck it. Prices have receded somewhat from those inflated values, but the normal value of real estate to-day is still very high and will be kept so.

It is, therefore, easy to see that the Yankee saw his opportunity and left. He would n't have been a Yankee if he had not. A little of the old New England stock still survives, but it is a remnant. A different order has come about. In place of the New England yeomanry have come the summer residents and the caretakers of the great estates. The whole personnel in the public places, in the churches, has entirely changed. The character and nationality of the citizens of Lenox differ *toto cœlo* from what they were fifty years ago. Municipal conditions have arisen more difficult to cope with, and the literary atmosphere once breathed in this old student-town has diminished. Another generation has arisen which knows not Miss Sedgwick, and which is a stranger to the intellectual and social prestige of the ancient Berkshire capital.

But if the unmaking of the old town has proceeded with the making of the new resort, it may with equal justice be said that the losses which Lenox has suffered have not been without compensations. Aside from the presence of great wealth here, as a source of patronage and as the element which contributes the most heavily to meet the town's annual budget of expenses, and aside from the many inspirations to right living which an affluent class "rich in good works" can and does present to those who are less favorably circumstanced, Lenox has enjoyed very many benefactions at the hands of those who have appropriated these heights as building sites. Fifty years ago Mrs. Fanny Kemble-Butler presented to the town the clock which, though it somewhat outlived its usefulness as a timepiece, graced the belfry of the old village church until recently. It has now been replaced by another, the gift of Morris K. Jesup, Esq. The purchase of the county Court-house by Mrs. Adeline E. Schermerhorn, in 1874, in order that she might present it to the town for a library building, has already been mentioned. Later a public watering-trough of beautiful design, in memory of Miss Emma Stebbins, was given to the town by Mrs. C. C. Tiffany and Miss Wheeler, and later still Professor Thomas Egleston erected to the memory of General Paterson a fine shaft on the green in front of the hotel. Some years after the gift by Mrs. Schermerhorn, her children, Mrs. R. T. Auchmuty and Mr. F. Augustus Schermerhorn, completed their mother's generous and useful present by adding to the library building what is known as the "Sedgwick Hall Annex," a most attractive assembly room and lecture hall. More recently Mr. John E. Parsons has given to the town a fine granite standard for a cluster of electric lamps. If we might include the gifts to the churches in the list of gifts to the town, it would be difficult to stop the enumeration of gracious and fragrant alabaster-boxes whose sweet perfume is the memory of saintly lives. Many are these "memorials": the font and tablets in the Congregational church, the gift of David Egleston, in memory of his mother; the campanile tower attached to the Episcopal church, the gift of Mrs. Auchmuty and Mr. Schermerhorn; the chancel given by the Kneeland family as a memorial to a member of their household; the choir room, the gift of Mr. Charles Lanier in memory of his wife; the sweet-toned chimes presented by George H. Morgan, Esq., as a memorial to his wife, and the Trinity Parish House, a most useful and attractive structure, presented to the Episcopal church by John E. Parsons, Esq., in memory of his wife. Mr. Parsons has, also, given to this church for its work in another part of the town, a handsome property with church (St. Helena Chapel) and parish-house in memory of his daughter. And, last, but by no means least, should be mentioned the generous donations of the summer residents, one and all, to the support of the Town Library, which contains fourteen thousand volumes, and which has greatly expanded its facilities through the active and munificent interest of its patrons who come to this hill-country at the annual hegira.

I cannot close this part of my subject without the fear that I have omitted the mention of some deeds from this list of sweet ministries, and so I will erect an altar " To the Unknown Givers," whose many charities have relieved distress, but have never been known by the general public. Lenox receives all these public donations in a deeply appreciative spirit. It can no more do for itself what it once could in the way of artistic adornment; but then it lacked the inclination; now, with a valuation of over three millions of dollars, it would seem as if it ought to lack neither the inclination nor the means. Modern Lenox should be the most beautiful town in the

A vista, Lenox.
Taghconics in the distance, Bald Head at the left.

world, with its superb scenery and magnificent estates. There is a susceptibility to adornment here as nowhere else. It will take all the polish wealth can put upon it. Its views should be treated artistically by cutting away some of its ornamental shrubbery. Its public buildings should be in harmony with their environment, rich and substantial. Municipal regulations of a far-seeing character should be adopted, looking to the preservation of all this natural beauty. Gifts to the town should be made by individual donors, following the examples of those who have in other days marked their affection for the place by public memorials.

But the greatest gift to a town is the public spirit of its citizens, and there have been some among those who have created beautiful estates here who have given *themselves* to the town. 'The best gift thou canst give to me," said Emerson "is a portion of thyself." It would be invidious to specify any when so many of the Lenox "cottagers" have taken such a deep interest in the town. Some men cannot live in a town without making themselves felt in it for good. Such men among others in Lenox were the late Colonel R. T. Auchmuty and Mr. Richard Goodman, Sr.; and there are many among the living whose public spirit is a precious and a potent testimony of friendship for their adopted town, vying with that of those who are " to the manner born."

Modern Lenox traces its beginnings as a place of fine estates and villas far back into the past. The magnificent prospect to the south, in which direction the town slopes down to two little lakes, with mountains rising beyond, could not fail to attract those who desired to erect summer residences. It may be doubted whether the physical loveliness of the region was the only attraction, or whether the charm of a literary town, an academic centre for the country lying between the Hudson and the Connecticut, did not lure some. As the shire-town, also, with courts, a regular weekly newspaper, and a perfected system of stage routes, all of which, of course, led through the county seat, it possessed certain facilities not to be afforded in an inaccessible and isolated spot, where the scenery might have been equally as fine. We have seen that Mrs. Kemble's first visit in Lenox was in 1836, and that in the Berkshire Coffee-House (now Curtis Hotel) as early as 1838 the summer boarder was *en evidence*. The first estate to be created here was that of Mr. Samuel G.

Modern Lenox

Ward, in 1846, afterwards sold to Mr. Bullard and known now as Highwood, charmingly located on the heights above the northern shore of Lake Mahkeenac (Stockbridge Bowl). Charles Sumner, who spent September of 1844 in Berkshire, recuperating from a severe illness, passed several days with Mr. Ward in Lenox, and writes his friend, Sam. Howe (September 10th): "Ward jolted us in his wagon to view the farms, one of which he covets." I take, also, this quotation from a letter of Oliver Wendell Holmes: "Pittsfield, August 17, 1849. Rode my little horse over to Lenox this forenoon. Mr. ——'s place is one of the most beautiful spots I ever saw anywhere. I visited it some years ago when it was building and it appeared to me perfect almost to a miracle"; and continuing the description of his visit at Lenox, Dr. Holmes mentions two other building sites which had been selected, "one by Mrs. Butler, 'the tragedy queen.'" Hawthorne, six months later (in the spring of 1850) came to this shire-town of the Berkshires, in the first glow of his literary splendor, occasioned by the creation of his masterpiece, which he had just completed, and his work here for a year and a half, unremitting, productive immortal, drew attention to the town. Anyway, in the next five years the sales of real estate must have disclosed to the town at least a hint of its changing character.

The beginnings of certain large estates which have remained practically intact until the present day are seen to emerge from that period, half a century ago; they are the Bullard and Tappan places, lying on the ascent from the north shore of Stockbridge Bowl, and just a stone's throw from the "little old red house" where Hawthorne wrought; the Schermerhorn and Haggerty estates in the village, the latter now owned by George W. Morgan, Esq., of New York; the Kemble place, known as "The Perch," and now the property of Mrs. William Thompson, of New York; the Aspinwall-Woolsey estate, now passed into the hands of a syndicate, and the Beecher farm, now a magnificent estate, for many years the property of General Rathbone, but at present belonging to John Sloane, Esq., of New York City. The locations of these estates will show that thus early in the history of the town as a resort, the beauty of the township *as a whole* was recognized.

Topographically Lenox is a sort of "saddleback," with the villa of Charles E. Lanier, Esq., "Allen Winden," high in the pommel, and the Congregational church at the other end high in the rear, or *vice versa*, whichever you choose to call it, the land sloping off to the east and west from these eminences. From either side of "Allen Winden," whose name suggests its elevation, the land descends, to the west to two little lakes, one of which is "Stockbridge Bowl," on which are two of the estates previously named, and on the east to another little body of water, Laurel Lake. It was on this latter side that Mrs. Kemble-Butler selected her building site in 1850, looking down upon the brightly glowing face of the mountain mirror as it caught the sun's rays in the morning, and beyond it to the Tyringham Pass, where the "Shadow Bridge," constructed by Richard Watson Gilder's poetic vision, spans the dell early in the afternoon. Fanny Kemble also looked off due east to the "Beecher farm," on rising ground a half-mile distant, purchased by the Rev. H. W. Beecher in 1853. Retracing our steps to the village, where Mrs. Adeline E. Schermerhorn bought in 1853 and built in 1859, we pass on and through, up the steep hill crowned by the village church, to the Woolsey estate immediately in the rear. On a little higher ground than that on which the church stands was situated this very large, thickly wooded, and handsome property, acquired by Mr. E. J. Woolsey and Mr. W. H. Aspinwall at nominal prices from those who sold to them the well-timbered heights of their side-hill farms. It commands a prospect to the south that beggars description: the town beneath, the glistening surface of Stockbridge Bowl far away to the right, and beyond, rising one above another as they recede into the farthest distance, the mountains, "Rattlesnake," "Monument," and "The Dome," the last 2800 feet in height, while close in on the western side of the landscape runs the "Taghconic" range, with the tonsured summit of Bald Head near by, where a fine view of the Catskills may be obtained.

This, then, was the beginning of the creation of large estates in Lenox. In twenty-five years, or at the opening of the year 1880, when the author first made the acquaintance of this ancient capital, there had been added to these seven properties, twenty-six; and since 1880 forty-two, making in all, not counting the same place twice where it has simply changed hands, during fifty years, seventy-five distinct places, showing an increased ratio of growth. Such an aggregate of private property represents many millions of dollars. Villas, surrounded by extensive, park-like grounds, overlook the landscape at different angles of vision, and dot the hillsides everywhere, many within a radius of a mile from the Lenox post-office. Some of the most beautiful estates are within a radius of two miles, including a part of the northern section of the town of Stockbridge, and cover large areas of territory; while a still longer radius would be required to include the handsome properties of all who belong to the Lenox colony. The author will not attempt to give with chronological nicety the order in the creation of these estates. When he knew Lenox first, in the spring of 1880, the town was in a chrysalis stage; it was becoming, it had not become. There were, it is true, many places here then, but the Berkshire Hills were attracting only those who were in the secret of their charm. The estates which were in existence then were, in addition to those already described, as follows; and it will be seen from their location that they were pretty generally distributed throughout the township. There was the property belonging to the late Mr. Robeson, who bought the old Ellery Sedgwick place, created in 1858 and greatly beautified by Professor Salisbury, its next owner, in 1870. Farther away to the south, on what was formerly known as Walker Hill, were two large estates: the Bishop place, marking like the Robeson grounds historic sites in the growth of the county and town, and the Goodman property (the old Judge Walker place), acquired by Mr. Richard Goodman from the Hon. Judge Pierpont in 1865, by whom it had been purchased from John Walker, Esq., in 1859. Farther away to the southeast was a cluster of estates grouped around Laurel Lake: the Schenck property then being laid out (for the last twelve years with other adjacent land merged in the Westinghouse estate), the Goelet farm, lately bought by F. K. Sturgis, Esq., and the Sargent and Dorr places, the latter now in the possession of Mr. R. W. Patterson. The old Beecher place was then owned by General Rathbone. Off to the west in addition to the Bullard and Tappan places were the estates belonging to Samuel Ward, Esq. (acquired and greatly enlarged ten years since by Mr. Anson Phelps Stokes) and the Geo. Higginson place. Within a mile of Lenox post-office at that time were the following smaller places, viz.: the properties belonging to Mrs. Joseph White, Mr. Alfred Gilmore, Mr. Parkman Shaw, Mr. Kneeland, Professor Egleston

Modern Lenox 175

(purchased by him from Judge Pierpont in 1859 for $5600), the heirs of Charlotte Cushman, Miss Furniss, Miss Carey, General Barlow, General Oliver, Mrs. Kuhn, Geo. W. Folsom, Esq. (the old Brevoort place); while off to the northwest were the three very beautiful estates of John E. Parsons (since very extensively enlarged), Henry W. Braem, Esq. (present Winthrop place), and Dr. R. C. Greenleaf. To the east two miles from the centre of the town was the Dana place; and to the north about the same distance the estate owned by Col. R. T. Auchmuty.

It may be said that if all these estates were in existence prior to 1880 substantially the same as to-day, Lenox could hardly have been obscure at that time; yet certainly it had not leaped into the world-wide notoriety it now possesses. In the last twenty-one years there has been going on an exodus of the Yankee farmer, and in place of his farms, great estates have come up as if by magic; and what is more, with each year the modest summer house which once satisfied the summer resident here has given way before the more stately type of villa. Some of the most beautiful estates here have been created within the last twenty years; many within the last ten. All varieties of domestic architecture are seen, from the Swiss chalet to the Tudor castle, from the colonial mansion to the turreted composite majestic in size and dignity, and from the plain summer house to the architectural perfections of the chaste Elizabethan structure or the grand and simple beauty of the Petit Trianon. Bridges of elaborate and solid pattern in granite grace the drives in some of the private grounds; monoliths from Egypt and marble antiques adorn others. Each villa commands its own charming landscape in which a lake is set as a pearl surrounded by emerald; and it is needless to say, as the surpassing charm of Lenox is in its drives, a system of road-construction on the highways has, at great expense, been made possible, thus preserving this pleasure as a permanent and delightful feature of the modern town. The Lenox of to-day, then, has the same old quiet dignity it always had, set in a lustre of glory; Nature perfected and adorned by Art; worth crowned with a resplendent wreath of favor from those who lavish upon it the substantial proofs of their affection.

And now I propose to take the reader with me on a few walks and drives about Lenox in order that we may see some of these estates with their charming villas. A convenient place to start from will be the Paterson monument, which stands at the "four corners" in the heart of the village. The adjacent elms of hoary age must feel lonely, indeed, as they have seen the busy generations come and go across the site now occupied by this granite shaft. A glance at its inscription is worth the while, and while we stand there I would like, though I forbear, to read you a page out of Fields's *History of Berkshire* (1829), or Holland's *Western Massachusetts*, to show the marches, the sufferings, the heroisms of the Lenox soldiers under Paterson in the Revolution. General Paterson's monument in the centre of the town is a mute bugle-call to patriotism. The "four corners" where it stands are the meeting-place of two intersecting streets, Main and Walker, though the southern prolongation of Main Street is called "Court-house Hill" (more properly Stockbridge Road), and the western extension of Walker Street is called from the monument West Street. Court-house Hill slopes off precipitously from Monument Square. West Street is a continuous but less abrupt descent for nearly a mile, and both these hills, with

"Church Hill" in the rear coming down toward the monument from the north, are merry with coasters in the season. Looking up from Monument Square toward the old village church-on-the-hill is one thing in June; quite another in December. Hither came in all winds and weathers for eighty years the yeomen and gentry of Berkshire for litigation, first to that little Court-house on the southeast corner which is now (1902) being moved off to make way for the imposing Town Hall in process of construction, and then after 1816 to that grandly simple and stately building behind us, and just the flip of a stone up Main Street from the square where we are standing, the second Court-house, now known as Sedgwick Hall.

The first walk one takes in Lenox is up the heights rising on the north of the town and known as Church Hill. On a typical "Berkshire day," clear, bracing, and exhilarating, one can walk miles with slight fatigue. An altitude of thirteen hundred feet, like that of Lenox at this Monument Square, where we are standing, is not too high for vigorous exercise. The first building on our right as we turn to go away from the Paterson monument is the Curtis House, which has recently been greatly enlarged, transformed, and modernized; and next beyond it stands Sedgwick Hall, where the Town Library finds ample housing in this ancient and classic building, once the county Court-house. Adjoining this edifice on the north is Mr. W. C. Schermerhorn's property, for many years in the possession of the county as the site of its jail. Twenty years ago the two modest cottages here standing were built in place of the old jail-house which had been moved off, and now the glow of altar fires replaces the glare of hate behind barred windows, greeting our fathers as they passed up and down the street. We pass on up Main Street noting, where Cliffwood Street runs off obliquely to the northwest, an old building on the opposite side of the street, with the date "1803" on its belfry, the venerable "Lenox Academy" to whose classic halls once came the youth within a radius considerably over fifty miles; and if we might reckon a few students from New Jersey and South Carolina, the area of its influence would be seen to be enormous. Midway between the Academy and yonder church-on-the-hill, we pass on our right the Roman Catholic church, built in 1873, though for twenty years before that the project of such a building was mooted. And here we are at the top of the hill, a half-mile from Curtis's, face to face with a rare and classic specimen of old-time church architecture, the ancient village church built here in 1805 and dedicated to the service of God January 1, 1806. This edifice replaced an older one that stood on the same site, a few rods farther south. Let us stroll out into the churchyard, or if you are not too tired climb the belfry tower. What a prospect! One can easily understand now why this church is so conspicuous an object for miles around — you practically never get away from it. I myself have seen it over on the heights of Monterey, fourteen miles away.

But we must not forget our quest, and so we will leave the scenery which has been so oft alluded to in this book, and try to locate a few of the "places" from our eyrie. It has been a favorite place for the generations to come, this church belfry, yet for the sake of a more extensive view, and the greater convenience of seeing it, I am going to ask you to accept a chair by my side on the piazza of the Aspinwall Hotel, which has recently been built a little farther up this hillside, and which with its extensive grounds, its magnificent situation, its ample accommodations and mod-

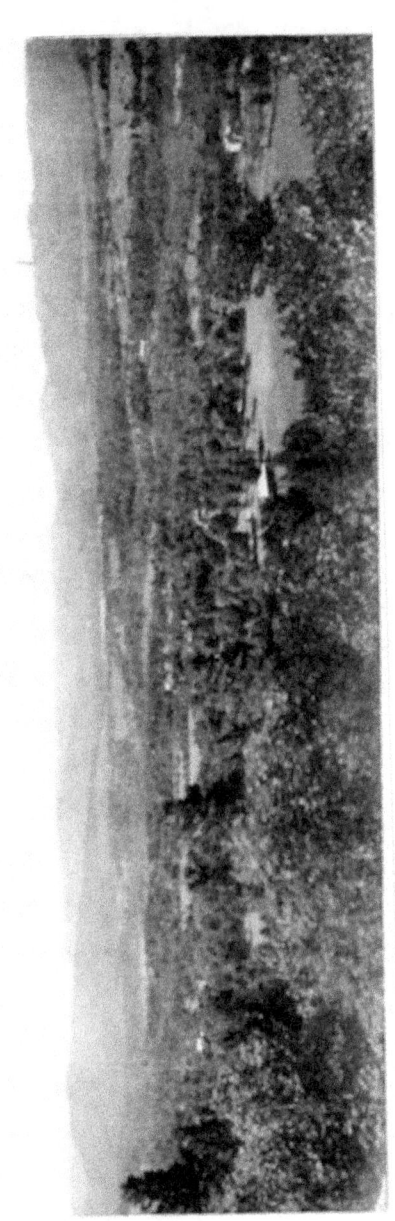

The view from the Aspinwall piazza.

Rattlesnake Mt.   Monument Mt.   Stockbridge Bowl.   Taghconics.

ern facilities enters this year upon its career of promise. By a "turn of the eyeball," as Mr. Beecher said, your eye sweeps the far-off horizon from Greylock to Taghconic Dome. Lenox lies down immediately beneath you. Our aërial point of view does not disclose the location of all the estates, but will reveal salient features. Out of Stockbridge Bowl, three miles off there to the southwest, rises on the right " Bald Head," on whose sides as they slope down many hundred feet into the lake we can see beautiful summer villas. Here is, among others much smaller, the nine-hundred-acre estate of Anson P. Stokes, Esq., "Shadowbrook," adorned with a grand and palatial castle in granite of composite architecture. On the other side of the "Bowl" rises "Rattlesnake," and between us and it a very high knoll on which is perched "Allen Winden," the charming villa of Charles Lanier, Esq., whose many acres adjoin some of the largest estates in Lenox. The land descends, as we have said, on either side of "Allen Winden" to two small lakes. Across the waters of the one, Lily Pond, on rising ground lies "Wheatleigh," owned by Henry H. Cook, Esq., with the belfry of the Curtisville village church in the far distance; at the steep western side of the other, Laurel Lake, stretches over a vast acreage "Erskine Park," the estate of the distinguished inventor, George Westinghouse, Esq., with the tall and slender spire of the Lee village church in the distance, erect and white against its mountain background, and the lake in the foreground. Between these two lakes lie "Interlaken," belonging to the heirs of the late D. W. Bishop, Esq., and "Elm Court," the property of William D. Sloane, Esq., either of which two last-named estates covers a vast area of territory. "Elm Court" was created by Mr. Sloane in 1887, though greatly enlarged since by extensive acquisitions of adjacent property.

Turning our eyes now far around to the left, on the ground rising out of Laurel Lake to the east and north, and touching the very waters themselves, are the Wharton, Sargent, and Goelet estates; while back of them on still higher ground, forming a sort of concentric quadrant, are the Foster, Barnes, John Sloane, and Paterson estates, all large and adorned with beautiful villas. We do not see all these places from where we are sitting; but we see pretty nearly where they are. We shall see them more closely when we come to go out to them in our drives about Lenox.

Modern Lenox

All of them are of comparatively recent construction, though one, that of John Sloane, Esq., "Wyndhurst," is on the old Beecher place. In a way it may be said that the ridge from our height of observation to the Lanier place and on beyond to the Westinghouse estate is a sort of divide, with the waters of one side flowing ultimately into Stockbridge Bowl, and those of the other side reaching at last Laurel Lake. Each of these two longitudinally divided sections of the town has its distinctive view; each was early recognized in the development of the place into the resort it has become. If now we turn our eyes to the northward where Greylock stands up clearly in the far-off northern horizon, we get another distinct section of Lenox, and here two miles away from the Aspinwall are the estate of the late Col. R. T. Auchmuty, "The Dormers," and, nearer, that of the late William H. Bradford, Esq., "Wayside." These are large estates, charmingly situated on high ground commanding views of Greylock, the Housatonic River up and down its tortuous course, the beautiful October Mountain rising abruptly from the opposite bank of the winding stream, and off in the opposite direction the massive mountain ramparts of the Taghconics, with "Yokun's Seat" conspicuous against them, as though that ancient chieftain were fortified by natural barriers against the dwellers in Mount Ephraim (Richmond) on the other side. Nestled under "Yokun's Seat," though itself on very high ground, is the estate of Thomas Shields Clarke, the sculptor.

But so far our glance has been out upon the township rather than down upon the town. Look down now, sheer down, say three hundred feet from this sightly piazza where we are sitting. We are upon the edge of a bluff. The golfers going the rounds in the links below us seem moving miniatures. Half-way down the steep bluff, and a little to the left, are two handsome estates commanding, though lower, much the same view as we are seeing, "Belvoir Terrace," the property of Morris K. Jesup, Esq., President of the New York Chamber of Commerce, and "Under Ledge," belonging to Joseph W. Burden, Esq.

Down there on the lower level, among many other smaller estates, all of which are situated on high enough ground to command prospects which vie with the one stretching out before our eyes, are three estates created twenty-five years ago : "Windyside," with its Swiss chalet, owned by Dr. Richard C. Greenleaf ; " Ethelvyn," the property of Mrs. Robert Winthrop, lately purchased of the Henry Braem estate,— another part of the same estate having been purchased by Dr. Henry P. Jaques and called 'Home Farm" (that is it that we see with its English manor-house yonder to the right); and the other one of the three estates named is 'Stonover," the very large and beautiful estate belonging to John E. Parsons, Esq. Mr. Parsons's property has been very greatly enlarged since his original purchases twenty-five years since, by the acquisition of a tract of adjoining marshland which has been drained and transformed into a park, which the public very generally and gladly avails itself of for drives. I think I have indicated the locations of the largest estates in Lenox with the exception of two which lie off to the east of us, the villas belonging to the same being in the heart of the town itself, but a stone's throw from the campanile tower of Trinity Church, yonder, far to the left : "Ventfort Hall," built by George H. Morgan, Esq., an Elizabethan manor-house, large, rich, chaste, and simple, and "Pine Croft," the summer home of F. Augustus Schermerhorn, Esq., whose long residence, extensive holdings of realty, and deep interest in Lenox make him, like so many others of the summer residents here, seem as much a part of the town as those who have been born and bred within it.

I have not tried to indicate with any completeness the locations of all the estates, villas, and summer cottages in Lenox; only what could be seen in the main from the lofty " Aspinwall," which crowns the crest of this bluff on the old Woolsey place, one of the oldest estates in the town. Let us now descend to the churchyard where sleep the generations of the Lenox dead; a cemetery whose prospect is hardly less entrancing than the one at which we have been looking from the heights above. The street which runs past this ancient churchyard is the base of an isosceles triangle with its apex in the village at the junction of Main and Cliffwood streets, and in each angle of this triangular section is a "summer-place": " Edge Road," in the apex, owned by Mrs. A. C. Kingsland, while up here at either end of the base line are " Hillside," purchased by Mrs. Hartman Kuhn, October 27, 1870, so the local press of that period stated, for $1600 (!), and " Breezy Corners," owned by Mrs J. Williams Biddle. Standing here at " Breezy Corners " with " Belvoir Terrace " rising high at our back we see up the road leading to the

illage, the Livingston estate with its pleasing
illa, "Osceola Lodge," "Sunnyridge," the
property of Geo. W. Folsom, Esq., "The
Homestead" the village property of Anson
Phelps Stokes, Esq., formerly owned by
Charles F. McKim, the architect, and in the
opposite direction "Deepdene," the estate of
Dr. F. P. Kinnicutt, while in front of us, at
the side of "The Homestead," whose villa is
of unique architectural design, opens Yokun
Avenue, with the estate of Mrs. E. G. Bacon
on the right, adjoining the golf grounds. As
we are out on this "walk" to get an idea of
the general location of the estates in Lenox,
our return to the Paterson monument will be
by the way of Yokun Avenue to West Street,
where turning to the left we soon arrive at the
place from which we started. On the way
tither from "Breezy Corners" we pass just
beyond the entrance to the golf links the entrances to "Windyside," "Ethelwyn," "Stonover," all of which we saw from above; and
now continuing our way we pass on the
right the entrance to the extensive "Stonover
Park" and on the left the two pretty and
modest villas of Miss Mary DeP. Carey and
Miss C. Furniss, "Gusty Gables" and "Edgecomb." It is still very high ground here,

although we have made such a descent to reach it, and the same enrapturing landscape has greeted and rested the eye at every step. We make our way on to West Street, where on the corner at our right stands the old "Charlotte Cushman cottage," given by Miss Cushman to Emma Stebbins, the sculptor, and on our left the newly created summer-place owned by Mr. D. F. Griswold, while right before us lies the Robeson estate with an old English type of Gothic manor-house, built of stone and rather low, standing at the far end of a large and level lawn bordered with ancient elms. This house was built in 1858 by Mr. Ellery Sedgwick, overhauled and repaired in 1871 by Professor Salisbury, its next owner, at an expense of $150,000, and after a few years' occupancy was sold to Mr. W. R. Robeson, who occupied it every summer until his death. The Robeson property is interesting as one of the historic sites in the days when Lenox was the county seat. Immediately adjoining this estate on the west is "Brookhurst," owned by the Shattuck heirs, but we turn and come up the hill, passing next beyond the Robeson place on the east a small estate owned by Mrs. Thornton K. Lothrop, and adjoining that "Cosy Nook," the summer home of Miss

Yokun Avenue, Lenox.

Helen Parish. Opposite is "Fairlawn," belonging to the heirs of Mr. Charles Kneeland, but one of the earliest "summer-places" in Lenox, having been originally owned by Mrs. Lee of New Orleans, one of the first comers to the Berkshire resort. Emerging from West Street on Monument Square, we pass on the southwest corner the beautiful property known as the "Bishop place," once the property of Judge Henry Walker Bishop, a prominent citizen of Lenox, who was elevated to the bench of the Court of Common Pleas. Since his death this estate has been owned by his son, Henry Bishop, Esq., of Chicago.

And now just to get a closer view of some of the outlying estates we have been looking down upon from our far-off eyrie, I want to take the reader for a couple of drives on, let us say, some beautiful day in June; one shall be in the morning and one in the afternoon. We will start for our first trip from the Paterson monument again, and driving up Main Street through Cliffwood, we pass on the left some small places, belonging respectively to F. Egmont Schermerhorn, Esq., B. K. Stevens, Esq., and Miss Anna Shaw, the latter the old Hotchkin place, for many years the residence of the cultured family of John Hotchkin, principal of Lenox Academy and founder of Lenox Library, and reach at length the entrance to "Stonover Park." It is the old "Belden Marsh" as the fathers knew it, but now the revelation of what a few tiles and the landscape gardener's art can do. We drive for a mile or more over perfect roadbeds, through wooded lanes and out in the "open," now a graded loop down some steep declivity, now a straight and level course between ranks of chestnuts, and at length reach the Stonover farm buildings under the crest of Bald Head. On we go over the country road to "Shadowbrook" a mile away and by an easy ascent through the Stokes estate are soon on the summit of the tonsured mountain, looking off on one of the loveliest landscapes in the world, with the picturesque and broken chain of the Catskills making a ragged sky-line fifty miles to the west. We descend to the palatial villa on this vast estate; large, turreted, baronial, from which the spacious lawns go sweeping down almost to the very edge of peaceful Mahkeenac,—everywhere the most transporting scenery, the fresh and luxuriant leafage, the liquid notes of the bobolink, the variegated carpet of the fields, all the rich shades and tints, the different hues of blue in ty, and lake, and far-off mountains, and the commingled perfume of lilac, syringa, and the wild flora of the region. Here at " Shadowbrook " we see, for the looking, a cluster of fine estates. Adjoining Mr. Stokes on the south is " Lakeside," owned by Charles Astor Bristed, Esq., while back of us on the higher slopes of Bald Head are " Bonnie Brae," owned by Henry Barclay, Esq., and " The Orchard," belonging to H. H. Pease, Esq.

We make an abrupt turn here and take the Hawthorne road, which runs on high ground along the northern side of Stockbridge Bowl, and almost immediately pass through the very heart of three fine estates on both sides of the highway, the villas being on the still higher ground on the left: " The Corners," owned by Geo. Higginson and acquired by him in 1860; " Tanglewood," which is the old Tappan place, a beautiful estate which was created more than fifty years ago; and " Highwood," owned by the heirs of the late Mr. Wm. S. Bullard, who bought this estate of Mr. Samuel Ward, by whom it was laid out in 1846, the oldest private estate in Lenox. This section of the town is trebly interesting; first, on account of its rare scenic beauty; again, because this is the starting-point of

Lenox as the resort of those who by affluence and rare taste have created magnificent estates; and still again, because of the memories of Hawthorne. We are passing now on the right the site of the "little old red house" where Hawthorne wrote his *House of the Seven Gables*. The genius of Hawthorne is here "writ large" on the landscape, on the very names of the estates, on the road along which we are being driven. A half-mile farther on, and around a picturesque turn through some tall pines, called "Lovers' Lane," we come to "Wheatleigh," with its spacious and stately Italian villa, — an estate of some hundreds of acres belonging to Henry H. Cook, Esq.; and here by a very steep grade and a spiral descent we reach the edge of the lake, across whose inlet we bowl.

Almost immediately we turn abruptly to the left, into the truly great estate of the late D. W. Bishop, Esq., "Interlaken." A secluded carriage road skirts the wooded bank of the inlet for a mile into the heart of primeval forest where the road winds steeply upward many hundred feet amid grand old trees, to the heights above, and the highway (Stockbridge Road). Reaching this point and turning to the south we drive on to "Erskine

ark," the extensive and beautiful estate of
Geo. Westinghouse, Esq., passing as we go
hither many fine places, — "The Poplars"
recently purchased of the Philip Sands estate
by S. Frothingham, Esq., "Merrywood" opposite, on the right, owned by Charles Bullard,
Esq., and the very extensive property of Wil-
iam D. Sloane, Esq., "Elm Court," a grand
estate lying along the road here, and the cross-
roads, for three miles, its beautiful villa,
built near an ancient elm, being charmingly
situated on a commanding eminence nearer the
village. We shall see it on our return. But
here we are at the junction of Stockbridge
Road and Kemble Street, where we enter the
Westinghouse grounds, lying in the extreme
southeastern part of the town. Miles of spacious white roads thread their way by graceful
urns through vast sweeps of lawn, dotted
here and there with most beautiful old elms,
and now the long driveways skirt, and now
they cross by massive bridges, an artificial lake
(in which are five *jets d'eau*), until they encircle
the handsome, white villa which stands half a
mile from the entrance on a high elevation of
land rising abruptly three hundred feet out
of Laurel Lake. What a charming prospect
is here! We have been for the most part

looking into the other valley where Stockbridge Bowl peacefully reposes at the base of the Taghconics. Here is another " mountain mirror," the beautiful Laurel Lake, which forms the centre-piece in the landscape for a dozen places grouped around it. Directly across the lake, as we stand here near the "Erskine Park" villa, the Hoosacs rise with an average altitude of two thousand feet, October Mountain lies empurpled in the evening glow, while on and on the mountains stretch toward the north where twenty miles away Greylock rises over all. Immediately beneath us lies the placid lake, around to the left rise the terraced heights of Lenox adorned with many beautiful villas, and as we turn to retrace our way to the entrance we see across the sunlit lawn the awesome majesty of Rattlesnake, fifteen hundred feet, darkly standing against a westering sun. Glimpsing the ever-present scenery through the trees as we return by another drive to the entrance, we see from one point the terminal mountains at either end of the county, Greylock and the Dome, and also look around the spur of Rattlesnake to still Mahkeenac at the base of Bald Head.

We make our way back to the village along Stockbridge Road once more in order that we

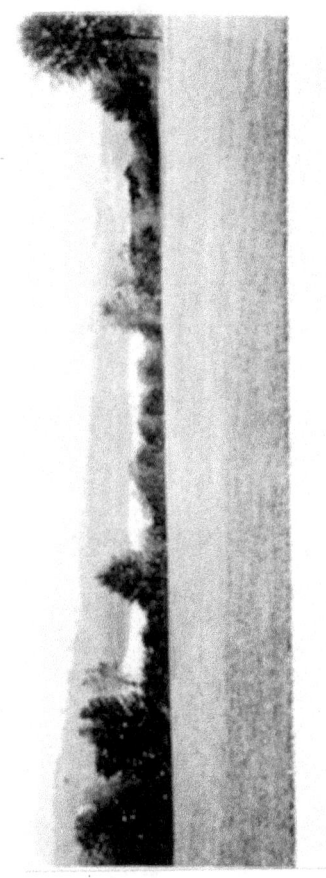

Laurel Lake.

Modern Lenox 195

may see at closer range some handsome properties and villas which on their very sightly elevations we have been seeing before at a distance. A short way beyond the place where we entered this highway by the steep wood-road through the "Interlaken" estate, we drive for a mile on Telford Road, built at private expense, along the ridge which divides Lenox into two valleys. This is all very high ground through here, commanding superb prospects. On the left we see "Elm Court," the spacious residence of Wm. D. Sloane, Esq., looking off on a most enchanting landscape, two lakes in the foreground of the picture and a background of mountains reaching up and down the valley for miles in either direction; on the right, opposite, the "Interlaken" villa which looks into the other valley and off upon its glistening lake, a most picturesque bit of landscape. Farther on we pass an old-time bit of domestic architecture, "Yokun," an eighteenth-century survival which was built in 1794 by Judge William Walker of Lenox, but for many years, with its fine acreage, was the property of the late R. Goodman, Sr., and now owned by his heirs. It is most sightly; almost as much so as its more fashionable neighbor "Allen Winden" farther up the slope. It looks off upon both valleys and the three lakes. Beyond " Yokun " on the left, high up on the very crest of the ridge, stands " Allen Winden," the handsome summer residence of Charles Lanier, Esq., whose wife was the great-granddaughter of General Paterson, and who himself has given proof of the depths of a long and sincere attachment for Lenox in many substantial ways. Across from " Allen Winden " is " Maplehurst," the beautiful estate of Mrs. Joseph M. White, whose friendship for Lenox extends over so many years, and who has endeared herself, as have so many others, by opportune ministries to the people of the town. Coming this way toward the village once more, we pass in order three places, " Lithgow Farm," " Plumsted," and " Redwood," belonging respectively to Clinton G. Gilmore, Esq., Joseph S. Whistler, Esq., and S. Parkman Shaw, Esq., the last-named place being within a stone's throw of the Paterson monument only a few rods down Courthouse Hill.

A fresh pair of horses in the afternoon, if you are not filled to satiety and fatigue by the morning's excursion, will enable us to "do" the rest of the town by a short drive in the direction of the neighboring town of Lee, along the new "State Road" and back by Kemble Street. We start once more from the Paterson monument in front of Curtis's, and take Walker Street out to the eastward. The new Town Hall stands on our right, opposite the hotel. We pass on the left Church Street, a little way down which is the Methodist church, organized early in the nineteenth century. On the right we see at once, here in the very centre of the village, not two hundred feet from the Monument, what was hidden before—the same lovely, far-stretching "view" which we saw from the piazza of the hotel on the high hill yonder. The "view" is everywhere; you have not to go anywhere to get it; it is always before you, except where the thick setting of ornamental hedge has shut it out, and then the enchanting prospect is aggravatingly just over the hedge. As we drive along Walker Street our attention is constantly arrested by the glimpses of the magnificent landscape through the trees.

On the right we quickly reach, where Kemble Street diverges, the handsome Episcopal church property, with its church edifice, parish-house, and rectory, all of blue Berkshire limestone. The ecclesiastical organization connected with this church is quite old. Services according to the Episcopal order of worship were held in the town as early as 1771, and regularly after 1793, though the "Mission" here was carried on jointly with the church in Stockbridge for some years. But Trinity Episcopal Church, Lenox, hardly became self-supporting until 1856, when its rector at that time, the Rev. W. H. Brooks, stated in his annual report : "In the summer season Lenox *being a great resort* our congregations during that portion of the year are always of good size and frequently fill the church," and he adds that the whole number of communicants belonging to the local church was at that time fourteen. To-day the condition of the Episcopal church is far in excess of the promise of fifty years ago. The present property was acquired in 1887, and with the phenomenal growth of Lenox as a place of resort and of fine estates, this church has greatly strengthened its stakes. It is the church of the summer residents, owns a valuable property with church edifice and parish-house in an outlying section of the town, helps liberally every good cause in the county, and has greatly increased its roll of communicants. It was only after a good deal of discussion that this site was

Trinity Episcopal Church, Kemble Street.

determined upon for the new church, but it is an ideal one.

Opposite the church as we drive on past "Trinity," down the beautiful State Road which leads over four miles of macadam to Lee, we pass on the left next to "Lenox Club" the cottage of Mrs. William C. Wharton, "Pine Acre," and still on beyond "Wynnstay," the property of Mrs. John Struthers. "Bel Air," next on the left and occupied for some years by Thatcher M. Adams, Esq., goes with the Morgan estate opposite, "Ventfort Hall," of which it is a part. "Ventfort Hall" villa is an Elizabethan architectural unity, as "Wyndhurst" is Tudor, and "Bellefontaine," French, the last being modelled after the Petit Trianon. Domestic architecture that embodies some one central idea is always pleasing, and "Ventfort Hall" has the advantage of crowning one of the oldest estates in Lenox, the Haggerty place; hence the avenues and trees have the dignity of age. Next beyond the estate of Mr. Morgan is the property of Mr. Schermerhorn, which extends from here two miles to the east and embraces many hundred acres. On the left, opposite, are "Sunnybank," owned by Mrs. Francis C. Barlow, and just beyond "Thistledown," the property of David Lydig, Esq. Passing

"Thistledown," the road turns abruptly to the right, and a mile farther on we reach five large estates. Immediately bounding Mr. Schermerhorn on the south is the hundred and fifty acre tract of Giraud Foster, Esq., while opposite this property on the left we are passing the estate of Mr. John S. Barnes, "Coldbrooke," beyond which we come to "Wyndhurst," the very extensive property of John Sloane, Esq. Mr. Sloane's property lies on both sides of the road, and the handsome villa in yellow pressed brick stands conspicuously to the left on high ground. On the next "four corners," two miles from the village of Lenox, three estates meet, "Wyndhurst," occupying two, and the properties of Mr. R. W. Paterson and Miss Sargent the other two. The Paterson place is, also, another one of the old estates of Lenox (the old Dorr place); and on the opposite corner looks off the modest cottage of Miss G. Sargent on the charming Laurel Lake in the near foreground.

We turn here and pursue our way along this northern side of the little lake, and are soon passing the estates of the late Robert and Ogden Goelet, Esqs., Robert W. Chapin, Esq., Mrs. John Struthers, and Edward R. Wharton, Esq. It is a drive of a mile from Miss

Modern Lenox

Sargent's cottage to the Wharton villa, and here we turn towards the village once more along Kemble Street, passing on the left "Interlaken," "Maplehurst," and "The Perch," the latter once the home of Fanny Kemble, and on the right the stately villa in white marble, "Bellefontaine," belonging to Giraud Foster, Esq. The property through this section, as indeed we might say throughout the whole of Lenox, is simply one of large contiguous estates. Hereabouts the little Laurel Lake forms part of the picture, with the long white chalk-line made by the Lee village church spire against the mountains; everywhere the rim of mountains; everywhere at night the brilliantly illuminated mansions thickly sown; everywhere beauty and restfulness. Passing the Foster estate we are soon ascending the hill, leaving on the left "Clipston Grange," owned by Frank K. Sturgis, Esq., and "Sunnycroft" just beyond, on the same side, the property of George G. Haven, Esq. On the right the hedge half conceals the palatial "Ventfort Hall," and here we have at length reached "Trinity" once more just as the melodious chimes are vying with the sylvan minstrels to usher in the evening's peace. Opposite the church the "Frelinghuysen cottage" stands with its rigid lines against the sunset and far off on Bald Head the observer would see it now o'ertopping like a house of gold the crest on which we are standing. Between it and "Sunnycroft" which we have just passed stands, among some pines, a house modest and old-fashioned enough to shrink from comparison with the modern villas about it, yet possessing the dignity and interest with which the memories of Catherine Sedgwick invest it. Here on this old Sedgwick property was Mrs. Charles Sedgwick's school for girls, and here in the half-hidden house through the trees was the residence for many summers of the gifted and voluminous author of stories which between 1822 and 1858 captivated the reading world on both sides of the Atlantic: Kate Sedgwick, whom Donald G. Mitchell in his *American Lands and Letters* has styled "the charming old lady of the Berkshire highlands."

We have returned again, passing on the left as we turned into Walker Street the fine old colonial cottage of the late Judge Julius Rockwell, to Monument Square and the Curtis Hotel. A hostelry on this very spot has dispensed hospitality for a hundred years, with a noteworthy succession of landlords during the

Modern Lenox 203

century, each having a long tenure of service. The present proprietor, Mr. Wm. D. Curtis, succeeded his father, William O. Curtis, in 1894. Through the proprietorship of father and son extending over a period of fifty years, this hotel has maintained and greatly added to the high prestige it enjoyed in the earlier days, and now its later glory outshines all its previous rivals on this same site. Its registers reaching back only through its present management would be valuable to autograph collectors, such names appearing here as those of Longfellow, Charles Sumner, O. B. Frothingham, Chester A. Arthur, John A. Andrew, Alfred Bierstadt, John A. Dix, George McClellan, Wm. T. Sherman, the Duke of Marlborough, besides those of ambassadors from all foreign courts, leaders in finance and social circles here and abroad, and many, many others equally distinguished in all walks of life. To-day this famous hostelry with its architectural simplicity, its homelike interior, its etchings, its afternoon teas, its large and fashionable patronage, seems to have but entered into the realization of the promise of its humbler predecessors, before whose doors the Hudson and Pittsfield stage with a winding of the horn, and a crack of the whip, and a circular sweep of narrow dimensions used to regularly but somewhat dramatically and perilously deposit its load of passengers. Verily the very ground on which Curtis's stands to-day in its simple magnificence seems a palimpsest, from which the earlier record will not be rubbed out.

The valuation of Lenox twenty years ago was a little over a million of dollars; in 1883, $1,599,411; and in 1900, $3,750,004, a phenomenal increase. With all this appreciation in property, due to the building here of great estates, has been going on a steady increase in population. The sturdy farmers of other days have been replaced by those who, as superintendents, gardeners, and care-takers of these vast properties, have made the flood-tide stronger than the ebb, and Lenox has thus been saved from the depopulation which has visited other Berkshire towns. The population of Lenox in 1800 was 1041; to-day it is not far from 3000. It was not till twenty years ago that the 2000 mark was reached, and though the original Yankee element has, during these last twenty years, disappeared as never before, Lenox has added in that time as many to the population as in the eighty years preceding. The business conditions in Lenox are such as obtain in a "resort." Great industries that once turned out here manufactures of iron, glass, tin and willow ware are dead and well-nigh forgotten. One industry, that of the manufacture of glass, gasped its last expiring breath within twenty years, but its history reaches back many years. Indeed far back in the eighteenth century, the General Court made a grant of 1500 acres in Berkshire to Mr. John Franklin and others, for the purpose of promoting glass-making at Germantown, near Boston. This is known as the "Glass Works Grant," and was confirmed by buying the right of the Indians in 1757 for £28 10s. It was located south of Lenox Furnace, and just east of the "Ministers' Grant" referred to in an earlier chapter. Glass was made at Lenox Furnace for years. Its budget of business, the making of plate-glass, bottles, etc., is a frequent item in the files of the county press, and specimens of its work may be seen in the patent office, Washington, D.C. The "Iron Works" went out of business some years before the manufacture of glass stopped, but its subterranean galleries and corridors actually honeycombed a section of the village on Main Street, so that on November 27, 1862, a house standing on one of the streets fell through the crust and was buried up to the second story. Modern industrial conditions, combined with the peculiar forces which were at work to make Lenox a place of resort, the removal of the courts in 1869, the proximity of a city on the north (Pittsfield, 25,000 population), and the coming of the trolley have at times affected the local business, yet the tax budget was never so large, and the improvements which the town has been able to have in recent years, through the presence here of a wealthy class, have made it privileged far beyond other towns with great municipal blessings: a perfect sewer system, water and electric-lighting, fine roads, good schools, a splendidly equipped library, and the Town Hall, which has been built this year (1902) at an expense, with the land on which it stands, of $80,000.

Such then is modern Lenox: beautiful for situation, imposing and impressive in its many palatial villas, and the park-like estates adjoining. It can be compared with so few places of its class that its rank and charm and fame have conspired to give it the name, among those who are its rapt lovers, "*Lenox, the only.*"

VI

THE VICINAGE

FROM GREYLOCK TO THE TAGHCONIC DOME ON
THE WHEEL

THE " Berkshires " are the foot-hills of the
Green Mountains, which fork at the northern end of the county, and, running down its
sides in parallel ranges,— the Hoosac and
the Taghconic, — make its eastern and western boundaries. Greylock, thirty-five hundred
feet, commands the northern approach and
salutes the rising morn on Monadnock and
" Tom " far away ; and the Dome, twenty-
eight hundred feet, stands sentinel at the
south. It is a country as prodigal of landscapes as of bracing air. Through the very
heart of it winds the Housatonic, deflected
often to a right angle by some mountain barrier as it makes its way to the sea, ever
deepening, ever broadening, turning the myriad

wheels of many industries, placid in the meadows, troubled near the towns.

One may moralize, dream, aspire, rest in such a country, but the heresy obtains that one may not ride the bicycle there. Canoeists have paddled its river with many portages, and bicyclists have coasted its hills which they have climbed with many dismounts and trundlings. But is there no compensation to the wheelman in the picturesque landscapes and exhilarating "coasts," in the pure mountain air and restful wayside inns? And where such views, such "coasts," such tonic in the air, such fine roads, and such ideal inns as in Berkshire! Is there no compensation in visiting a section of country rich in historical and literary associations, studying its folk and customs, viewing its fine estates and villas? And where such gratification as in Berkshire!

Bicyclists, so far as Berkshire is concerned, may be divided into two classes: the sacred and the profane; the first-named being those who are in rapt oneness with the loveliness and the traditions of the region; the latter, those who worship their wheels, are oblivious to scenic beauty, and are attracted hither only to see fine estates. I was standing one day at a bend in the road where all of a sudden a burst of entrancing landscape opens out to the beholder, and then is partly screened from view by two rows of trees so placed that what part of the scenery one does n't shut out the other will, when along came a party of bicyclists riding for dear life. The leader, who was familiar with the region, shouted, as they passed — or rather fairly whizzed — out of sight: " Now, boys, keep your eyes peeled. This is the finest scenery in Berkshire County!" And then a cloud of dust hid them from view, and I was left with the charming vision blurred by man's inappreciation.

A wheelman in a hill-country should always pursue the general tenor of his way with the view before him rather than behind his back, and consequently Berkshire should be traversed from north to south. We will enter it through the Hoosac Tunnel, — that colossal feat in engineering, — at the northeastern end of the county. The tunnel is four and three quarters miles long (next to the longest in the world) and was finished in 1874, after nineteen years of toilsome labor, the loss of 136 lives, and an expenditure of $12,000,000, for which the State gave its credit. We emerge from the tunnel directly upon the beautiful manufacturing city of North Adams, the largest city in Berkshire County; city of prints and shoes and many industries; home of the State Normal School; a thriving and attractive *urbs in rure*, right at the foot of Greylock. A day must be taken to make the ascent of the mountain, and though there are carriages in waiting to take you to its summit, we push on down the valley road to the smart manufacturing town of Adams, made notable by the stay of President McKinley during a week he spent in the Berkshires the summer after his first inauguration. Leaving our wheels and liberally provisioning ourselves against the sure access of fierce hunger awaiting us on the peak of Greylock, where the means of gratifying the inner man have until recently been limited by what you carry, we eagerly enter upon the laborious ascent. It is a rough and tortuous climb of four hours, allowing for rests by the way, following now a wood-road, now the dry bed of a mountain brook, now a somewhat uncertain opening through the forest, over logs and boulders, up steep inclines, tilted to nearly forty per cent., on and on with many rests until the top is reached, a weary climb of five miles, taxing every atom of strength and endurance, but more than compensated for in the grandeur

Greylock from Onota Lake, Pittsfield.

The Vicinage 211

of the prospect when once we stand upon the summit and scale the last staircase of the skeleton tower which rises there sixty feet.

Berkshire lies beneath us, its lakes seeming like silver maple leaves fallen to the ground, its heights stunted; and immediately below us are the towns we have left, with their busy looms too far away to hear, and farther around at the base of the opposite slope, Williamstown, whose far-famed college and classic retreats await us on the morrow. Far away to the north, and reflecting a slanting ray of the sun, the Bennington monument catches the eye against the blue background of the Vermont hills, out of which rise individual peaks; to the east, over the Hoosacs, appears the observatory-capped summit of Mount Tom; southward stretches Berkshire, while in the west appears a faint streak of silver, the mighty Hudson, and beyond, making a saw-toothed sky-line, the jagged chain of the Catskills. It is a good introduction to a Berkshire trip, wedged, as the country is, into three States, Vermont, Connecticut, and New York; and gives us a sort of bird's-eye view of the country we are to cover. Let us say incidentally as we descend to our bicycles in Adams, that we shall see no sublimer thing in

Berkshire than the prospect we have left; though many more picturesque bits of scenery, the filling in of the picture so vast and grand on the heights of Greylock, charm and inspire the wheelman as he rides from town to town; now a vista opening here, now a pastoral with village-spire in the distance, now a mountain lake of pearl set in its emerald enclosure of mountains, now a path between the arching elms along the river side, now a magnificent expanse from some hill he is about to "coast," now an olden mill by the bridge, a deep fissure in the rocks, a beetling and overhanging cliff, now a peaceful dale where the sun early sinks to rest, now a neat trim farmhouse, now an abandoned group of buildings in the many "deserted villages" which abound in the borders of Berkshire, and now expansive manors with well-kept grounds and parks stretching away from palatial mansions, commanding superb views and arresting attention by the diversity in their architecture.

It is only a short easy distance along a macadamized State road from North Adams to Williamstown, so we decide after wheeling in from Adams to push on to the college town for the night. It is the week after Commencement, and the village is bereft of its student-colony, but its hilly street, on either side of which are the substantial and handsome college buildings, presents an attractive prospect, and tired as we are, though refreshed by supper, we set out to stroll in the grounds. The Mecca of all pilgrims is, of course, the "Haystack Monument," erected to perpetuate the memory of those valiant youths who here gave themselves to Christian work in foreign lands ; and with the thought in our minds that the movement of foreign missions in America was born on Berkshire soil, we return to the inn and to the dreamless sleep of the wheelman.

Williams College cannot be written about in a paragraph. It has passed its century mark ; its graduates are in all lands, doing efficient service ; its standards and results place it in the first rank of American colleges ; its condition is always prosperous and progressive, its location is perfectly entrancing ; and after another look about the buildings — and into them so far as we can — we turn our faces southward. It is a run of five miles to South Williamstown along the side of Greylock, and over a level piece of road, but thence on through the adjoining town of New Ashford to Lanesborough the grade is up, with many dismounts, but with ever-increasing loveliness of scenery as the higher levels are reached. The country through here is not yet pre-empted by the summer resident, and land is almost given away. Land which sells in Lenox at prices ranging from $1000 to $20,000 per acre sells in some parts of the county at from one dollar to four dollars per acre! Almost one whole township in Berkshire has been bought by a well-known citizen of New York, at less than an average price of five dollars an acre! Lanesborough, through which we are now wheeling, and where we are shown the birthplace of Josh Billings, is one of these decadent towns, and yet only four miles from the city of Pittsfield, the county seat. On we push past placid Pontoosuc Lake, known to the Indians as Skoon-keek-moon-keek, and Pittsfield is soon reached. A morning's work has been accomplished, and after dinner we are at liberty to look around the city.

Pittsfield is a distributing centre for miles around. It is six miles north of the geographical centre of the country, but it stole the courts and county seat away from Lenox, thirty years ago, after trying in vain for fifty years before success crowned its efforts.

The Haystack Monument at Williams College, marking the birthplace of American Foreign Missions, Williamstown, Mass.

The Vicinage

Every one is glad now that Lenox is rid of the incubus of court-week, county jails, and hangings, and Pittsfield can take care of all that with no perceptible disturbance on the surface of its life. It is a beautiful city, with handsome edifices and residences, many industries, and dominated by a spirit of culture and refinement such as few cities possess. We wheel out to Dalton, four miles away, a beautiful manufacturing village, connected with Pittsfield by trolley, the seat of the paper-mills which furnish bank-note paper to the United States Government, and the home of the present Governor of the State, W. Murray Crane; and then we wheel to Lenox, skirting Pittsfield on the east in order that we may pass through that section justly noteworthy on account of its being for seven years the home of the humorist and poet Dr. Holmes. We reach Lenox, twelve miles from Dalton, in the evening, having covered in the day's wheeling about forty miles; and, as we wheel up to the Curtis Hotel, the village band, under the electric lights, is giving its regular out-of-doors concert, the piazzas of the hotel swarming with guests in dinner dress, and the streets filled with people and equipages.

To reach this point of our journey it has

been a gradual climb all the way from Williamstown; henceforth there will be nothing but a steady descent, even when we cross Monument, whose approach on the Stockbridge side is an easy rise, but whose southern slope towards Great Barrington is a " coast " straight down of over a mile. From Lenox to Stockbridge there are many ways to go; all beautiful enough, but one surpassingly so, viz., the road that leads by Stockbridge Bowl past the Hawthorne site, and thence on into the village-on-the-plain by the heights where stand the residences of Mr. Choate, our Minister to England, Dr. Henry M. Field, and others. It is worth the while of the wheelman, however, before leaving Lenox, to see its beautiful places, whose superintendents are trained English gardeners for the most part. These grounds need not be entered to see them, as they lie on slopes easily seen from the highway. The villas themselves are conspicuous, and may be viewed at a distance. They crown the crests and swells in the land; their velvety lawns are on the slopes and terraces; and the great desideratum of a country-seat hereabouts being a " view," the house is always on a knoll or spur, so that the wheelman can take it in as he passes along the highway.

The Vicinage

It may not be amiss to say to the wheelman, *en passant*, that in going from town to town it is well not to be too slavishly tied to the *Road-book* issued under the authority of some State association of bicyclists, whose study is often a matter of levels rather than of landscapes. In the temple of Berkshire loveliness no foot is profane but that of him who hurries through her courts. Her symphonies fall upon deaf ears, her visions waste their prodigal beauty on sightless eyes, unless one stops to admire, and stopping, finds his admiration turn to aspiration. If bicycling is a matter of levels in such a country, then Niagara is only so much horse-power, and all sentiment valuable only as a marketable asset. I have actually seen many bicyclists avoid the hilly road with its transporting apocalypses. The *Road-book* says: "From Lenox to Stockbridge go through Curtisville" (now Interlaken). We do not. Leaving Curtisville on the right, we wheel into Stockbridge over Field hill and then on through the charming village under the high and white-faced crags of Monument, which we ride without a trundle, though perhaps a little out of breath when we reach the highest point of the pass over the mountain's eastern slope. A sign, "Wheelmen; Dangerous!" informs us that other wheelmen have been lured to these heights; indeed, one was killed here last summer.

We decide to leave our wheels in the thick forest-growth everywhere about us, save where a vista in front reveals the height to which we have climbed, and to make the ascent of this far-famed mountain immortalized by Bryant. A little foot-path marks the way to the summit, and soon we are sitting in the "Devil's Pulpit," with the entrancing landscape at our feet: in the north Greylock, far up the county, in the south the Dome, whither we are tending; off to the far west the ragged and graceful Catskills (graceful in their raggedness); below us the winding Housatonic and the manufacturing village called by the name of the river,— the only town in the county to preserve the Indian nomenclature,—and everywhere the pastoral beauty of field, and farm, and meadow, stretching forth to the bases of the distant Taghconics. It is a charming by-path excursion, and we are all the more ready, returning to our wheels, for the "coast" down Monument into Great Barrington, four miles away.

Great Barrington invites a rest after a good

morning's work. The inn where we stop is filled with summer boarders and the heights around us are crowned with country-seats. It is the "season" in Great Barrington, while that in Lenox begins in May and ends in November, reaching its greatest intensity in September. The fame of the lesser of these resorts is much enhanced by its having been for a few years the home of William Cullen Bryant. A truly palatial castle is also here, with atrium of African marbles and doors from Windsor and walls hung with masterpieces of modern art. It is all very beautiful from the piazzas of the opposite inn, but refreshed we push on to Sheffield, six miles over a perfectly level road of ideal hardness. It is swift and constant pedalling unbroken by dismount or "coast." We have now reached the southern end of the county and have been having on our right for some time the near view of the Dome, called by the people who live in this region "Mount Everett." Sheffield enjoys the distinction of being the oldest of the Berkshire towns. It has been the birthplace of some notable men : Dr. Orville Dewey, the distinguished Unitarian divine of the ast century, President Barnard of Columbia, Mr. George F. Root, the well-known musical composer, and others. The chief attraction the little village possesses is its long, wide street bordered by overarching elms. We have left now the region of the summer cottager for that of the summer boarder, of which latter genus there are many lodged here and there throughout the entire township. The "season" here is very short, yet, by the modish attire of the "boarders" going to and from the post-office, resting lazily in the hammocks, or playing at tennis and croquet on the lawns, we are pleasantly impressed with the social standing of the village among those who seek relief in the summer from the heat of the city.

It is a pedal of about six miles, at the northern base of Everett, to the little village of South Egremont, and we decide to wheel there for supper and the night's lodging. The sole attraction here, aside from those beauties of landscape with which the whole Berkshire region abounds, is the inn. It is filled with guests, some being "colonized" out of the house. We are now, at South Egremont, only four miles from Great Barrington and not much farther from the New York line: way down in the extreme southwestern corner of the State of Massachusetts. Did you ever notice the jog in the southern end of that divisional line between Massachusetts and New York? It would take volumes to tell the story of the running of that dividing line, which was finally determined by a Federal commission. Its course was a slant from southwest to northeast at a pretty nearly uniform distance of twenty miles from the Hudson River. At any rate here we are at the southern point of that line, the "old corner" or jog as it looks on the map. On the morrow we make the ascent of Mount Everett, and survey the country over which we have come,—rightly compared to Switzerland. Far in the distance rises Greylock in the form of a colossal saddle. Monument, Rattlesnake, Tom Ball, Perry's Peak, Bald Head, and the Lenox heights are in between. It has taken four days to see the Berkshires by our leisurely itinerary, and when we part on the summit of Everett, two of our party descend into Connecticut by way of the Salisburys, two take the New York side, descending by way of Bash-Bish Falls,—a beautiful cascade over the precipitous cliffs of Everett, falling for more than a hundred feet,—while I retrace my way to Lenox.

Berkshire then is the cycler's paradise. Its hills, if a little difficult to climb, are fine to coast; its roads are always in prime order; its views fascinate; its air exhilarates; its history stimulates; and its ideal hostelries are no small part of the charm of the region. A flat country makes constant pedalling, and the horizon hems one in so that the eye is given nothing to do. In Berkshire, the landscapes and the "coasts" repay all the climbing, and if one will not slavishly follow the itinerary of the *Road-book*, he will fasten upon his mind an ineffaceable picture of loveliness.

PITTSFIELD, THE HEART OF BERKSHIRE

Industrially and socially Pittsfield is the heart of the Berkshire region. Though on high ground itself the city lies in a slight depression among the hills, the grade out of it on the east being nearly two per cent., along the railway, and on the south by the carriage road leading to Lenox, six miles distant, not far from one per cent. It was doubtless this fact, among others, which influenced the location of the Boston & Albany Railroad, which describes an ox-bow as it crosses Berkshire. Pittsfield in 1800 was but little larger than Sandisfield, at the far southeastern limit of the county; it progressed proportionately and normally during the first half of its present existence, but with the acquisition of the railroads in 1840, and the courts in 1869, it has shot way ahead of all the other towns of the county but one, changing to a city charter in 1889, and having now a population of nearly twenty-five thousand and a valuation of $16,000,000. It is to-day the very heart of Berkshire mercantile life, though this by no means implies that there are not in other parts of the county great and profitable industries; indeed, North Adams, Adams, Dalton, and Housatonic are factory towns (the first-named a prosperous city itself and larger than Pittsfield, with large outputs). Still, Pittsfield with its electrical, woollen, and other industries, its stores, its dignity as the county seat, and its location on the great highways of railroad traffic is *facile princeps* among smart Berkshire towns and one of the most attractive cities in the whole of New England. Two beautiful lakes, a fascinating environment of hills with Greylock lifting its saddle-back against the northern sky, a mountain atmosphere, impart to this city all the necessary essentials for a "resort"; and Pittsfield does annually entertain hosts of summer visitors. Its air is as bracing as any of the Berkshire towns; it is easy to get to and get away from; it has the most enchanting prospects and drives, less beautiful than those of its southern neighbors, still delightful in the prodigality of rich landscapes; its facilities in the way of stores, shops, library, churches, and society are all that could be desired; its hotels, like all the other inns of Berkshire, make ample provision for the comfort of summer guests; and last, but by no means least, its unique and homelike "House of Mercy," with the best of medical attendance and an efficient school of trained nurses, appeals to tourists who make provision for the exigencies of illness.

But the purpose of this short bit about Pittsfield, as we might say of the whole of this book, is to make part of the Berkshire region intelligible and enjoyable to those who are not familiar with its story. It is not to write history only so far as it explains the Berkshire picture, and this chief city of the Berkshires could not be understood without a glance into its past.

It becomes interesting to us at once when we know that Oliver Wendell Holmes said: "the whole of the city of Pittsfield, consisting of a section of land six miles square, was,

"*Somewhat back from the village street
Stands the old-fashioned country-seat.*"

The home of Longfellow's wife, Pittsfield, where stood the "Old Clock on the Stairs," the original of the well-known poem by that name.

with the exception of a thousand acres, the property of my great-grandfather, Jacob Wendell." This ancestor of the humorist bought the land of the Province and the first settlements were begun in the years 1749-52, when (1753) the little frontier hamlet was known as the township, or plantation, of Pontoosuck. It was incorporated with its present name, Pittsfield, April 21, 1761. It was the fifth town to be incorporated in the county, the others having been in the far south, and there were yet to be twelve before the break with the mother-country. The names of all but two of these ante-Revolutionary towns in the Berkshires are English; afterwards the town nomenclature is conspicuously patriotic,—"Hancock," "Adams," "Washington," "Lee," "Dalton," "Otis," and so on. Pittsfield is one of the towns named before the Revolution; hence the name after the Earl of Chatham, at that time England's leading statesman.

I have already indicated briefly in other places the Indian occupancy of this region before and during the progress of the early settlements, and I have hinted at some of the leading causes which conspired to augment the material prosperity of Pittsfield. The

history of the town is the history of the
Church until Congregationalism was disestablished in 1834, and so when we think of the
early period in all the New England towns,
it is the Church which looms up big. Moreover, as the meaning of the word "parson"
is simply our word "person," or the man who
in his *person* represents the Church, so it may
be said as the town was the Church, so the
Church was the parson,— and in this case
"Parson Allen," better known as "Fighting
Parson Allen" of Bennington fame, a graduate
of Harvard, 1762, and pastor of the First
Church, Pittsfield, 1764-1810, his only pastorate. Two of Mr. Allen's successors in this
parish are as well known, Dr. Heman
Humphrey (1817-23), called from here to the
presidency of Amherst College, and Dr. John
Todd (1842-72), whose *Index Rerum* and
Student's Manual used to be an indispensable
part of every scholar's outfit; but the lustre
of romantic and intense patriotism, as well as
the ardor of a perfervid Democratic partisanship in the midst of Federal New England,
have made "Parson Allen" one of the most
interesting figures in all American history.
He has been rightly styled a "revolutionary
and democratic zealot." He went with the

Berkshire troops to Bennington as chaplain, but he levelled his musket at the foe with a keen relish in addition to his regular ministerial duties. After the nation was constitutionally organized Jefferson was his political idol, whom all the rest of the New England clergy, with few exceptions, execrated. The First Church bell-rope broke with the violent and exultant ringing at Jefferson's election in 1801. Dr. Belknap, writing of his trip July 4, 1794, from Pittsfield to Northampton, says :

" Independence Day. From Pittsfield to Northampton ; from Democracy to Federalism! When we left Pittsfield great preparations were making to observe the day. The inhabitants of this and neighboring towns were to meet to-day at Richmond. When we came to Northampton we found that not a bell had been rung ; nor a gun fired, nor a bowl of punch drank in that very federal town to celebrate the day." — Massachusetts Historical Society Collections.

It is interesting to read that although Parson Allen's intense make-up was behind all this riotous political enthusiasm, yet his sermons in shorthand were read with " but little action."

Pittsfield had by 1794 developed into a place of such importance as to necessitate the location here of a post-office, the first in the county having been located at Stockbridge in 1792; and the third, fourth, and fifth were located respectively at Great Barrington (1797), Williamstown (1798), and Lenox, (1800). Previous to 1792, Springfield was the one post-office for the whole of Western Massachusetts. In other chapters I have described how Pittsfield with its newspapers (continuous files of some of which may be seen in the Athenæum) and with post-riders and stages fell naturally into its position of purveyor of news for the whole Berkshire region. It was always a trade centre; and later became an educational centre, having at one time the Berkshire Medical Institution, established in 1822, and the Maplewood Young Ladies' Institute, started in 1841, both of which institutions were vigorous, efficient schools for a long time, but are now defunct, yet always full of pleasant and inspiring memories to their graduates. Pittsfield also inaugurated a new era in the interests of agriculture by the formation in 1807 of the Berkshire Agricultural Society, making the annual exhibition a sort of gala-holiday and so setting a type for all similar societies for all time to come.

If we add to all these claims to eminence the great men who have been identified with

The Vicinage

the town in one way or another our interest in the Berkshire city is enhanced. It is no small honor that it has been the home of Allen, Humphrey, Samuel Harris, and Todd. Pittsfield early attracted to it Elkanah Watson, the accomplished and versatile gentleman, publicist, friend of Washington, and promoter of agricultural enterprise. The Berkshire capital also vies with its neighbor, Dalton, in giving a Governor to the commonwealth, Governor George N. Briggs, seven times chosen Governor of Massachusetts (1843–50). It gave a distinguished Senator to the United States Senate, Henry L. Dawes, *nomen clarissime*, and he and his brilliant daughter, herself a woman of letters, are residents in this charming city in the highlands of Western Massachusetts. It was the home for seven summers (1849–56) of Oliver Wendell Holmes, who loved the ancestral estate in the Berkshires and here three of his children were born. The street on which he lived is known as "Holmes Road" and is full of memories of the poet-humorist. Pittsfield was also the home of Herman Melville, whose sea-stories were in their day very popular and still find admiring readers. It is the home to-day of a distinguished writer of present-day fiction, William Stearns Davis, author of *A Friend of Cæsar*, and *God Wills It*. If we scan the annals of patriotic devotion we see beside many others the names of the gallant General W. F. Bartlett, Colonel of the 49th Massachusetts in the Civil War, General Henry S. Briggs, and Colonel Henry H. Richardson, the latter still living. Indeed, where shall we stop in the enumeration of the great men whose names are inseparably linked with the county seat of Berkshire!

Pittsfield has an air of refinement and culture befitting its pre-eminence. The spirit of the motto *noblesse oblige* is always in the ascendant. Its public buildings and private residences are becoming more and more stately and handsome year by year. It has a beautiful housing for its library and art gallery, the "Athenæum," built in 1875 of blue granite. It has a round dozen of strong, efficient churches. It is soon to have a new art museum, the munificent gift of Mr. Zenas Crane of Dalton. Trolleys lead from the city in all directions. The main streets of the city cross each other at right angles, and are known by the rather unattractive names of the points of the compass. Pontoosuc Lake, the old Indian "Skoon-keek-moon-keek," is an out-

The Vicinage 231

ing place in the summer months, with two steamers, pavilions, and cottages. Excursions to Greylock are frequent by carriage drive. Dalton with the very interesting Wahconah Falls is five miles to the east, Lenox only six miles to the south, and Lebanon Springs past the placid Onota only nine miles to the west. One of the old "institutions" of Pittsfield, a beautiful custom, still survives: a sunrise prayer-meeting on New Year's Day, when all the citizens come together to render thanks for the blessings of the past year and to supplicate mercies for the year to come, a custom which has survived since the pastorate of Heman Humphrey.

HISTORIC STOCKBRIDGE

Have you heard that old saw that down in Stockbridge all the crickets chirp "Sedgwick! Sedgwick!"? Donald G. Mitchell gives it a classic setting in his *American Lands and Letters*. It has now passed into folk-lore. Stockbridge, the home, during the latter part of the eighteenth century, of the Hon. Theodore Sedgwick, one of the most distinguished of our Massachusetts statesmen at the time of the birth of the republic, was the birthplace of his brilliant daughter, Catherine Maria, who reflected upon her native town, as well as upon Lenox, the place of her adopted residence, the dazzling glory of her name in literature as a pioneer in American letters. In fact, the township has never been since those early days without a representative of the Sedgwick family; and the adage about the crickets is only another way of expressing the delicate homage this charming village pays to a name which gathers into itself the dignity, culture, and worth of this old and far-famed town.

There is an air of classic stateliness and repose about Stockbridge. Its wide, elm-bordered street, adorned at intervals with appropriate memorials in stone, and lined with beautiful residences, is a perpetuation of the old New England idea of laying out towns, and vies with the celebrated street in Old Hadley-on-the-Plain. To the north of the village rise rather abruptly the heights which are crowned by magnificent villas, and which, overlooking the town and the winding Housatonic, which flows through the heart of it, catch the reflection of the sun first on the chalky cliffs of Monument, which rises 1640 feet in the southern extremity of the township. It is, indeed, an ever-to-be-remembered view, the very same as that which Bryant, who spent his early years in this region, has sketched in his poem on *Monument Mountain:*

> " . . . the scene
> Is lovely round; a beautiful river there
> Wanders amid the fresh and fertile meads,

> " . . . On each side
> The fields swell upward to the hills; beyond,
> Above the hills, in the blue distance, rise
> The mountain-columns with which earth props up heaven."

Stockbridge is, in a way, mortised into Lenox, the heights we have described receding back and up into the more commanding eminences of the last-named town, to which it is contiguous, so that a very considerable part of the summer residents who have made for themselves country-seats in this region actually pay taxes in Stockbridge, but in everything else are identified with Lenox. The northern end of the Stockbridge township is less than a third of a mile from the Lenox post-office; indeed, the first-named town pays to the latter nearly two hundred dollars per annum for the education of children living near Lenox village. Topographically, Stockbridge is a rectangle on a series of terraces, with the tilted end, where the villas are, in the Lenox heights, and the low end, where the village is, at the base of Monument. It is an old town, one of the very oldest in Berkshire, and was incorporated in 1739, though the Congregational church of the village was organized two years earlier, 1737, when the Mohican Indians, the aborigines of the county, were here collected and educated by John Sergeant. The records of Stockbridge are thus almost synchronous with the beginnings of the county itself.

The history of Stockbridge is little more than that of an Indian town until the outbreak of the Revolution. The Indians were docile and friendly, were ministered to successively by John Sergeant, Jonathan Edwards, and Gideon Hawley, and were removed in a body to a reservation in New York in 1785-87. An appropriate monument — a simple monolith of field-stone — has been erected in the village of Stockbridge to the memory of these red men; not far away is the shaft in memory of Edwards, who was called from his pastorate here in 1758 to the presidency of Princeton College; while a little farther down the wide village street was standing until two years ago the house in which he wrote the *Freedom of the Will.* It is a pity that this ancient building was not preserved: a priceless possession, which might have been removed to another part of the village when its site was wanted for a modern residence. On the eminence north of the town stands the Missionary Building, where the savages were instructed, their education being to a certain extent industrial, even in that day of religious scholasticism and catechisms; and in the village, near the Congregational church, stands the Field Memorial Tower, with chimes, perpetuating the name of one of the best-known Stockbridge pastors, the Rev. David Dudley Field, D.D., and marking the place where the first church edifice stood.

But the story of the "Stockbridge Indians," as they are now called in the asylum they have found in the far West, and who never numbered more than four hundred at any period of their sojourn in the Berkshire village, is only one element of interest in this historic town. What vivid pictures from the olden days throng one's steps in the quiet village street as he looks out upon the stylish equipages, the golfers on their way to and from the links, the groups of "resorters" on the piazza of the "Red Lion," the occasional *bon vivant* in white flannel negligee! Here the

Indians were taught, and Sergeant wrought his labor of love, finished all too early by his untimely death. Here Edwards "shaped his creed at the forge of thought," while over Monument at frequent intervals came from the adjoining town his friend, Samuel Hopkins, who moulded into credal forms (so long the galling chains of the free religious spirit) the theology of New England. Here succeeded to the mighty Edwards the faithful Dr. West, who enjoyed a pastorate of fifty-eight years, longest on record in the county. Miss Sedgwick has drawn him to the life in many of her stories, just as Mrs. Stowe has Dr. Hopkins in her *Minister's Wooing*. One finds much to love in the amiable " little Dr. West," "an Apollo in little," as Catherine Sedgwick describes Parson Wilson in *The Linwoods* from the original of her girlhood's pastor, "being not more than five feet four in height, and perfectly well made, with well-turned leg without the aid of garters, three-cornered hat, gold-headed cane, and buckskin gloves," and whose first act, on the occasion of a pastoral call, was to " smooth his hair to an equatorial line around his forehead " and then to help himself to the decanter.

Here in Stockbridge the Revolutionary spirit

The home of Catherine Maria Sedgwick, Stockbridge.

The Vicinage

rose to the highest pitch of indignation and enthusiasm, sending its choicest sons to Bunker Hill, and boycotting goods of English manufacture. Here in the War of 1812 some French prisoners of war were quartered during a memorable winter, much to Catherine Sedgwick's delight, then a young woman in her early twenties. Here in 1819 came the Rev. David Dudley Field, D.D., as pastor of the village church, the father of one of the most distinguished families in American history, and here he ministered until 1837. Here Mrs. Jameson and Miss Martineau visited Miss Sedgwick; and through these village streets have passed at one time or another those who have had the most honored names in the world's statesmanship and literature. And what shall we say of the natives themselves? What would any town be without its local heroisms and sacrifices and its sturdy yeomanry? It is no wonder the pride of residence is developed in one who lives in Stockbridge perhaps more than in one who lives in any other town. Its history, its scenery, its dignity, its quiet give it a unique charm. It vies with Lenox in attracting wealth to its sightly hillsides.

Stockbridge includes within the limits of

the township the outlying hamlets Glen Dale and Curtisville. At Glen Dale there is a fine water-power from the Housatonic, and until within recent years this little village was the seat of woollen and paper industries. It is through the burning of its two mills paralyzed industrially, but here the great American sculptor French has made himself a "summer-place" with studio, and it was here his heroic figure of "Washington," lately presented to France, was wrought out. At Curtisville is located St. Helen's Home for the Fresh-air children, an institution of the most beneficent character, provided through the liberality of John E. Parsons, Esq., of New York, and his practical philanthropy not only has blessed many squalid tenements and joyless households, but has yielded him, in the happy faces and merry hearts of the children, the best return upon his investment.

THE STOCKBRIDGE INDIANS

A solitary monolith of rough field-stone stands at the western end of Stockbridge, overlooking the river flats and the different golf links which cross and recross the winding stream, and bears this inscription: "The ancient burial-place of the Stockbridge Indians.

The Friends of our Fathers." At the other end of the village, on a rising piece of ground, converted fifty years ago into a pleasure park through the munificence of the heirs to the Sedgwick estate, of which it was a part, is "Laurel Hill," once the Indians' place of meeting and council. Between these termini, nearly a mile apart, stretches the beautiful village street, broad, perfectly level, and bordered by ancient elms; a street which breathes its historic associations, its classic dignity, its repose into the beholder, causing it to stand out as distinctly in his mind as any of the famous streets of the world. Along it are other memorials of the Indian period: the monument to Jonathan Edwards, pastor here among the aborigines 1751–58; the "Field Memorial Chimes," which mark the spot where the first meeting-house stood, where some redskinned brave "wound the horn," so to speak, by announcing through a huge conch shell, as through a megaphone, the stated hours of service; and not far away, on the same street, was, until within two years, the house which Jonathan Edwards occupied, and where he wrote his famous treatise on the *Will.* Another sacred relic, still surviving, is the "Mission House," standing on the heights to the north of the village. It is a sacred period, that of the Indian occupancy from 1736 until 1785-87, during which all the Indians of Berkshire were collected here in this broad plain, surrounded by dense wilderness, through which a trail led by Maus-wa-see-khi and Skatekook winding in and over the mountain passes of the Hoosacs to Westfield, and another in the direction of the setting sun through the forest to Kinderhook. As in a palimpsest, we read distinctly beneath the surface of modern Stockbridge the record of that missionary predecessor, the village of Wnogh-que-too-koke, with its wigwams, its savages, its belts of wampum, and its pipes of peace.

Early Indian Settlers

It is not known exactly when the Muh-hekan-e-ok (or *Mohicans*) came into this valley of the Hoo-es-ten-nuc (Housatonic). They were here in the seventeenth century, and there is a record of a fight with Indians on the banks of the Housatonic in "King Philip's War" in the year 1676, but these hostile Indians were covering their retreat from Westfield to the Mahecannituck (Hudson), and were not the peaceful aborigines of this valley. This is believed to be the first historic mention of this region, and the name of the river, called by some of the early chroniclers "Ausotunnoog," and by others "Ousetonuck," would seem to indicate that the Indians who gave it this name must have been here before this date. Whatever may have been the date of the coming hither of the Mohicans, it is certain that the earliest settlers did nothing, nay, even they did worse than nothing, for the regeneration of the debased savages in whose midst they were preparing to make homes. The Dutch trader with his "fire-water" and the first settlers with their greed were not adapted to impress upon the savage mind the immense superiority of Christianity from an ethical standpoint. And besides as the theology of that day was fatalistic to the non-elect, in which class were doubtless numbered many of their savage neighbors, it would be worse than useless to offer the Gospel; nay, even, would be an affront to the Deity, whose decrees were fixed! Moreover, there is no reason for supposing that frontier settlements then were unlike what they are now; and, indeed, we have positive evidence from Dr. Hopkins, pastor at Great Barrington, 1744–69, that "vice and licentiousness were everywhere prevalent." The days of "the fathers" would not seem so gilded with the lustre of other-worldliness, if we could get back there. The Indian was not deceived by a nasal piety, and yet we read that Konkapot, the chief of the Muh-he-kan-e-ok, wanted to have the Christian religion taught to him and his people. Settlements had begun in 1722, but it was not until 1734 that anything was done to promote the well-being of the aborigines. It was then that the Indian mission was started, prosecuted for the first two years in the north parish of Sheffield, and transferred in 1736 to Stockbridge, which remained the missionary town as long as the Indians stayed in Berkshire.

The Indian Mission

And so Berkshire, which was to become celebrated in history as the birthplace of the great foreign missionary movement in America, is also known through this early experiment in home missions, with which the names of Sergeant and Edwards are so prominently identified, to whose memory tablets have been placed on the walls of the village church. The saintly Sergeant gave it fifteen years of his life, coming here from his tutorship in Yale, then in the first twenty-five years of its splendid career, and was succeeded by Edwards,

The Vicinage

who had graduated from Yale in 1720, nine years before Sergeant, but who came to Berkshire from his long and troubled pastorate in Northampton. Sergeant died in 1749, but he had established the mission on a sound and firm basis, industrial education playing no small part in his sensible scheme. His was the pioneer work — organization, building, translation, preaching, and a sort of general oversight of the Indians and their needs in the surrounding country. David Brainerd came hither to Sergeant for instruction in the Indian tongue, and made frequent visits to Stockbridge before taking up his work among the Delawares. Jonathan Edwards, Jr., who was a boy of six when his father came to Stockbridge, says the only English he heard spoken during his boyhood was in his father's house. There were a few white families in the township, but the younger Edwards says his playmates were all Indian boys, and consequently he himself came to have great facility in the Indian language, becoming later an authority on the Mohican dialect. Stockbridge was, indeed, a centre of instruction for other tribes than the Muh-he-kan-e-ok, some of the Mohawks coming here for instruction from the region about Schenectady. The town was an inviting place for all those schemers who make up Indian "rings" and grow rich off the Indian's necessities, and more than once the righteous Edwards burned with holy anger against their iniquitous doings. An Indian party and an anti-Indian party at length began to appear in the town, during the long pastorate of Dr. West, who succeeded Edwards in 1758 and remained pastor until 1816, when he died. But long before his death the Indians had taken their departure for Oneida, New York, and thus ended the period of the Indian occupancy. Dr. David Dudley Field says "the average number of Indians was four hundred as long as they remained in the town," but a writer in the Collections of the Massachusetts Historical Society says that the number of Indians in the town was continually "wasting away." One authority says that in 1736, when the mission moved to Stockbridge, the number "was ninety persons; in 1752, 150 families; in 1764, 221 persons; and in 1786, when they migrated, one-third that number"; and another still that "in 1736 the number was 90 individuals; in 1740, 120; in 1749, 218; and in 1786, 400."

There are many points of interest in connection with the "missionary" period in the history of Stockbridge. It is noticeable that industrial education, which is so prominent a feature in modern methods, was then a main part of the work. Possibly that idea may have been born on Berkshire soil, too. It would also be worthy of note if the report of a commission sent out to Oneida, N. Y., in 1796, to inquire into the condition of the Stockbridge Indians, could be summarized here, showing in its conclusions how faithful and efficient had been the labors in the Berkshire village during the Indians' stay there. It is also pertinent to state here that the subsequent history of the Stockbridge Indians, who removed to Green Bay, Wisconsin, in 1829, later to Lake Winnebago, then to Minnesota, and lastly to a reservation, I believe, in the Indian Territory, has fulfilled the hopes and promises of their early education; their general character is industrious, temperate, honest, intelligent, and peaceful. It would be interesting to study some of the prominent members of the tribe. Chief Konkapot for example, and Umpachene and Occum, remembering that a race can only fairly be judged by the finest specimens. Certain it is that the seeds of that work by Sergeant, and Edwards, and Woodbridge, and West, and later by the son of the saintly and sainted John Sergeant, possessed the germs of immortality.

Jonathan Edwards's Memory

But doubtless the point of keenest interest to the general public in connection with the missionary labors on behalf of the Mohican Indians in Berkshire is the part taken in that work by Jonathan Edwards. When he was called from here in 1758 to the presidency of Princeton he almost declined, and his letter asking for time to consider the "call" and lay it before a council tells how much he will sacrifice in a literary way by leaving Stockbridge, the many books he had it in his mind to write for which there was leisure in his Berkshire parish. He burst into tears when the council decided that he ought to accept the "higher call" and reluctantly left Stockbridge in January, 1758, being inaugurated at Princeton the next month, and dying the month succeeding of inoculation to prevent smallpox, or vaccination. Those seven years in the heart of the Berkshire wilderness were practically his last on earth, and one almost wishes the mighty brain might have been spared to work out, in the Berkshire surroundings he loved, the seed-thoughts and the teeming concepts with which it was filled. His Stockbridge life was not without its romance as well as its work and its friction. Here in 1752 President Burr of Princeton College came for the hand of his daughter, Esther, and was married, a child of their union being no less a person than the distinguished Aaron Burr, once Vice-President of the United States and the slayer of Hamilton. Here in Stockbridge Edwards bought the house formerly built and occupied by Sergeant, the house which came down two years ago. I think of no more fruitful scene for the painter's brush than that of the philosopher among the savages, a picture, indeed, of what foreign missions will become when to the benighted heathen go the brightest intellects, ready to cope with the sophistries of a strange religion and seeking to evolve therefrom all that is true and immortal. Jonathan Edwards, a missionary, suggests infinite possibilities.

A word about the house where he lived and its razing. Jericho's walls were not flatter than it is to-day, but the enterprising pastor of the village church, to which his sometime predecessor Edwards ministered a hundred and fifty years ago, having failed to persuade his flock to raise the necessary thousand dollars to preserve the historic edifice where the *Freedom of the Will* was written, has hit upon the novel scheme of making up its fallen timbers into various objects of vertu and bric-à-brac, brackets, candlesticks, etc. One such souvenir in the shape of a substantial chair made from its oaken beams was the gift of the originator of this interesting conceit to the author of this book. As oft as I sit in it I congratulate the world that it has escaped from the tyranny of Edwards's theology. Take this passage from his "Sinners in the hands of an angry God," preached in 1741: "The God that holds you over the pit of hell much as one holds a spider or some loathsome insect over the fire, abhors you and is dreadfully provoked; you are ten thousand times so abominable in his eyes as the most hateful and venomous serpent is in ours." And then follows a pitiless description of millions of ages in hell, which when they have been passed will be only a "point to what remains."

Nevertheless, I sit in the quaint chair humbly when I think that it once formed part of the rafters that sheltered "the mightiest intellect America has produced."

GREAT BARRINGTON OF OLD AND OF TO-DAY

One of the beautiful villages in the Berkshires is Great Barrington, lying in the southern part of the county, with Monument Mountain (Maus-wa-see-khi) rising in the northern part of the township and the Dome (Taghconic) ten miles away in the opposite direction. The village is built on an old Indian site, by the side of the Housatonic River, whose waters to-day turn the wheels of many prosperous industries within the precincts of the town. It was here in this part of the county, in the township of Sheffield, which originally included that of Great Barrington, that the settlement of Berkshire commenced, and until Lenox became the shire-town in 1787, Great Barrington was the county seat. The present Congregational church stands on, or near, the site of the " Great Wigwam," one of the settlements of the Mohican Indians when the white man first crossed the Hoosac range to take up his home in the Housatonic Valley, about the year 1725. Indeed, the Indian mission, under the auspices of a Scotch " Society for the Propagation of the Gospel in Foreign Parts," was here undertaken by John Sergeant in 1734, and prosecuted by him for two years, when the mission was removed to Stockbridge, where it remained and prospered until the close of the American Revolution. Sheffield, including what was then its "north parish" (now Great Barrington), was incorporated in 1733, but in 1761 this northern part of the old township of Sheffield had grown large and strong enough to seek and obtain incorporation under the name it now bears, after one Viscount Barrington, and it was called *Great* Barrington to distinguish it from another town of the same name on the line between Massachusetts and Rhode Island, at that time a disputed boundary.

The town of Great Barrington, which, with its outlying and extensive manufacturing district known as the village of Housatonic, has a population of nearly six thousand, has suffered less, being on the river and on the railroad, from the vicissitudes of fortune than many another Berkshire town. It is the business centre of the immediate vicinity; both sides of its main street being crowded on any afternoon, but particularly on Saturday, with wagons and teams from the surrounding country hitched to posts close together on the edge of the sidewalk. Yet despite this survival of distinctive rural customs, perhaps because of it, the town is well patronized; it is,

The Vicinage 251

also, well patronized by summer visitors when the annual exodus from the heated cities occurs. Many estates have already been created within the confines of the town, and the country houses built here by many who are well known in the large cities are beautiful specimens of rural architecture.

Great Barrington is charming in its drives, which lead north over Monument to Stockbridge, eight miles away, and back by the tortuous Housatonic through the villages of Glen Dale and Housatonic; west through South Egremont, a charming hamlet always well filled with summer guests, to Bash-Bish Falls, a cataract whose small stream of water falls a hundred feet down the cliff on one side of the Dome, and south, six miles, to Sheffield, another town which has its quota of visitors and is rich in interesting associations. Eastward from Great Barrington the road is a constant ascent to New Marlborough, where summer guests abound and where some of the finest views in Berkshire are to be obtained. Midway between Great Barrington and New Marlborough, on this last-named road, is the beautiful Lake Buell, on either side of which a drive passes close to the margin of the lake, making it accessible for camping and pleasure parties.

Great Barrington enjoys eminence among the towns of the country as having one of the finest parsonages in the world, the "Hopkins Memorial Manse," built by the late Mrs. Hopkins of California in honor of her husband's ancestral relative, the Rev. Samuel Hopkins, D.D., pastor in Great Barrington 1744–69. It was built in 1887, and is of solid granite, having cloisters which connect it with the church. The cost was nearly a hundred thousand dollars, and, as can be easily imagined, the expense of maintenance made an increase in the village pastor's salary imperative. To this munificent gift to the Congregational church Mrs. Hopkins superadded the present of a magnificent Roosevelt organ, having nearly one hundred stops and five thousand pipes, with electric echo-organ attachment and water-motor power; one of the great organs of the country. It is, perhaps, necessary to say, in order to complete the story of Great Barrington's eminence, and Mrs. Hopkins's regal wealth, that the house — palace, rather — she built for herself after her marriage to Mr. Searles, the architect, is one of the most costly and elegant of private residences in the United States, if not anywhere. It stands almost directly opposite the "Inn," and the high wall which

The house where William Cullen Bryant lived when he was a lawyer and town-clerk in Great Barrington, 1816–1822.

The Vicinage

borders the Hopkins property shuts the house off a little from the view of the street. A description of its palatial interior; its atrium and massive columns of African marble; its elegant rooms, filled with rare and costly works of art; its music-room, with another grand Roosevelt organ; its furniture, books, pictures, Windsor-Castle doors, busts, and medallions, would make an interesting story by itself.

The fame of this beautiful Berkshire village rests upon the securest foundations, since within its metes and confines once lived two of the greatest men America has produced — Dr. Samuel Hopkins, the father of New England theology, an ultra-Calvinistic "system of divinity" that relaxes its grip and its gloom only under the sledge-hammer of modern criticism; and William Cullen Bryant, the poet-journalist. On the extensive grounds in the rear of the Berkshire Inn still stands the house in which Bryant was married, when a young lawyer and the town clerk of the village.

SAMUEL HOPKINS, THE EMINENT THEOLOGIAN AND ABOLITIONIST

The arc that spans the distance of thought from Samuel Hopkins to Miss Catherine

Sedgwick measures 180 degrees. Berkshire has the honor of having been the residence of extreme thinkers of the Hopkins-Edwards type, and those of the Sedgwick-Dewey order; and perhaps it may be said with perfect truthfulness that if we had never had Hopkinsianism we would never have had Unitarianism. Who, then, was this man Hopkins, and what was his system?

In general, it may be said he was one of the greatest theologians that New England has produced. His system of theology dominated the creeds of Congregational churches, and to a certain extent also the Presbyterian, for half a century and more. He became after leaving his twenty-five-year pastorate in Great Barrington the doughty foe of slavery in its then stronghold, Newport, where he was pastor thirty-three years, until his death in 1803, covering the Revolutionary period and the trying times in that exposed and beleaguered city. Born in 1721 in Connecticut, and graduating at Yale in 1741, a pastor at Great Barrington, Mass., 1744–69, a period exactly synchronous with the early development of Berkshire, and dying at eighty-two in Rhode Island, his long and eminent life was known throughout New

England. The intimate friend of Edwards, whose pupil he was and whose biographer he became, he differed in some particulars from his great teacher, and in 1793 gave to the world his *System of Divinity*, a work in two volumes whose speculative and dogmatic positions were designed to be the most ultra reaffirmation of Calvinism against a growing Arminianism. Mrs. Stowe has made this man, Samuel Hopkins, the hero of *The Minister's Wooing*, and her picture of him shows that a man may be better than his creed. Whittier in his essay on Hopkins says:

"There are few instances on record of moral heroism superior to that of Samuel Hopkins in rebuking slavery in the time and place of its power. It may well be doubted whether on that Sabbath-day the angels of God in their wide survey of his universe looked upon a nobler spectacle than that of the minister of Newport rising up before his slave-holding congregation and demanding in the name of the Highest the 'deliverance of the captive and the opening of the prison doors to them that were bound.'"

This was the man, then, who for twenty-five years was the pastor at Great Barrington, and who is, next to Edwards, the most prominent of the Berkshire clergy. He was ordained, a boy of scarcely twenty-two, over the church in North Sheffield (now Great Barrington), on the day that the church was organized, December 28, 1743, having studied theology, between his graduation and settlement, with Jonathan Edwards at Northampton. His salary in this frontier settlement of the Berkshires was £65 per annum, and almost twenty years after, June 4, 1762, I find this entry in the Great Barrington Town Records:

"Voted that £80 lawful money shall be the annual sallery [*sic*] for the Revd. Samuel Hopkins when the necessaries are bo't and sold at the following prices [scale named] and As those necessaries of life shall fall or rise his sallery shall fall or rise accordingly or in proportion."

Notwithstanding this advance in Mr. Hopkins's salary, it was not paid, and in 1768 he brought suit against the town to recover "arrearages for 1761, 1762, 1764, 1765, and 1766. The town voting to defend itself against the suit, Mr. Hopkins in 1769 resigned, and was dismissed, because the church could not support him. It was a godless, frontier community," and vice and licentiousness were prevalent. Five years after Mr. Hopkins had been settled he had married in his parish, and by the wisdom or unwisdom of our forefathers' custom a large family was the result, so that Mr. Hopkins was obliged to support his household of wife and eight children by devoting considerable time to agricultural pursuits.

Meantime, he was a vigorous opponent of the loose Half-way Covenant of the time, and so dissension got into the parish. One year the town cut down his "sallery" to £45, and decreased the amount of firewood, evidently trying to freeze him out in more senses than one! His church, which at the first only consisted of thirty families, was weakened; "scarcely any one," he complained, "comes to my house for instruction"; "I study but little" (he was rising each day at four A.M. for sermon and other literary work), "and devote much time to my wordly concerns"; and on May 8, 1751, he records in his diary: "One soul converted through me; this is the first evidence I have had of the conversion of any one since I have been in this place, and surely it is well worth while to preach seven years to be in any ways instrumental in the conversion of one soul." The bright spot in Hopkins's Berkshire residence was the coming to Stockbridge in 1751 of his old friend and instructor, Jonathan Edwards, and until 1758, when

Edwards was called to Princeton, their friendly intimacies were re-established. Edwards died in 1758, and his friend became his biographer, a task as colossal as it was painful to him. One loves to think of these two mighty men riding back and forth across Maus-wa-see-khi to discuss their scholastic dicta. A scholastic age splits hairs. Every religion and every church has its scholastic period. It is small wonder that Hopkins had only one convert in a heptade of years. Edwards and he forged the chains that Channing broke. Hopkinsianism was formulated as a system in 1793; Unitarianism was distinctly organized and avowed in 1819, and Miss Sedgwick's *A New England Tale*, in 1822, was not only associated with the rise of American fiction, but it was fiction with a purpose, and that purpose was the merciless exposure of a narrow orthodoxy.

But Hopkinsianism as a system had some peculiar tenets, which may have been inferences from, but were not an integral part of the older Calvinism, such as the divine authorship of evil, the willingness to be damned for the glory of God, and the doctrine of disinterested benevolence. It was the last that attracted Channing as much as the former repelled him. Hopkins was dismissed from

Great Barrington January 18, 1769, and was not settled at Newport until April 11, 1770. He was then a man of forty-nine, and in the full vigor of his powers, but the immediate questions on hand were national for the next few years. In the great struggle, and in the greater crises during "the critical period of American history" (1783-88), Hopkins was occupied with the measures and events that marked an old order making way for the advent of the new republic. Accordingly, it is not until 1793 that the *System of Divinity* appears. It was as Whittier says, "a system which reduced the doctrines of the Reformation to an ingenious and scholastic form, and had the merit of bringing those doctrines to the test of reason and philosophy." It will be remembered in the popular mind longest with the question which it propounded to all candidates for the Church: "Are you willing to be damned for the glory of God?" a question which was seriously asked far on into the present century. It was the highest reach of the submissive spirit to be able to answer that question affirmatively; then regeneration might be expected to take place. It was on a par with all the grosser features of the reigning Puritan theology.

The movements of religious thought in New England are interesting and profoundly instructive to trace; from the Mathers to Edwards and Hopkins, with the variations of Emmons, Bellamy, Taylor, and Dwight; the mighty cleavage of Channing's protest; the reconstructive system of Bushnell, in whose footsteps we are walking to-day. It is a hundred years since Hopkins's "system" appeared, and its reactionary conservatism was destined to be only the leading of a "forlorn hope." Hopkins was hated and fought in his day, but he was triumphant, if that can be called a triumph which in crushing an enemy does not subdue his spirit. Hopkinsianism spread through eastern New England but now nothing is left of it but a name. The breath of the progressive spirit passes over it, and it is gone.

Of Hopkins as a man enough cannot be said. Read Mrs. Stowe's beautiful portraiture of him in *The Minister's Wooing*. After his dismissal at Great Barrington he regrets that he went away, "considering the unhappy consequences to that people by my leaving them"; and in 1794 he revisits his Berkshire parish only to find the most pitiable religious destitution; no minister, the meeting-house the resort of bats and sheep, and the Sabbath given over to horse-racing, sitting in taverns, and not enough interest in religion to even fit up a place in which to hear their old pastor preach. Whittier says that on leaving Great Barrington he "sold a slave whom he had himself owned," but assuredly the great heart of Hopkins was stirred to deepest hatred of the slave-traffic, and even the money which he received for his slave he devoted to the support and education of a negro. He was the proto-abolitionist of America, and he only assented to the Constitution in 1789, which granted the right of existence to slavery for twenty years, because he preferred that to anarchy. "Still," he said, " I fear." Hopkins was a man, said Jonathan Edwards the younger, "of immeasurable influence over men," yet he was meek, always preferring others to himself, seeking the advancement of Edwards, when it would have been to his own selfish interest to have pushed his own claims for the Stockbridge parish on Sergeant's death. Mrs. Stowe's story is founded on a true fact in the early love-experiences of Dr. Hopkins, whose conduct in the affair was so honorable as to have suggested to the novelist her charming romance. He refused "calls" away from his Newport parish, and stayed on "one fifth of what the Boston ministers were receiving," and refused to take up collections for his support, but lived on what was given him. He was swift to apologize for errors in his own conduct, and out of his meagre pittances gave generously to all good causes. His novelist-biographer, Mrs. Stowe, says "that a little child once described his appearance in the pulpit by saying, 'I saw God there and I was afraid.'" Others saw God in the man, and loved, because they saw love and sympathy and benignity.

THE OLDEST TOWN IN THE BERKSHIRES

Where the Housatonic glides past the towering "Taghconic Dome," in an area of broad meadow lands, there lies the ancient town of Sheffield, just three hours from Manhattan. The little unpretentious railroad station, through which pass the summer tourists, is alive only at intervals. Otherwise everything is slumbrous. There before you rises the lofty "Dome," and behind you stretches the sleepy town, whose very wide, elm-bordered, and densely shaded street is a dream of quiet, restful beauty, with the golden shower of sunbeams falling through the leaves of the trees

upon the road below. Sheffield is the paradise
of the weary. It has no villa of the wealthy ;
no social conventionalities ; no fashionable
mandates to obey; society's giddy whirl and
the Ixion-wheel of business are stopped ; " early
to bed and late to rise" is the improved maxim
of daily practice, and with this distinctive and
sole asset of restfulness as its stock-in-trade,
Sheffield receives a very large patronage of
summer guests from the great cities. "Country board" is the desideratum, and hence, although a second hotel has just been built and
is filled with guests, the villagers and the farmers in the vicinity reap a very large harvest
by entertaining summer visitors. Good whole-
some food, plenty of cream, fresh air, green
pastures, and early hours, and no noise more
disturbing than the chanticleer's summons to
waken, or the cricket's lullaby to sleep—these
are the attractions which have made Sheffield
hold its own relatively with the other resorts
of Berkshire.

But these are not all the attractions. Sheffield, as the oldest town in the Berkshires,
possesses a historic interest.

The tide of settlement flowed over the Hoosacs soon after 1725, and it came by the way
of an Indian trail which led from Westfield

through a region now occupied by the towns of Blandford, Otis, Monterey, Great Barrington, and North Egremont—all in Berkshire—to Kinderhook and Albany. This trail came through what is now the village street of Great Barrington, and, as Great Barrington was not set off from Sheffield, of which it was originally a part, until 1761, it will be seen that Sheffield, in the extreme southern part of Berkshire County, was, during the early years of settlement, the important town, as its "North Parish," or Great Barrington, was later the capital, remaining such until 1787, when Lenox was made the shire-town. The story of the early settlement of Sheffield, which was incorporated in 1733, is not unlike that of many another New England town. Between Sheffield and Westfield as late as 1735, it is recorded, there was only one house. It was wilderness "vast and primeval" all about. In 1735 the present Congregational church of Sheffield village was organized, and to the council which installed the first minister of the church came delegates "from the neighboring [!] churches." Jonathan Edwards rode hither to that council from his Northampton parish fifty miles away!

The story of the church is the story of the

town in New England until the disestablishment of Congregationalism in 1834, and so the village church is the centre of interest in those early days. Everybody was taxed to support it and had a voice in its affairs, unless he "certificated," *i. e.*, obtained a certificate from the civil officer to the effect that he, the holder thereof, had other religious preferences, and so was excused from the village tax for the support of the Congregational church. The amusing story is told that in one of these Berkshire towns a person having Episcopal preferences applied for the usual certificate, and it was made out in this way: "This is to certify that A. B. has renounced the Christian religion and joined the Episcopal church!" It is all amusing and very interesting how at the raising of the church in Sheffield so many "gallons of rhumb" were drunk; how one of its ministers, the eccentric Dr. Ephraim Judson, pastor here from 1791 until 1813, used sometimes to deliver his sermons sitting, and occasionally, when the heat was intense, would give out a long hymn of ten stanzas, and then leave the church to get some fresh air while the singing was in progress; how intense a Jeffersonian Democrat he was in a Federal stronghold yet making no enemies by his partisanship because he never preached politics "in the pulpit," and never alluded to political matters except in the presence of his loving kindred! In the adjoining "North Parish" of the town, now Great Barrington, was preaching contemporaneously with the first pastor of the Sheffield church the illustrious theologian, the Rev. Samuel Hopkins.

Meantime the town was growing, helped by the increased immigration hither at the close of the French and Indian wars. The news of the surrender of Louisbourg, 1745, and of the fall of Quebec in 1759 brought no small joy and relief to the Berkshire settlers, who had been harassed by the incursions of marauding bands of hostile Indians in league with the French. "Church services," a local historian says, "were interrupted to give thanks." It must also have been an occasion of interest to the people of Sheffield when Ethan Allen led the captured train of artillery from Fort Ticonderoga through the town of Great Barrington, and when Burgoyne encamped there on his way with his disheartened troops to Boston after his ill-luck at Saratoga. Here the Revolutionary spirit ran high, as in other parts of the country, and here, later, the disgraceful Shays' rebellion reared its viperous head.

Otherwise, the progress of the town was normal, quiet, and steady; farms tilled, population growing so that at the beginning of the first century after its settlement it was about two thousand, and the church and its minister the centre of village life in the piping times of peace.

Sheffield is noted as the birthplace of some great men in different walks of life: George F. Root, the noted composer; President Barnard of Columbia University, and Dr. Orville Dewey, the distinguished Unitarian divine. Orville Dewey's change of faith from orthodoxy to Unitarianism was one of the stirring events of the day in his native village, where an intensely Calvinistic theology was dominant, but the people have long since forgiven him his defection, because their own standards have broadened, because he became a distinguished leader and a famous preacher among the early Unitarians, and because his descendants, loving the town their fathers loved, have established a local lyceum, "The Friendly Union," whose beautiful stone building, built in modern style, furnishes a place for the regular winter courses of lectures and entertainments, as well as for the housing of the town library.

Each town of Berkshire has a picturesque

beauty, a historic interest, a peculiar claim and hold upon those who know the story of its rise and development, and it is not strange that all this is causing the region to be more eagerly sought out from year to year. The summer season in Sheffield is short, usually the brief period of the vacation in the schools, July and August, but while it lasts it is intense, and many of the guests there have been coming to this quiet old place for several seasons. It is only at the gateway of the Berkshires, but its convenient access from New York brings to it an increasing patronage.

BERKSHIRE DESERTED VILLAGES

Berkshire has many "sweet Auburns," only they do not "lie on the plain." They are the hill-towns, inaccessible, exposed, desolate, yet once teeming with life and animated with the moving pictures of profitable industries. To-day the once verdant pastures and meadows have literally grown up to timber again; the weather-beaten outbuildings "filled with plenty" once are now crumbling to their ruin, and the plain farmhouses where dwelt a pious, hard-working, and simple yeomanry are untenanted, while in many a field the implement is rust-eaten where it was left when the final chapter in the book of the Berkshire exodus was written.

I visited one section of this region one bitter midwinter day not many years ago, driving through—perhaps I should have said scaling—the southeastern portion of the county, which lies seven hundred feet up from the villages along the Housatonic, and in which are the towns of New Marlborough, Monterey, and Sandisfield. My companion, the minister in two of the places named, said to me as we neared Sandisfield: "You will not know when you get to it." Yet here in 1800 was a population of nearly two thousand, and the fourth town in size and importance in the county. Now "the decent church tops the neighboring hill," lonely relic of a former grandeur, but that is all that remains! And here we are almost as much higher than Great Barrington as Great Barrington is higher than New York, on the tip-top part of this ridge, which runs along the eastern part of Berkshire and is the water-shed of the Connecticut and Housatonic rivers. Here was the one main and central street of the village, the "four corners" hard by, and around this church-crowned mount streaming from all directions upon the Sabbath days towards this sacred peak was gathered an industrious and thrifty people. The town lay on the highway from Westfield over the Hoosacs into Berkshire, the thoroughfare that was originally an Indian trail and led to Sheffield in the Housatonic Valley. Along it bowled the ancient stage-coach past Three-Mile Hill and Six-Mile Pond, which have now been rechristened with a more ambitious nomenclature.

I find this note in the account of some travels of Professor Benjamin Silliman, the distinguished physicist, who in a journey from New Haven to Lenox and beyond passed through Sandisfield, September, 1819: "It was quite dark before we arrived at Sandisfield, but our road was good and the welcome light of the inn at length caught our eyes. We slept in a great vacant ball-room." The church which stands on that Sandisfield hilltop now is the lineal successor of the ancient edifice, and the site is a good place to pull out Goldsmith's *Deserted Village* and reread its lines, which glow with a vivid light in the midst of the thronging fancies the place awakens,—

"Sweet was the sound, when oft at evening's close
Up yonder hill the village murmur rose,"—

and are literally true when, describing the village pastor, Goldsmith says:

The Vicinage

> "A man was he to all the country dear
> And passing rich with forty pounds a year."

As a matter of fact, that was just what was voted the first pastor of the Sandisfield church, the Rev. Cornelius Jones. Here is the record at his settlement, May 19, 1756: "Voted to pay £40, and the minister's lot,"—which was usually a piece of wood-land which furnished "fier-wood," and was given in fee to the first settled minister. It may be added that an interesting feature of the ordination of Mr. Jones and his settlement over the Sandisfield church was that the services were held in a barn, and the moderator of the council was Jonathan Edwards, another member of the council being Samuel Hopkins. Mr. Jones, a graduate of Harvard, 1752, remained only a short time, and was succeeded by the Rev. Eleazer Storrs (Yale, 1762), who served here in the ministry for thirty-one years, and was followed by the Rev. Levi White (Dartmouth, 1796), who continued in the Sandisfield pastorate thirty-four years, from 1798 until 1832.

Goldsmith's original

> "Unpractised he to fawn, or seek for power,
> By doctrines fashioned to the varying hour,"

doubtless survived in any one of this apostolical

succession, but I fear the poet's description of "sweet Auburn's" pastor as a man who "quite forgot the vices" of his people "in their woe" would hardly apply to any New England ministry of the period named. They were men, those eighteenth-century Berkshire ministers, cast in a heroic mould; poorly paid, supplementing their stipend often by farm labors, grounded in the bed-rock principles of an intolerant Calvinism, yet sincere, sacrificing, zealous servants of their fellow-men, and in many of these parishes through the county are buried near the churches to which they ministered so long and well.

New Marlborough, once an educational centre, is the next town to Sandisfield, and ideally located, with views rivalling those of Lenox, but is only a shadow of its former self, with property selling at a song. It is now looming up a little into prominence as a quiet resort, and there is a project on paper, if not on foot, to connect this beautiful town with Great Barrington by trolley. Its old academy is now in the season a commodious and comfortable hotel, and there are other inviting boarding-houses in the village. Monterey, Otis, Becket, Washington, Peru, Windsor, Florida, Savoy, are all towns of which Sandisfield and New Marlborough are types, dreary and desolate if one considers merely their inaccessibility and isolation, but each one having individual excellences and very interesting histories. Tyringham has alluringly appealed to not a few literary workmen of note, and affords an ideal retreat. New Ashford, Cheshire, Lanesborough, Hancock, and Alford on the opposite side of the county belong to the same class of "decadent" towns, *i. e.*, towns which have been left stranded by the opening up of the Great West, by the coming of better means of transportation into the lower levels along the Housatonic, and by the ruinous competitions of modern industries. At Alford may still be seen the saw left in the block of marble with a slab half sliced off, just where the implement stopped when the marble works were abandoned years ago.

The problems which these towns present are peculiar along religious, educational, industrial, and social lines. They are not different from other parts of "decadent rural New England." Religiously the Berkshire decadent villages do not suffer so much as they do educationally and socially. Two county missionaries regularly visit these towns, in addition to the regular services of resident pastors. All of these villages have a long and honorable history going back into the eighteenth century, and many a one has been the birthplace and home of some who have risen to distinction in letters or finance. Their isolation has meant for them desolation. Indeed, it would seem that those who have become eminent and affluent and who trace back their beginnings to any of these towns, could not better pay a debt to the place of their nativity and childhood than by establishing travelling lectureships and libraries. Intellectual vacuity is the great curse of these towns, and as "nature abhors a vacuum," an empty mind is pretty apt to be the depository of all sorts of vagaries, isms, and trivalities.

VII

THE GENESIS OF VILLAGE IMPROVEMENT AND THE LAUREL HILL ASSOCIATION, STOCKBRIDGE, MASS.

MY theme, "Village Improvement," has a technical meaning, inclusive of hardly more than the hygienic and external conditions of the village: sanitation, good water, neat streets, trim sidewalks, handsome roadsides, attractive dooryards, shrubbery-hidden objects of offence, and an agreeable look to the town as a whole, by the planting or removal of trees, by preventing unsightly "dumping places" in the outskirts of the village, and by a general oversight in the matter of the streets, their roadbed, their sprinkling, and the lighting of the same. And I am to give as a concrete example of all this, a Berkshire village, viz., Stockbridge, known far and wide as one of the loveliest villages of America, and its village improvement society, the Laurel Hill Association, which has been the parent of upwards of a thousand similar organizations scattered throughout our country as far as the Pacific. But "village improvement" as an ideal is something more than this technical conception of it. A good library, well-appointed schools, a Law and Order League, a Citizens and Taxpayers Association are prime requirements and essentials in the general idea of village improvement. The health of the village must be considered, its appearance beautified, its mind fed on the best literature, its pauperism and pauper spirit decreased, its social life infused with inspiration, with sympathy and benevolence, its morale improved, its administration made economical and effective. Village improvement as a final ideal means all that. It is not decorative; it is regenerative. It is not to beautify simply but to beatify. We have been handicapped long enough by the tyranny of that olden line, "God made the country; man made the town"; and now we are trying to get more of God into the city and more of man into the country. Village improvement is not something laid on from the outside, but the working out of mighty principles from within. It does not have in mind a single object, but it takes in the whole village structure, its health, its appearance, its administration, its life. And yet I wish in this chapter to treat village improvement in its partial and technical sense; though the reader will not forget its larger and truer meaning.

Village improvement in this narrower signification is of comparatively recent origin; and it may fairly be said that not yet has it attained wide acceptance. An article appeared in *The Atlantic Monthly* for 1858, on "Farming Communities in New England," by J. G. Holland, and I have just read that protest against the unsightliness of farm villages. It evoked a good deal of feeling, adverse and favorable, and inspired some books. Five years before that the Laurel Hill Association (the village improvement society of Stockbridge, Mass.) was started, though with the idea first of beautifying a village pleasure ground and caring for the cemetery. I presume none would claim that "Laurel Hill" started with the very definite and well-mapped-out idea of what it subsequently and very soon became, and what it now so eminently stands for. Almost all great movements are the accretions of littles. The idea works out more clearly with more intelligent discernment of new needs. To Stockbridge, however, justly belong the authorship and the sponsorship of the village improvement idea; an idea which is scarcely yet fifty years old in America; for it may be said that the "Common" which was a feature of New England villages in the earliest days was more practical than æsthetic; a place of common pasturage rather than of pleasure; for cattle more than for men. Boston "Common" was so used until well into the last century, and now its forty-six acres make the beauty and charm of the city. The Amherst "Common" is another instance, and there are a few others, yet even these spacious commons were not objects of beauty as pastures. The modern spirit transformed them into parks. Would that there might have been more of them!

The farm village of fifty years ago—yes, much less time ago than that—was absolutely a stranger to æsthetic ideals and aims in its appearance, and hundreds and thousands of villages still are. Go into any one of these towns and see the general indifference to external attractiveness,—carriages and horses hitched to the curbs along the streets, papers and refuse heaps lying in the road, grass by the roadside uncut and white with dust because the streets are never sprinkled, unweeded walks and unshaven lawns in dooryards, and so on. We are gradually awaking out of all this, but it is recent. Some of our villages have taken the matter up vigorously, and the intensity of our present devotion to æsthetic ideals is in inverse proportion to the lethargy and reluctance we showed in coming to them. In the village of Lenox, where there has been a village improvement society for about a score of years, we have recently taken up the beautifying of the grounds about the railroad station, pulling down an unsightly shed and planting flowers and shrubs; and the latest thing has been the adornment of our school grounds here and there in the township and the decoration of school interiors. This latter work has been aided by the Village Improvement Society though springing from the town itself. The contagion of the spirit of village improvement spreads. There is an awakening appreciation of the ministry of the beautiful everywhere. Some benevolent circles exist simply to hang pictures on the walls of the poor, and to beautify their tenements with flowers. It would seem strange, indeed, if this growing recognition of the power of the beautiful in our lives did not reach our farm villages. It has reached them, but only within recent years. The old type of farm village is slowly changing. The leaven of "Laurel Hill" is working, and the lawn-mower has supplanted the old scythe and sickle, which made a lawn look like quadrants of close-cropped stubble wherever the knife had been. The farmer is beginning to have more use for the ornamental, because the ornamental is proving itself more useful to him in selling his property. Our New England villages, which always have been far ahead of most European villages, because of their intelligence and thrift, have nevertheless fought the spirit of improvement. In the place where the horse-rake stopped in mid-August there it stayed through the winter and spring, and in the place where the bob-sleighs scraped the ground last in the March days there they rested through the long summer. "Why put away tools! What use to make any extra steps! There are weeds in the walk, yes, but you can walk there can't you? Cut the grass in the dooryard? Why man, that grass means a few more foaming pails of milk to me!"—so said the farmer of yesterday. And his farmer-neighbor down the road a piece did n't agree with him, but kept his fences in repair, his walks weeded, his lawn mowed, his tools put away, his outbuildings painted or hidden by trees and shrubbery, and one day sold to great advantage, while the other, with a finer outlook or a better soil, went grubbing along, unable to sell. Village improvement appreciates real estate, and this is the sovereign argument that is changing the face of things.

J. G. Holland, in the article in *The Atlantic* to which we have referred, said that the reason why the boys left the farms and went to the cities was because farm life was unrelieved dulness—nothing but a grind; the same dull monotony staring at one daily; no place for the agreeable, the pleasant, the ornamental. It was so then; I guess it is still so. It was a stock phrase in his day, "How shall we keep the boys on the farms?" And his answer was practically along the lines of village improvement; and that was forty-four years ago. Make villages pleasant to the eye. A beautiful exterior goes far to redeem the hardest lot. The sentimental uses of the beautiful are as distinct and valuable as its commercial uses. It was difficult to make men see this, brought up as all our New England villages have been, on ideas of thrift and economy, "plain living and high thinking," simplicity and utility. "Laurel Hill" voiced a needed reform; is voicing it to-day. Twenty years ago its daughters had become so numerous that a national association of village improvement societies was formed at Greenwood, N. J. (1882), and many interesting papers were read.

So much for the history of the movement and the need of it. Let us come now more closely in touch with the movement itself and study its workings in the parent society; and then we will ask ourselves a few general questions growing out of our study of this theme.

To understand "Laurel Hill" one needs to know Stockbridge, its quiet and classic dignity, its beautiful environment in the Berkshire Hills, its inheritance of rich traditions, its spirit of village pride, not to say hauteur.

To the Athenian all the world was barbarian, and it was imagined that if Jove came to earth he would reside in the many-templed and altar-strewn city of Athens. I was present once at an anniversary of "Laurel Hill," not ten years ago, when one of the speakers, a gentleman well-known in letters and in the church, a far-famed traveller, absolutely capped the climax of village pride by asserting that

The Indian Monument, Stockbridge, Mass.

Laurel Hill Association

"Heaven was but another Stockbridge." This was rather rankling to the mind and heart of a Lenox man, for he has been inclined to shape his dreams as to what Paradise is from his own exalted visions on the heights. But after all village pride is as good a thing for a community as self-respect is for the individual. Stockbridge shows the dignity of its antecedent years in the step of its citizens on the street. It is the old axiom *noblesse oblige* working out; a walking worthy of its history, its traditions, its beautiful location. The village lies in the heart of the mountains; the winding river meanders through it; a wide elm-shaded street passes through the length of it; at one end of this street is the Indian burial-ground with its appropriate and beautiful monolith; at the other, a half-mile distant, is the pleasure park, a wooded hill, in the early years a place for council to the Indians and deeded in trust to the town in 1834 by the Sedgwick family. Later this park was made over to the "Laurel Hill Association," which takes its name from the abundance of laurel growing in this park. It is in this park that the annual meetings of "Laurel Hill" are held, when, with speaker (often a distinguished man), with band, and simple refreshments, the work of the year is celebrated. I have often been present at these meetings when the villagers turn out *en masse*, and I honestly believe "Laurel Hill" owes something of its success to this yearly assembly. The Lenox Village Improvement Society has never observed this feature of "Laurel Hill," partly from the trouble of the thing, partly from scepticism as to its practical value. Stockbridge, on the contrary, never omits it. It is the yearly village festival, and now and then when a speaker like Edward Everett Hale is secured, as two years ago, the surrounding towns send large delegations. Everybody goes for miles around, and the address is always pertinent to the day and theme. Really Stockbridge ought to preserve and publish these addresses for distribution or sale.

"Laurel Hill" began, then, forty-nine years ago; its first distinct aim being to put the recently bestowed pleasure park in good shape, then the village cemetery, then as the work opened out before it, it extended to the whole village.

"Trees," says one of the early workers, "were planted by the roadside wherever trees were lacking. The children were made helpers by calling trees by their names if they would watch and care for them for two years. Others were paid to pick up loose papers and unsightly things in the streets. Then the broad village street was graded to a uniform level; walks pushed out to the remoter parts of the town, and property-owners encouraged to keep their grounds and walks in order."

And then the work enlarged so upon the hands of the society that special committees were appointed to look after separate parts of the township, which was mapped out for that purpose, and now every square inch of ground in the limits of the town is under the eye of its special committee; and finally, the work still enlarging, each department, sanitation, finance, trees, lamp-lighting, etc., has its separate committee. The district comittees taken together make up the executive committee of the whole, never less than fifteen, hold monthly meetings, and this larger committee has power to appropriate moneys, direct all improvements undertaken by the society, arrange for annual meetings, and offer prizes, or premiums, to the villagers who shall make the best showing or the most improvement on their places during the year. This is a good deal of an incentive on some streets.

The money for the work of "Laurel Hill"

comes from the interest on investments (it has a fund of $5000), an annual appropriation from the town, from private subscriptions and life memberships. But it must be remembered that a village improvement society could be started anywhere without a cent of money in the treasury; in fact much of its work does not call for money. As Mr. Waring says, "What most detracts from the good appearance of any village is the slovenly look which comes from badly hung gates, crooked fences, absent pickets, and general shiftlessness about private places." The spirit of that remark is true, even if we have given up fences and gates now, because we no longer pasture horses in the open streets. Little improvements by private owners are what make a village beautiful. One place in neglect can ruin the appearance of a street. Money will prevent this by offering a premium, but village and neighborly pride ought to go far to remedy it. I was talking with a gardener of one of the large estates in Lenox last month and I asked him how it was that almost all the gardeners in charge of the elaborate "places" on these heights were Englishmen. He replied, "Why! every Englishman is a gardener; every English village provides commons where the poor are assigned places to cultivate. But I presume the great reason," he said, "is because we have lived all these centuries side by side with a noble class, whose fine estates are graced by gardens, and the long familiarity with flowers and hot-houses and magnificent grounds has insensibly worked far into the English character. An Englishman loves flowers and likes to care for them." And then I remembered what Miss Sedgwick, the American writer of the middle of the last century,— herself a Stockbridge woman,— wrote in 1841, in her book of travels in England, how she was impressed all through England among all classes, even the poorest of the poor, with the way every square inch of ground was put to flowers; and she contrasted again and again these two-by-four courts of the poor or middle class, bright with flowers, with her own dull villages in Berkshire; "land, land, land everywhere and never a flower!" I have often wondered if "Laurel Hill Association" did n't after all owe much of the praise of its origin to the gifted author, whose chaste, refined taste and free spirit won the immortal laurels of authorship by the very message of her books, which was to make life beautiful. It is said that "Laurel Hill" owes its origin to a woman, Mrs. J. Z. Goodrich, who did indeed write and labor for it until she got it started, and who kept it going during its early infantile years; but how much did she owe to her townswoman's books, read at that time all over the world, passing through many editions and making Stockbridge famous by the people they drew to the home of Miss Catherine Maria Sedgwick? Miss Sedgwick's message was to the villages, how to make them beautiful with pleasant, ideal homes. But, however that may be, Mrs. Goodrich was the organizer, the anointed apostle of village improvement, the "stirrer-up of things" generally; and thus "Laurel Hill" in a way is another indication of the manner in which woman can serve her town, as a humble but most efficient citizen. Before woman clamors for "rights" she has not, let her use the "rights" she has. Village improvement is within her sphere and influence; many believe that this is her work, a work she can do best, and certainly "Laurel Hill" believes that, as a glance at the personnel of its committees attests.

The success of "Laurel Hill" is due to a good many causes. It has, in the first place, a distinct idea of what it wants to do. It systematizes this work so that all the interests of the village are covered by appropriate committees. It interests the whole village by putting itself, through district committees, in touch with all parts of the township. Taxpayers living in the outskirts of a town naturally protest against all the improvements being made in the central part of the village. "Laurel Hill" has also owed something of its success to its success. The town is interested in keeping alive and effective its own peculiar institution, which has given birth to a thousand and more similar ones. "Laurel Hill" owes much to its own anniversary meetings, to keeping itself out of the hands of politics, to getting the town to refrain from organizing a "fire district" by which money now expended by "Laurel Hill" would then be expended by the town, to interesting the women, and so on, but its chief success arises from the results as seen in the village itself. It has justified its right to be a thousand times. One cannot be an hour in Stockbridge without being impressed with the work of this society. At the railroad station, as one gets off the train, the flowers, the *porte cochere*, the handsome structure itself, the signs, "No dumping here," as one comes to a spot that otherwise would be the depository of cans, bottles, papers, and refuse, the absence of unsightly objects in the streets, the beautiful cemetery scrupulously neat (and who has n't seen country cemeteries in shocking neglect?), the broad street faultlessly graded, elm bordered, and always wearing a charm of repose and quiet grandeur, the houses and lawns — all these tell the story of public spirit and village pride. But they only tell part of the story, though a great part. "Laurel Hill" is a centre of creative impulses which express themselves later by town action in practical measures of sanitation and water supply, and it has so preached the gospel of beauty all these years as to have evoked in the entire township a sense of the beautiful.

Let us come then to a few general reflections as growing out of all this, and the first is this: The success of any work of this kind depends upon a general interest on the part of the entire village. How arouse and maintain that interest? Follow the example of the parent society. Interest all classes, even the children. Offer prizes for the best places and most improvements. Map off the entire township into districts, so that the whole village shall come in contact with the work. Have annual meetings, yearly village festivals. Show the landowner that village improvement enhances the value of his property. Devise ingenious schemes to arouse interest and to avoid ruts. Show work done as a specimen of what can be done. Study the bibliography of the subject and have the books bearing on it in the town library. I am quite sure that in Stockbridge the work is done by the village. It is the "fad" of none. It should be everybody's work and everybody should be drawn into it. But secondly, every village improvement society will have its own peculiar local problems. In Lenox, one is how to discriminately and reverently apply the axe to some of the trees. A good sewer system, the best of water from mountain springs, Telford roads, a splendid library, electric lights, efficient schools, good sidewalks pushing out gradually to the remote sections, liberal appropriations; all these should be supplemented by that vigilance which conserves the "views" for the pleasure of the passer-by in the streets, and prevents the landscape from being absolutely shut off by ornamental or wayside shrubbery. Some tree cutting has been done in recent years under the direction of Mr. Sargent, of New York. Three lakes are visible from Lenox, but the trees at their borders have been allowed to grow so that now these placid bodies of water embosomed in the hills are actually dwindling in size to the far-off observer, and the view, as we say, has grown up and out.

I am conscious that I have dealt with my subject in a fragmentary, partial way, but let it be said in conclusion that plainly the curse of the country towns is in their *emptiness*,— nothing to engage the mind, which thus becomes vacant, a capital place for all mischief and evil to find lodgment. Village improvement should always work up to its higher and larger and truer sense; and aside from the provision of a good library, keeping taxes down, cultivating a high morale, killing the pauper spirit, and demanding good government, which go with the larger meaning, something should be done to relieve this vacuousness of country towns, by entertainments, lyceums, lecture courses, gymnasium, socials, and what not. In the village there is nothing to think about, nothing to take up the eye, and so the youth are on the streets at night with nothing more lively than a prayer-meeting to attend, and usually line up around the post-office and stare into vacancy. That sort of thing is perilous. Their minds will not be vacant long. It would, in my opinion, be an act of religion for the church to amuse this class. At any rate to improve the village will be to strike at this spirit of vacuousness someway.

Let me then sum it up by saying : The ideal village is one whose health is conserved, whose appearance is tidy and handsome, whose mental life is fed on the best books, whose morale is self-respecting and law-abiding, whose administration is honest, efficient, and economical, whose children have careful instruction in good schools, whose pauper spirit is killed, whose taxes are not burdensome, and whose social life is kept fresh and healthful by entertainments, lectures, and pleasant gatherings ; and to the attainment of all this, "Laurel Hill" points the way. It is one of the many original movements conceived and cradled on Berkshire soil.

VIII

THE CHURCH OF BERKSHIRE UNTIL THE DISESTABLISHMENT IN 1834

THE aim of this chapter is not so much to write history as to present retrospective sketches. History implies continuity in the narrative; retrospection is a sort of general survey at a glance. History is the completed picture, down to the minutest detail; retrospection is only the rough outlines of the picture, faintly sketched in.

Berkshire, lying spread out upon the tops of the foot-hills of the Green Mountain range, lay unscaled by those who came either with missionary or domestic intent until towards the middle of the eighteenth century. It was in 1734, after a futile attempt at colonization a few years previous to this, that the first settlers crossed the Hoosac range, in what is now the southeastern part of the county, and took up their abode in Sheffield. It will be remembered that within twenty-five years after the Pilgrims first set foot on these shores Springfield was settled, and yet for almost a century longer those who lived to the east of the Hoosacs sat down in grim despair before the mountainous barrier that separated them from this beautiful and inviting region.

There were good reasons for this as we have stated, but it is important for us to note the fact that these early settlers who took up claims and began to form communities in Berkshire not only brought their Church, the Congregational, with them, but they brought a Church of a settled policy and splendid history. Harvard College was already a hundred years old; and Yale, though more recently founded, was yet strong and of mature growth. Cambridge and Savoy with their formularies were far down the years and the Mathers had wielded their influence and gone. Even Saybrook with its unifying trend—an early step in the direction of welding the churches more closely and firmly together — was far enough in the past to have become a historic fact, and a strong factor, in the Church these settlers came to plant "in the wilderness."

It is noticeable, then, that with this aureole

of history about them — and true to the Germanic idea of a close cementing of the ties between State and Church — they scarcely put an axe to a tree, with which to build their rude cabins, ere they had appropriated money for the hiring of a minister and the support of the gospel. The incorporation of the town and the organization of the church went practically hand in hand. It is significant, perhaps, that the first man to have preached the gospel in this county, to whom Sheffield extended a call June 7, 1734, was one Ebenezer Devotion, and as I read the records of the work, the trials, and the results of Congregationalism in this county, it has been one ever-glowing and ever-eloquent sermon upon such earnestness and faithfulness as can be called by no other name than devotion, devotion that vies with, if it does not pale, the annals of many another sublime epoch in the history of the universal Church.

It is scarcely needful for me to say that Berkshire County was settled from the south toward the north, and as the centre of population was tending northward, so the courts were moved first from Great Barrington to Lenox and finally to Pittsfield. It is this fact of the early settlement of southern Berk-

Established Church of Berkshire

shire which gives some of the churches in the southern part of the county a greater antiquity than any in the northern. Ten years after the very first settlers had crossed the Hoosac ridge of the Green Mountains,— emigrating from Westfield to Sheffield by the most direct route as a glance at the map will show,— there were still very few settlers in Berkshire; and what few there were were clustered in the south and southeastern portions of the county. Yet in the first decade of growth, four churches — of the Congregational order of course—had become organized and were efficiently at work. The beloved Sergeant was fluently and earnestly proclaiming the gospel to the Indians at Stockbridge, the second church to be organized in the county, that at Sheffield having been organized in 1735, two years before the Stockbridge church. In Sheffield was Jonathan Hubbard, to whose installation over the church there the great Jonathan Edwards came, making his way from Northampton doubtless for the first time into this valley where he was afterward to be a pastor himself.

In Great Barrington, eight years after the church in Sheffield was organized, a young man of twenty-two years, fresh from his studies under Edwards, and who was to leave a marked influence on New England thought, namely, Samuel Hopkins, was beginning his long pastorate over that people; and in New Marlborough, where the church was organized in 1744, just one year after the church in Great Barrington, Thomas Strong commenced his labors, which, if we except the adoption of the "Half-way Covenant" (1769), were to be a blessing to that parish, for the record reads that he labored there exactly a third of a century. So far as I know, the church at New Marlborough was the only one in Berkshire County to adopt the "Half-way Covenant," so provocative of mischief, so derogatory to Christian principle, and yet so thoroughly sanctioned by no small part of the New England ministry. It is worth noting in passing that these four men, the pioneer pastor-preachers in the county,— Sergeant, Hubbard, Hopkins, and Strong,—were young men, aged twenty-four, thirty-two, twenty-two, and twenty-five respectively. They labored side by side in harness for a considerable time, Sergeant the first to break the circle, his death occurring when he was only thirty-nine. Eleven years after Sergeant's death Hopkins removed to Newport. Three years later Hubbard died, and after four years more Strong passed to his reward.

Established Church of Berkshire

But in the meantime other churches were springing up,— in the next decade and a half three, Tyringham (1750), Sandisfield (1756), and Becket (1758); all, it will be seen, in the southern part of the county. It should be observed that this Tyringham church is the same in continuity of life as the present church in Monterey, the town having been divided fifty years ago, and what was South Tyringham became Monterey; and it should also be observed that he who first ministered to this church, from its organization until after the war of the Revolution, a period of thirty-four years, was Adonijah Bidwell, one of whose descendants is a deacon of the church in Monterey and an honored man in the county.

The population of the county was now (1760) rather rapidly increasing. The military defences of Berkshire were being strengthened and repaired; and with the feeling of greater security came a decided increase in the number of colonists. In the next decade (1760-70) five churches are organized, four of which are in the north part of the county, namely, Pittsfield (1764), Lanesborough (1764) Williamstown (1765), Richmond (1765), and Lenox (1769). Of the first-settled ministers over three of these churches, namely, Williamstown, Richmond, and Lenox, we know little more than that they were graduated at Yale College: Rev. Whitman Welch in 1760, and pastor at Williamstown 1765-76, from which place he enlisted as chaplain of a regiment in the war of the Revolution and died of smallpox at Quebec while in service, leaving his church pastorless; Rev. J. Swift, graduated at Yale 1765, and pastor of Richmond eleven years (1765-76), when he was dismissed, becoming distinguished afterwards as one of the most useful and eminent ministers of Vermont; and Rev. Samuel Monson, graduated at Yale 1763, and becoming pastor at Lenox in 1770, where he remained twenty-two years, having a difficult and uneventful ministry, ending in some acrimony on both sides.

The other two churches organized in this decade, namely, Pittsfield and Lanesborough, had as their first settled ministers two men who, though differing *toto cœlo* politically,— Dr. Allen being a rabid Democrat of the Jeffersonian type, and Dr. Collins a Federalist, with Tory leanings it was thought,— yet enjoyed exceedingly prosperous, useful, and long-continued pastorates in their respective parishes.

Established Church of Berkshire 301

Of "Fighting Parson Allen," forty-six years pastor of the Pittsfield church, one could write a book, and we must compress the volume into a sentence. Up and down the county, rousing to democratic white heat every town, praying and shooting at Bennington, beset by factions in his parish, which toward the very close of his life became torn and rent on account of his political thrusts — he feared not man or devil, only God. It is no wonder, when Jefferson was elected, that the bell-rope of the Pittsfield church broke through violent ringing! Dr. Collins of the Lanesborough church was, next to Dr. West of Stockbridge, the longest settled minister in the county, Dr. West's pastorate being fifty-nine years, Mr. Collins's fifty-eight. In the very last of Mr. Collins's pastorate the church gave him a colleague, who became his coadjutor and successor. The elder pastor ministered in holy things, however, until the very last, when in his eighty-fourth year he died, full of years and honors and of seals of his ministry.

In the next decade (1770–80), the period of the outbreak of the war of independence, six churches were organized,—Peru and Egremont the first year of the decade (1770), Windsor (1772), Washington (1772), Adams (before 1778), and Otis (1779). Of these churches much could be said as to their early history, but time and space prevent. The churches at Egremont and Adams sustained troublous and short-lived careers, and died; the Adams church having only, as it were, a momentary existence, "appearing for a little time and then vanishing away," and the Egremont church having a little longer lease of life, its pastor, Rev. E. Steele, being settled over it twenty-four years, when, between the upper millstone of the Shays rebellion and the nether one of sectarian rivalries, the little church feebly gasped its expiring breath, knowing, however, a resurrection a score of years later, when it reappeared as the present South Egremont church. The early history of the Otis church formed at this period is not worth speaking of, as it hardly got on to its feet for a score of years. Of the first settled ministers over the churches of Peru, Windsor, and Washington much might be written, particularly of Mr. Avery of Windsor, who though only just out of college (Yale, 1769), and hardly more than two years in Windsor, nevertheless gathered a company of his parishioners and, four days after the battle of Lexington, marched off to Cambridge with his troops, of whom he himself was chosen captain. He was dismissed from his pastorate to take a chaplaincy in the army, and afterward served at Trenton, Princeton, and Bennington and Saratoga. John Ballantine, the first settled minister over the church in Washington, which was formed during this trying decade, is entitled to the distinction of being the fourth longest-settled minister in the county, coming next to Dr. Shepard, who is the third. Mr. Ballantine was a Harvard graduate, nearly all of his contemporaries in the ministry in his region being from Yale. This church really began to wane during Mr. Ballantine's ministry of forty-six years, owing to divisions and departures, and this candlestick, once so light-giving, seems to have been removed out of its place, only to be reset by Time's beneficent changes.

In the next decade (1780–90) the churches organized were Lee (1780), Alford (1781), Dalton (1785), and West Stockbridge Centre (1789). Two churches of this period, Alford and West Stockbridge Centre, have had fitful lives, one, Alford, becoming extinct shortly after its formation, and only kept alive by the forbearance of the Lord and the endurance of one Rev. Aaron Kinne, who kept a good many candlesticks from falling in those early days, and the other, West Stockbridge Centre, which, though it has never been vigorous, still is in a better condition of work and promise than in some other years. The other churches of this period, Lee and Dalton, organized five years apart, have in their early history the distinguished names of Hyde, the second pastor of the Lee church, and remaining there forty-one years, and Jennings, the second minister of Dalton, whose pastorate there was prolonged thirty-two years. Of Dr. Hyde, one of the most influential men Berkshire ever had, what can one say in a single sentence! A young man like all the rest,— scarcely out of their teens and fresh from college and private and short readings with Drs. Edwards, Bellamy, or West,—he began as a comparative boy a work in Lee that was to engage him forty-one years. He must have been a man to whose opinions his contemporaries paid great deference, because we find him prominently engaged in every good work throughout the county, in county societies as well as among his ministerial brethren in their regular associational meetings, in the councils of the State as well as his own town—a veritable leader, albeit a quiet, modest, faithful minister to the last. It is said that Dr. Backus, with whom Mr. Hyde read theology, said to him: "Why, Hyde, I sin, and repent, I sin, and repent; but you don't seem to have anything to repent of." Dr. Hyde was an exception to the Yale rule, he himself being a graduate of Dartmouth.

The churches organized in the next decade, the last of the century, when the population of the county had increased to over 30,000, were Southfield (1794) and Hinsdale (1795). Neither of these churches started off brilliantly; and indeed the Hinsdale church was badly handicapped with debt, owing to shrinkage of values from the sale of pews, which were paid off, as the chronicler states, "under the influence of the ardent," and afterward it was found that the bibulous purchasers had not the wherewith to pay. Churches were raised, pews sold, doctrines discussed in those days with the ever-accompanying supply of spirits.

From the beginning of the century until the division of the Berkshire Association—October, 1852—twelve churches have been organized; and in the following order: Savoy (1811), Florida (1814), neither of which ever had any life to speak of, having been extinct almost from birth; Mill River (1820), Curtisville (1824),

North Adams (1827), Mount Washington (1831), extinct, West Stockbridge (1833), South Williamstown (1836), South Adams (1840), Housatonic (1841), Pittsfield Second (1846), North Becket (1849), and Pittsfield (South) (1850). It can hardly be said that all of these churches are strong and efficient; though some of them are notably so, and others are doing faithful work up to the measure of their ability. Four of them have died, Savoy, Florida, Mount Washington, and North Becket, the last merging with the Methodists. They were, but are not. Of the two churches organized since the old Berkshire Association divided, namely, White Oaks (1868) and New Boston (1874), it may be said that their feebleness is due to environment and causes wholly beyond their control, as is the case with many another church of our order in the county.

To retrace our steps, then, to that period which might be termed the Golden Age of Congregationalism in this county, let us lose ourselves once more among those distinguished men whose successors we are. We have mentioned some whose names are in close connection with the very earliest history of the churches, but there are others equally and

Established Church of Berkshire 307

more renowned. It is certain that the modern Berkshire pulpit has no reason to lightly esteem the work or the worth of some who have only lately gone from us — Mark Hopkins, Gladden, Munger, and Parkhurst, leaders in the world of thought to-day, and wearers of the mantles of the prophets; and, moreover, we would not be understood as diminishing aught the earnestness and efficiency of the present Berkshire ministry because we hold up to view the colossal labors, the faithfulness and earnestness, the sturdy character, the mighty influence, and the eminent distinction of those who once labored here, as pastors of the Congregational churches. We shall only repeat the names we have already mentioned, which belong not only to the planting time but to the period of the growth of these churches as well, as many of these first settled pastors remained until death at their posts, as we have seen: Hubbard and Sergeant, Strong and Bidwell, Allen and Collins and Hyde and others. Their immediate successors evidently prized their inheritance of entering into the labors of these proto-preachers and upholding the dignity and fame of the Berkshire pulpit. Here wrought Edwards seven years, writing his treatise on the *Will* amid the labors of his Stockbridge pastorate, from which he was called to the presidency of Princeton, and to which he reluctantly went. Here wrought that other mighty theologian, Samuel Hopkins, whose impress was felt for a century or more in all our churches and throughout our whole pale; and it is pleasant to know the generous rivalry between these two pastors of neighboring Berkshire churches. Hopkins on the death of Sergeant recommended Edwards for the Stockbridge parish, and thus their earlier friendship was renewed; preceptor and pupil once more together and under what peculiar circumstances! Theologians of the highest rank, original students of whom subsequent men for a long, long period were to be echoes or interpreters — out here on the frontier, missionaries, so to speak, their lives often in jeopardy from the savages, hampered with difficulties, Edwards smarting under the memories of his Northampton parish, Hopkins unable to get his meagre salary, and forced on that account to leave Great Barrington; yet pursuing quietly and persistently those studies which enchained them by the recondite mysteries and boundless questions they unfolded, studies which were to make their names famous throughout the world. It is pathetic to read in Hopkins's autobiographic memoirs, after he was appointed the literary executor of Edwards and at Mrs. Edwards's express request had agreed to write the life of her husband:

" As these manuscripts were in my hands a number of years, I paid my chief attention to them, until I had read them all, which consisted of a great number of volumes, some of them large, besides sermons, of which sermons I did not read the whole. In doing this I had much pleasure and profit. My mind became more engaged in study, rising, great part of my time, at four o'clock in the morning to pursue my study, in which I took great pleasure."

Only a little less galactic than these are the names of West, the minister of Stockbridge for fifty-nine years, longest settled of any minister in the history of the county, and Catlin, who was the minister at New Marlborough thirty-nine years. I have myself conversed recently with an aged lady in Stockbridge who remembers Dr. West, with his short clothes, silver buckles, hair braided down his back, and three-cornered hat. With this the account of Miss Catherine Sedgwick exactly tallies. Dr. West was a precisionist, an exquisite and a mighty theologian. Over eighty young men preparing for the ministry read theology with him and they became many of them noted preachers. His home became a sort of theological seminary. West came into the county ten years before Hopkins left it; and under the influence of this friendship West became an ultra-Calvinist, and his school a foremost and strenuous advocate of what was known as Hopkinsianism. Dr. West was consulted as to the foundation of Andover, and was the biographer of Hopkins. He was also chaplain at the Hoosac fort; and like Allen's prayer at Bennington, to which the soldiers attributed our victory (although Allen fought as well as he prayed), so at the Berkshire convention which met at Stockbridge in the early days of the Revolution and resolved to "boycott" all goods of British manufacture, West's "animated prayer" lingered long in the hearts of those early patriots of the county, which was one of the first to throw down that gauntlet of revolt. This action of the Berkshire men, not unworthy to be classed with the Boston Tea Party, was abetted and sanctioned by their youthful religious leaders and teachers.

Over in New Marlborough there was, as a contemporary of Dr. West, though not of Hopkins, a man, Jacob Catlin, whose *Theological Compendium*, a work much prized in his day, lies before me as I write. He was a pupil of West, and he in turn became an instructor of many young men about to go into the ministry. It is said of him and of Dr. Hyde that they almost never laughed. Dr. Catlin was known to laugh once, and Dr. Hyde never laughed loud enough to be heard in the next room. Catlin, owing to his small salary, carried on farming on an extensive scale, making worldlings envious of his success in tilling the soil, and yet he always found time to write out two sermons a week, conducted numerous meetings every week, and between services on the Sabbath carried on a sort of Bible school and parochial bureau of information. He was, like others of his brethren, an ardent lover of the Berkshire Association, which was a sort of advanced Bible class, lasting two days or so and devoted to spiritual and biblical exercises mainly. Yale gave him a D.D.

Another minister of this period was E. Judson of the Sheffield church, who, like West, changed from the Arminian to an ultra-Calvinistic theology, and, what is more, changed his church, too, for as one said: "We were made Calvinists before we knew it." Mr. Judson was himself an instructor of theological students, and, though eccentric, was "esteemed highly for his work's sake." We mention him here because he was the "faithful personal and political friend" of Thomas Allen of the church in Pittsfield, both of them being intense partisans of the Jeffersonian type, though Judson was far more adroit than Allen. The Berkshire Association deeply offended Dr. Allen, toward the very last of his life, by sanctioning the new church enterprise which split off from the First Church owing to Allen's political sermons; and the chronicler of Allen's funeral tells a volume between the lines when he says:

"His funeral sermon was preached by his faithful personal political friend, the Rev. E. Judson of Sheffield. . . . Other clergymen who took part were Rev. Mr. Marsh of Bennington and a Mr. Hall, who was preaching as a candidate." And then the historian adds: "Many of the neighboring ministers were, however, present."

And what shall I more say. For the time would fail me to tell of William Allen, called from Pittsfield to the presidency of Bowdoin; of Humphrey, called to the presidency of Amherst; of John DeWitt, long a prominent teacher in the New Brunswick seminary, once a colleague of Mr. Collins; of John Todd and his thirty-one years' pastorate in Pittsfield; of James Bradford and his thirty-nine years'

Established Church of Berkshire 313

pastorate in Sheffield; of Dr. Shepard and his fifty-one years' pastorate in Lenox; of G. Dorrance and his thirty-nine years' pastorate in Windsor; also in more recent years of Twining, of Hinsdale once, for many years on the *Independent;* of Alden, formerly of Lenox and long-time the Secretary of the American Board of Foreign Missions; of Harris, formerly of the South Church, Pittsfield, long a most distinguished teacher and leader at New Haven. Thirty-six ministers have served the churches of this county, by reason of their long pastorates, a grand total of eleven hundred years. It will be permitted me, perhaps, to speak specially of two ministers, Dr. Field of Stockbridge, and Dr. Shepard of Lenox. Dr. Field was the author of a very valuable history of Berkshire, and was no mean successor of West, Edwards, and Sergeant, though his pastorate was not as long as that of others in the county. Dr. Shepard of Lenox, nearly fifty-one years pastor of the church, was not as great a theologian as West, with whom, as well as with Dr. Field, he was contemporary, yet a powerful and useful preacher of great ability; blessed with frequent revivals; the very opposite of Hyde and Catlin in outward mien, for Shepard was very sociable and jolly; with a voice which Dr. Todd pronounced "the most wonderful he ever heard." He was a man of marked influence in the county. His remains lie in the churchyard near the church, like those of many of the older preachers, who became so attached to their parishes by long service as to wish interment amid the scenes of their labors.

It may not be inappropriate, having viewed these ministers singly in their several parishes, if we take a look more closely into their associational gatherings and see them together; though it will be very hard to digest the contents of three leather-covered volumes into a paragraph. By associational vote when the division was made, the records and files of papers, etc., were ordered to be preserved and consigned to the care of the South Association. They are most carefully kept in the vaults of the Stockbridge bank, and with something like eagerness, fascination, and awe I have gone through these ancient records, glistening with the blotting sand which still adheres, yellowed with age, and containing autographs of many of these olden pastors. The Berkshire Association was organized in 1763, but for thirty years the records were not kept; or

Established Church of Berkshire 315

if kept, were lost. It was organized with the following personnel: The Revs. Jonathan Hubbard of Sheffield, Thomas Strong of New Marlborough, A. Bidwell of Tyringham, Samuel Hopkins of Great Barrington, and Stephen West. Meetings were held three times a year, and as the number of ministers grew we find for a series of years only two meetings a year; but it must be remembered that the ministers of neighboring parishes used to have meetings once a month; certainly in the vicinity of New Marlborough in Dr. Catlin's time.

The regular meetings of the Association were almost always two-day affairs, and scattered through the records for twoscore years are many such notes as this: "Adjourned until 5 o'c. to-morrow morning"; almost always "5 o'c.," sometimes "7 o'c.," and once till sun "is $\frac{1}{2}$ hour high." The place of meeting varied and the exercises were the same for many, many years: namely, public service with sermon, afterward criticised, discussion of some question of theology, a study of the Bible in course, question box on questions of discipline, experience and polity, and business— coupled with anniversary meetings of various county societies. The Association was a sort of appellate court for the churches, and was almost always busy examining and licensing candidates. It had in after years a regular yearly narrative of the state of the churches. It was foremost in helping various causes, often initiating them : Bible, temperance, Sabbath observance, Sunday-school, and anti-slavery. It made recommendations and issued pastoral letters to the churches. It assigned pastoral visits to the churches, making out schedules for ministers to go by twos to various parishes, for pastoral and preaching work. It employed itinerant missionaries for the weak and feeble churches. It inaugurated conferences or fellowship meetings. It appointed many days of fasting and prayer for spiritual refreshment. It was executive, studious, spiritual, and it compelled attendance of members by exacting excuses for absenteeism before the whole body.

Many interesting minutes could be brought to view from the old records, as they show the state of thought and feeling among the "watchmen on the hills of Zion" regarding the various questions which swept, like cloud shadows, across these vales and hills. The change in relation to connection between Church and State, exempting non-communicants of one order from taxation,—in short the disestablishment of Congregationalism,—the work of missions among the heathen, the temperance cause, the anti-slavery movement—all these questions in the ethical realm, and those in the civil realm from the Revolution down show a state of mind, as revealed by these minutes, at once noble and far-seeing. I think one of the remarkable things is the suddenness and thoroughness of the temperance reformation in the county. Let it be remembered that drinking was universal, the sin only lying in excess: that Dr. Shepard and Dr. West and good and holy deacons and many of the rank and file were users of liquor; that the Hinsdale pews were sold to the accompaniment of the glass that cheers and inebriates; that the Sheffield church-raising had a town appropriation of "three barrels of beer and twenty gallons of rum" with which to put up its sacred timbers; that in Gordon Dorrance's ministry of thirty-nine years up in Windsor the only records are of about thirty church meetings or so, twenty-five of which are of discipline for drunkenness; that every sideboard had its decanter and ministers were accustomed to quaff a social glass at the pastoral calls; and then think of the thoroughgoing character of that reformation which, through the examples of these ministers largely, was wrought in the county. Our fathers handled with dexterity the flip-iron which has entirely gone out of our knowledge with the crane and the pillion; yet that flip-iron was the symbol of our shame. I find many a minute as to temperance on these pages. The first that I discover is of date June 10, 1828, and reads: "The report upon the subject of temperance, pledging entire abstinence on our own part and recommending the same to all others, was accepted and ordered to be printed." Seven years later (1835) the pledge is renewed and recommended again. In 1851 this minute appears: "In some of our communities no liquor is sold openly and in one none is openly drank, nor can a drunkard be found." It is but fair, however, to state that the hold of strong drink was not so relaxed that every community was a unit in this matter. Lieutenant-Governor Hull of Sandisfield, writes in 1854: "The male portion of our customers, including the aged minister, indulged liberally in the rations of strong drink." The minister here referred to purchased his liquor by the quart, and rejoiced in many a gracious season of revival, too.

The impression, I am quite sure, obtains

that someway the religious life of the fathers and of the time in which they lived was of a higher order than now. An impression of that sort does honor to our affection, but is not, I venture to think, quite in accord with the facts; at least if we may judge from what our fathers themselves said concerning the life and morals of their own age. Their sermons are full of the bitterest arraignment of the world in which they lived; its degeneracy, its lapse, its trend. We have lauded "the good old times" too much; though I doubt not they were better than their records and sermons make them out. Read Dr. Hopkins's sermon entitled "The author's farewell to the world," preached just before his death in 1803 — two or three years before, at the turn of the centuries; it breathes denunciation in every line, and seems to be modelled after the most fiery invective of the minor prophets. Read the magazines of the period, *The Panoplist* and *The Evangelic Magazine*, published in the first decade of the nineteenth century; Dr. Catlin's sermon on a fast-day in 1812, and the "Records" of the churches themselves. See the world of our fathers' day through the eyes of our fathers as revealed in their sermons and letters, and our affection will not usurp the place of our judgment. The world is improving, like good wine, with age. We live in better days than our fathers; and our sons will no doubt keep up the pleasant fiction that ours is the Golden Age, and theirs the Age of Stone; and so on and on, while time lasts and God works out His purposes despite human unbelief.

I wish to pass, then, directly into the subject which in the most signal way marks the difference between the age of our fathers and ours; viz., the theology of a hundred years ago, and less, contrasted with the belief in the churches to-day. I think few of us would be willing to assent to what Macaulay says about theology,— "that it is not a progressive science like pharmacy, geology, or navigation; and a Christian of the nineteenth century is no better or worse off than a Christian of the fifth, providing each is possessed of candor, for both alike have the Bible in their hands." The greatest progress imaginable is seen in the way people conceived of truth during this last century, and I pray for that wisdom in treating this subject which Lowell says Emerson had, "who took down our idols with so much grace that it seemed an act of worship." Let us come right to what the fathers taught about God, man, and destiny.

They taught that God hated sinful man, that man was only vile in His sight, and that the body as well as the soul of the sinner would burn in real fire endlessly. Dr. Hopkins begins his *System of Divinity*, published in 1793, as follows:

"Mankind needs to know the method God has appointed in which *He will be reconciled* to them"; and a little farther on we read, "this displeasure, anger, and wrath of God toward the sinner is just, benevolent, and kind"; and I quote again: "He who has a new heart must be a friend of God and must be pleased with His infinitely benevolent character, though he has not a thought that God loves him; and if he could know that God designed, for His own glory and the general good, to cast him into endless destruction, this would not make him cease to approve of His character: he would continue to be a friend of God."

What would Dr. Hopkins have said if he could have known that the Church a hundred years from his time would be singing:

"O Love Divine that stooped to share
Our sharpest pang, our bitterest tear,"

and that we would be throwing all the weight of our emphasis on the great cardinal doctrine of God's love as a means to awaken loyalty and service among men?

To-day the reconciliation of man to God has taken the place of the reconciliation of God to men. I know a lady — she is still living — who has told me how when she joined the Church, somewhere about 1833, the minister asked her, "Theresa, are you willing to be damned for the glory of God?" and she said, "No, sir." Even Mrs. Edwards, the wife of the distinguished Stockbridge preacher of old time, reluctantly yet eagerly accepted the idea of God's Fatherhood as a *new* revelation to her soul, when the prevalent doctrine was that he was a Sovereign, a "hard and austere Master," an offended and unreconciled Deity having a sort of consuming hatred for the human race; and all because through one man came sin.

And now look at the picture of that "first sin" in Eden, and the consequences of it as pictured upon the olden page; and not so very long ago, either, for this teaching of a hundred years ago comes way down well into the second quarter of this last century. It is incredible that we are only just emerging from the shadows. The creation of the world in six literal days, and, as Dr. Catlin, in an old manuscript ser-non lying before me says, of man "on Saturday at sundown"; the bringing of the universe into shape in 144 hours, a mighty, instantaneous work of the great Demiurge, with angels looking on and singing as on the first day they saw Europe, Asia, Africa, and America rise out of the waters, and all this "at the autumnal equinox" (see Hopkins, *System of Divinity*, p. 33); the Paradise of our first parents, in which, before their sin, serpents WALKED, for Mr. Hopkins takes pains to tell us that the serpent who tempted Eve "had an erect and very beautiful form, and had nothing of the appearance and form of serpents since the fall of man," and Dr. Catlin says of the serpent, "he walked erect *with great vivacity*, and was the most lovely and beautiful of all the brutal creation, until he was doomed after the fall of man to go upon his belly and lick the dust of the earth"; and finally the sin of Eden with the "revelation of the plan of mercy immediately after the fall of man, so that doubtless Adam and Eve embraced the Saviour and the plan of redemption by his blood";—how primitive all this appears to us! We wonder that only yesterday, so to speak, we believed all this.

Yet this theory of the creation and fall of

man is only trivial compared with the erroneous and mischievous doctrines built upon it. "Total depravity" followed, then original sin, and the doctrines of the "Decrees," by which God was said to damn some in infancy. Dr. Catlin speaks of the "universal sinfulness of infants": "infants are in a lost and perishing condition"; and farther on he proceeds to clinch the argument by this same doctrine of "original and innate depravity" due to Adam's sin. Is it any wonder that the fathers complain of "deadness and unbelief" in their churches, particularly when they made the acceptance of these doctrines a condition of salvation? Every mother bending over her sweetly sleeping babe in the cradle ought to have taken counsel of her heart and refused to listen to such counsel from these pseudo-interpreters of the Divine grace and nature. But this was only the beginning, the first step in carrying out the doctrine of "total depravity." Man was hated of God, vile, and so despicable in God's eyes that those who were "impenitent and unconverted" could do nothing good: "all their deeds of justice, of mercy and charity, *are perfectly odious* in the sight of a holy God" (see Catlin, *Compendium*, p. 195). "Sinners in many duties are constant and persevering: the external duties of religion, for example; the devotions of the sanctuary, reading of Scriptures, attending the Gospel ministry, meetings for prayer, and so on; they embrace and defend the doctrines of the Bible; even engage in family worship and the religious training of their children, well knowing these things are of infinite importance to their children, but all these external duties and sacrifices of the wicked are an abomination to the Lord"; yet they "must not renounce the externals of religion, lest they become barbarians." "A sinner ought to pray, but *his prayer is an abomination* unto the Lord"; *whatever good he does "is sin";* yet he must not omit doing good, even if it be "perfectly odious in the sight of a holy God."

Now it is very evident that this conception of man which our fathers entertained would lead to a doctrine of "conversion" which would be little less than awful. What it was many of us remember, or have heard. In some instances men were weeks and months in the grip of melancholia until they could get an overwhelming sense of their guilt and approve God's wrath; and this was encouraged. It was a trophy of true conversion to be able to have some *shuddering* experience to relate, and the magazines of the day are filled with these accounts. Every man's sin was a sin against an infinite God and therefore an infinite sin, no matter how small it was; and because it was an infinite sin demanded endless punishment. God was angry with men, and if He were to forgive He must have infinite satisfaction for His wrath; and so He appeased His wrath as He watched the sufferings and blood of Calvary. His vengeance demanded blood, and so Jesus turns away wrath, vindicates broken law, and the sinner gets off.

In the former days everything, incarnation, atonement, conversion, regeneration, must be worked out by a sort of primal conception that man was not loved by God, that on the contrary he was the one object on which the hate of God was focussed. And the wonder is how men read the Parable of the Prodigal Son, for example. It seems as if they must have stifled all their nobler feelings as interpreters of God; indeed they did do just that. One minister, living in West Stockbridge, the Rev. Mr. Camp, did venture to deny that man was so bad as the prevailing theology made him out, but he was "labored with," then suspended; and finally he "retracted." The "plan" was inexorable. To

Established Church of Berkshire 327

disbelieve the ruling creed was to invite excommunication; and Hopkins expressly declares that the Church must treat the man thus cut off "with peculiar neglect and slight, avoid his company at all times, and never so much as eat with him at a common table." The story of *John Ward, Preacher*, is sober realism. And as if that were not enough Dr. Hopkins consigns all those who differ with him to endless destruction; and what he means by hell is *real fire* as well as the bitter anguish of remorse. I quote:

"God will render a future separation of the bodies and the souls of the wicked impossible, and so form the body, as that it shall continue in *full* life, and with *quick sense* in union with the soul, in the *hottest fire* that can be imagined, or exist, through endless ages. . . . God will show his power in the punishment of the wicked by *strengthening and upholding their bodies* and souls in suffering torments which otherwise would be intolerable.' (*System of Divinity*, vol. 2, p. 253).

And this, he taught, was what all must come to who did n't hold the faith as he taught it, no matter how excellent and exceptionally moral their lives! To-day not only his doctrine of a physical hell, but an endless hell as well, is repulsive to the Christian consciousness; and is cast off.

I cannot dwell on our fathers' emphasis of the "Decrees of God"; of election and preterition; of the sovereignty of the great God, who disposed all events in the arbitrary way by which His glory would be best subserved; or of the doctrine of the perseverance of the saints; but one can but do these spiritual teachers honor for their extreme humility in rather timidly "entertaining a hope," only, of their salvation. Their stern doctrines smote them with godly fear and humbleness of mind. There never was a godlier race; sure they were right, yet never sure they themselves were saved, though we know they had an "abundant entrance" ministered to them as they "crossed the bar" into the beatific harbors. I cannot dwell here on their conception of Jesus Christ, whom they robbed of his humanity, making him forbidding in his holiness, a Deity on earth in whom temptation found no response, a Teacher of an impossible human goodness, a Being more in league with heaven than in sympathy with mortals; but who can withhold from our fathers their just meed of praise for the Christ-spirit they so largely expressed? If they regarded a Sabbath-breaker as worse than an adulterer or murderer — and they did (see Catlin, p. 217);

if the "Records of these Churches" are filled with quarrels and trials; I think we do wrong not to see how noble a motive often animated their sternness toward their fellow-men, viz., to save their souls from the inevitable and terrific fate, unmodified, unceasing, awaiting the wrong-doer,—and this, no matter how mistaken we see it to be now, was the Christ-spirit. I cannot dwell now on their conception of the work of "Foreign Missions," of which they thought as saving the heathen from an impending fate because they did not know of Christ—a work they prosecuted as life-savers the rescue of men from conflagration or shipwreck, because they felt no heathen could be saved without personally knowing Him of whom they had never even heard! But shall we see the mistake in their idea of "Foreign Missions" and not see their motive, the sublimity of their hope and sacrifices in establishing a work so momentous, so magnificent, so lasting? If they reasoned out "Trinity" on the basis of a text not in the Revision,— "There are three that bare record," which Hopkins makes an "express declaration" of the doctrine, and Catlin says "states the matter very clearly,"—we may smile but we do not therefore read out the term "Trinity" from our modern theology, though we put an altogether different meaning into it. And who can read this passage from Hopkins without honoring his simple reading of the Scripture :

"The spirits of departed saints when they leave the body do not go into some dark corner of the universe, or out of sight of heaven, of Christ, his Church, and this world, but they rise into light and take a station from which they can see all these things and all worlds, and have a perfect discerning without the least cloud or darkness." (Hopkins, vol. 2, p. 223.)

Of course our fathers believed in the resurrection of the body — now pretty generally given up; and I think this passage from Hopkins's "Farewell to the World" is rather a unique expression of the former belief concerning the "Last Judgment": "I am sure to meet not only all who are now in the world, but all the countless millions who ever have lived, or shall exist hereafter to the end of the world at the day of judgment, *when I shall know the character of every individual person*" (*Sermons*, p. 358). Dear, dear! And as if it were not enough to picture in so realistic a way that "Day of Wrath," and frame a mighty philosophy of human belief, conduct, and destiny, Dr. Hopkins plays the seer, and says that

> "the sixth vial is now running and began to be poured out at the beginning of the eighteenth century, or some years before, and will run some part of the nineteenth century, perhaps near fifty years of it. . . . And then the 'seventh and last vial,' the most dreadful calamities and destructions will be poured out, ushering in the millennium."

Nine pages of Dr. Hopkins's *System* (vol. 2, p. 290-299) are filled to prove that the Sabbath begins at sundown; one of his sermons is devoted — the one entitled his "valedictory" — to a general wail and denunciation, in which the only thing which has any vein of cheerfulness to his mind is this, that God will make his (Hopkins's) system of thought to stand : " I stand as a brazen wall, unhurt and not moved by all the shafts of opposition and reproach which have been levelled at me, and at the system of truth and religion I have espoused, being *assured it will stand forever.*"

Scarce a hundred years have elapsed, and lo! we look to-day upon the ruins of that system known in religious thought as "Hopkinsianism." Its author, he himself tells us, was regarded as "narrow and bigoted in his sentiments." The Berkshire ministry of to-day has broken away from his dogmatic chains, yet it reverences Hopkins as a man and as a reformer, but not as a teacher of truth. The catholic and broad spirit began to overspread the face of things soon after he died, coming to us from Coleridge, not to go farther back, then through Maurice, Robertson, Tennyson, and Browning on the other side, and through Channing, Bushnell, Beecher, and Munger on this side; the great law of evolution and the origin of species through Darwin, Spencer, and Huxley found place in human thought; the telegraph made all the world one, and so broadened our horizons; education has cleared away the cobwebs from our seeing; and above and beyond everything else the spirit of God has been brooding quietly over the mind and heart of man; and so it is not in the power of any old system of truth to hold us. That power to hold lies in Truth, not in a system of truth, and Truth is of God, a " system " is of men. Hopkins's system contained a great deal of sublime truth that will remain; but its reactionary Calvinism was its main feature, and this has been sloughed off.

Sergeant, Edwards, Hopkins, Catlin, Allen, Judson, Shepard, West, Hyde, Humphrey, Field — I am sure as I speak the names, they

Established Church of Berkshire 333

evoke a response from our hearts, prompt, grateful, and enduring, and more thrilling than the name of many a hero of Jewish and sacred story. Through faith they came into this Berkshire wilderness, and pioneered; through faith they taught the Mohican Indians they found here, and for fifty years gave these friendly savages a practical Christian education; through faith in knowledge they, all college men and by a very large majority from Yale, reared here their monument, Williams College, their creation, their care, and the loved object of their sacrifices, when to sacrifice was to yield almost their very life-blood; through faith they planted churches, and cared for them in long and happy and useful pastorates; through faith in their country's cause they offered themselves on the altar of sacrifice in the nation's peril, Avery of Windsor leading a Berkshire regiment to Boston after the news of Lexington came by fast couriers to the county, and Allen leading another to Bennington where the "fighting parson" shot as well as prayed and ministered to the dying; through faith they broke the rocks and felled the trees and tilled the soil, many of them toilers with their hands; through faith they carried on in their corporate capacity the vast interests of this region so far as concerned religion, morals, missions, education ; through faith they wrought wonders, preached the truth as they conceived it, lived pattern lives full of the spirit of their Master and Lord, ministered to the needy, and saw their work often mightily prosper. And these all, having " witnessed a good confession," died as they had lived ; and just outside the door of how many a village church in this county, or in the quiet cemetery not far away, is the precious dust of these venerated fathers, their graves the sacred shrines of the children and great-grandchildren of those to whom they ministered. Dr. Shepard's grave at Lenox is hardly a step from the church-door he so often entered, and almost on the exact spot where, as a mere boy, he was inducted into the sacred office of pastor, at a memorable open-air service in 1795. And here is the inscription on a stone in a quiet corner of the Stockbridge cemetery :

> " Here lyes
> the Body of the Rev. Mr. John Sergeant
> who dyed the 27th Day of July A. D. 1749
> in the fortieth year of his age.——

Where is that pleasing form I ask ? Thou canst not show.
He's not within false stone there's nought but dust
    below.
And where is that pious soul, that thinking, conscious
    mind ?
Wilt thou pretend vain cypher that's with thee in-
    shrined ?
Alas my friends, not here with thee, that I can find,
Here's not a Sergeant's body, nor a Sergeant's mind,
I'll seek him hence, for all's alike deception here,
I'll go to Heaven and shall find my Sergeant there."

I want if I can to bring up one or two of these men, and get a look at them in flesh and blood. Miss Sedgwick in her tales and sketches has left us many a portrait of Stephen West, who was just finishing his pastorate at Stockbridge as she was reaching the threshhold of her literary career ; and it may not be amiss to notice that what often and often has happened, happened here. We would not have had Miss Catherine Sedgwick's charming stories arraigning the awful, the dry and barren theology of her day if there had been no theology to arraign. It was the teaching of West and Shepard—the one the pastor in the home of Catherine's girlhood, Stockbridge ; and the other in the home of her womanhood, Lenox —and of such as they that gave us *A New England Tale*, which in its day was almost as popular as *Uncle Tom's Cabin* in its day, or as *Ben Hur* in ours. And yet Miss Sedgwick loved Dr. West as a man, for he was vastly better than his system, for she says, "beneath a stern and precise exterior, he was social, tender, cheerful, with a disposition like sunshine, warm and genial." Every morning he greeted each member of his family with "good morning prefaced with a broad sunny smile." He was an eminent theologian, having always in his household some student to educate for the ministry; a very pious, rigorously precise, man; an indefatigable student; rigidly Hopkinsian in his theology; and a man of tremendous influence. And yet I am bound to say that I think he rather "lorded it over God's heritage." A widow who was a member of his church married an immoral, unchristian man, and was excommunicated; a council was called, but Dr. West, then a man of forty, defended his action in a published sermon I have just read on "The duty of Christians to marry only in the Lord." The arguments are not worth consideration to-day; though doubtless in their day were plausible with many because the skilful advocate tried to bring the Scriptures to his defence.

But let me call up before you two other men:

Dr. Catlin of New Marlborough, the author of a popular work on theology; and Mr. Collins of Lanesborough,—both Yale men. Here is the way Dr. Catlin is described: "Of medium height, not fleshy but strongly made; of grave, manly countenance, and a kindly bow of the olden time for all whom he met. Dressed always in black; short clothes buckled at the knee; a white stock buckled behind; hat turned up at side and behind." It is said that he never laughed but *once* in his lifetime. One likes to imagine what that one joke could have been. Mr. Collins is thus pictured: "Tall, erect, quick in his movements, and wore to the close of his life the ministerial wig and three-cornered hat. He expected and exacted a bow from every child he met." It may be remarked in passing that Mr. Collins as a loyalist was profoundly incensed at his neighbor, Mr. Allen of Pittsfield, the "fighting parson," the intense patriot, and a Democrat of the Democrats, all the rest of his ministerial brethren being Federalists but one, Judson of Sheffield. Mr. Collins, however, took it upon himself to be so severe on "Parson" Allen, that the town of Pittsfield voted to ask Mr. Collins to desist from his course of "censuring and disapproving their reverend pastor"; and indeed his own town of Lanesborough condemned him for his Tory sentiments.

Let us take another couple of these olden ministers, Shepard of Lenox, and Hyde of Lee,— exact opposites :—Hyde, a reactionary orthodox; Shepard, orthodox, very, but progressive: Hyde, a man of sad and serious demeanor, never laughing, or if he did once in a great while, never loud enough to be heard in the next room; Shepard, a teller of funny stories and always jolly, though he knew when to be dignified: Hyde, a man to whom Dr. Backus once said, "You never have anything to repent of"; Shepard doing, I presume, a hundred things a day he felt sorry for: Hyde, a close, quiet manuscript preacher with almost no gestures, and Shepard an extemporaneous, vehement one, though both preached to a churchful: one having a ministry of forty years and a few months in Lee, and the other fifty years and a few months in the county seat, preaching to lawyers, students and faculty, and his own distinguished and cultured parishioners. Or, take another two, Allen of Pittsfield, and Judson of Sheffield, both the intensest kind of Jeffersonian Democrats, when their brother-ministers were regarding

The Rev. Samuel Shepard, D.D.,
Pastor Congregational Church, Lenox, Mass. [*1795–1846.*]

Thomas Jefferson as anti-Christ, the enemy of religion, and the defamer of God and all that was good. Yet even Allen and Judson differed markedly in the emphasis they laid on their political convictions in public. Judson, as intense a Democrat as Allen, never mentioned his politics even in conversation, except at home or among congenial partisans who thought as he did. Allen took the stump in exciting periods of great public questions; finally rent his own church in twain, and when he died the other ministers were a little scant in courtesy to his memory. He had a pleasant, affectionate countenance, which took on a most benignant expression in the pulpit. He read his sermons from manuscript in short-hand, having himself devised his own system of stenography.

To Sergeant, Hopkins and Edwards, all Yale men, I have already sufficiently referred. Sergeant lives on the pages of the great missionary record of all time. Hopkins and Edwards rank with the Augustines and Calvins of the Christian Church in all ages. Of Dr. Heman Humphrey of Pittsfield, or of Dr. David Dudley Field, two other Yale men, only passing mention can be made :—the first, one of the best known of college presidents (president of Amherst College 1823-45); and the second, the historian of Berkshire and the father of a most remarkable family, distinguished alike in American jurisprudence, science, and letters,—Stephen, long-time a justice on the bench of the United States Supreme Court; David Dudley, Jr., an authority on international law and a most effective advocate; Cyrus W., whose name will be imperishably associated with the Atlantic cable; and Henry M., minister, editor, and traveller, whose books are widely read. The Rev. Dr. Henry M. Field is now passing the evening of his days in his beloved Stockbridge.

The Congregational Church was disestablished throughout Massachusetts in 1834, up to which time all citizens were supposed to be taxed for its support, unless they had "certificated," *i. e.*, obtained permission from the proper town authorities to attend worship elsewhere by certifying their preference for other religious denominations. Some availed themselves of this privilege to escape the rigors of the dominant theology; more to escape taxation for the support of the local church; and thus other churches than the Congregational, with splendid histories and increasing efficiency, came into existence on New England soil. My space avails not to write of them though the lustre of brilliant achievement crowns their efforts and brightens the daily living of all. I have written of one Church only, because the thread of its working is a very distinct and integral strand in the fabric of state in the days when the Congregational was the established Church of New England; and I have confined myself to the workings of that Church in Berkshire.

IX

EPITAPHS IN BERKSHIRE CHURCH-YARDS

I CANNOT quite say with Whittier, at least so far as Berkshire is concerned, that "our fathers set apart to Death the dreariest spot in all the land." The Lenox Cemetery has the choicest landscapes, evoking the admiring gaze of thousands who annually visit it simply for its magnificent scenery. It lies on the summit of the hill adjacent to the old church, and its long-time pastor, Dr. Shepard, who ministered here for half a century, is buried just outside the door. It is only fair to say, however, that to test the truthfulness of the poet's description we need to divest this exalted and celebrated burial-place of its modern features, and see it as it was before "summer-places" grew up around it; a "lonesome acre," doubtless, dreary and bleak. If to-day then these

Berkshire Epitaphs 343

ancient burying-grounds have an inviting appearance, it is unquestionably attributable quite as much to a change of belief concerning death as to a change of sentiment concerning the adornment of cemeteries. The grim and gloomy grip of a stern theology has left its palpable impress on the moss-grown slabs; the sheer and downright contradiction to the "larger hope" of the present. Betwixt the theology of Watts and that of Whittier is fixed a deep gulf; from Edwards and Hopkins to Bushnell and Munger is a transition from the tomb into the living realities of a beautiful May morning.

It will be impossible for me to present with any completeness the quaint epitaphs in Berkshire churchyards; I must confine myself to types. I may say by way of preface that I do not think so rich a "find" is to be expected in Berkshire as in the older portions of the State. Still the age of epitaph-making had not passed away, and the "grave and the gay," the hortatory and the laudatory, the sentimental and the practical, the despairing and the hopeful, the sincere and the hypocritical are all here. I regret that in the limits of this short chapter I shall only be able to present typical specimens, but I shall be abundantly satisfied if I can induce any to turn aside from their excursions here and there through the county in order to decipher the memorials of another age.

> " For thus our fathers testified, —
>   That he might read who ran, —
> The emptiness of human pride,
>   The nothingness of man.
>
> " They dared not plant the grave with flowers,
>   Nor dress the funeral sod,
> Where, with a love as deep as ours,
>   They left their dead with God."

To begin, then, with some of those commonplaces which show the poverty of intellectuality, the Berkshire burying-grounds have their full share of those crude jingles designed to remind the beholder of his mortality. They are to be found throughout the whole region, such as:

> " Behold, my friends, as you pass by,
>   This stone informs you where I lie;
> As I am now soon you must be,
>   Prepare to die and follow me."

or this:

> " Friends, nor [*sic*] physicians could not save
>   This mortal body from the grave,
> Nor can the grave confine me here,
>   When Jesus calls I must appear."

or this:

> "Nor sex nor age can death defy;
> Think, mortal, what it is to die."

These are the common epitaphs, often associated with winged angels' heads and draped urns sculptured on the stone, perhaps now and then having, in addition, the motto "Nascentes Morimur," to intensify the depressing sentiment in the vernacular.

Here are two epitaphs to babies, the first a babe of nine hours, who died 1799:

> "Ye active babes and children all!
> Behold the scene of children's fall,
> My day was short, my hours few,
> And bid this world and all adieu";

and this, from another burying-ground, revealing a resignation hard and unnatural:

> "Happy the babe who privileged by fate
> To shorten labor, and a lighter weight,
> Received but yesterday the gift of breath,
> Ordered to-morrow to return to death."

It is comforting to read as a firm dissent from the theology of the times, when, by the "decree" of preterition, it was asserted that "hell was paved with the skulls of infants not a span long," this mother's assurance, engraved on another stone in a Berkshire churchyard:

"I know my babe is blest."

Rash woman she to defy the "doctors in the temple" and court the charge of heresy from her friends and neighbors. Oliver Wendell Holmes says Jonathan Edwards must have read that invitation of Jesus to children, "Suffer the little vipers to come unto me, and forbid them not," and I feel very sure so triumphant an exclamation as this parent's was not suffered to pass unchallenged.

A death in youth or in middle life or from accident was an opportunity not to be lost, and many are the stones which narrate in compact detail the actual circumstances by which the deceased lost his life, with sundry moral reflections based on the same. Sometimes one sees on the Berkshire roads the very spot on which a fatal accident occurred marked by a stone. Here is one on the road from Lenox to Lee:

> "On this spot was found the lifeless corpse of Mr. D. Blossom of Lenox, May 8, 1814, in the 22d year of his age. Walking here he was suddenly called into eternity without any earthly friend to console him in his last moment or to close his dying eyes. Reader, pause and consider the vast importance of being prepared to meet thy God. For thou knowest not the time, the place, nor the manner of thy death."

Here is another inscription on the slab to the memory of a man in middle life :

> " Repent, repent now you have time
> For I was taken in my prime."

And here is this rather unexpected philosophy from the lips of a youth who died 1791 :

> " In the twenty-third year of my age
> I quit this tirsom [*sic*] pilgrimage."

Bad spelling, omitted letters and words indicated by carets, and non-syllabic division of words at the ends of lines are to be found in all the Berkshire churchyards, but how far these things reflect on the average educational standards of the age and how far on the general schooling of the stone-cutters alone cannot be entirely determined from these epitaphs.

Here is one (1796) :

> " Cum all you living that me survive
> Unto these lines attend
> Walk in the paths of piece and truth
> And piece shall be your end."

Here is another (1798) :

> " O may this be your happy case
> That he who gives you length of days
> May raise you to his corts above
> There to pertake of boundless love."

The romance of the Berkshire epitaphs is a story all by itself. I give one. It is the lament of a young widow:

> "Hervey with thee I'd walk the narrow road
> That leads far hence to yonder blest abode.
> Grant me his faith, O Lord our God most high,
> Let me like Hervey live, like Hervey die!"

Often as I have gone reverently yet curiously among the mounds and ancient slabs of these burying-grounds a sense of life has seized me, *their* life, their living sorrows, trials, loves, and hates.

> "Oft did the harvest to their sickle yield,
>   Their furrow oft the stubborn glebe has broke;
> How jocund did they drive their team a-field!
>   How bowed the woods beneath their sturdy stroke!"

Here are simply "annals," as the classic elegiac calls them, but a life-story is "between the lines," always full of interest, sometimes surcharged with romance. Humanity with its needs, its aspirations, its jealousies, its strivings, its purposes and aims is the same from age to age.

I found this epitaph in one of the Berkshire cemeteries:

> "Her thinkings and achings are o'er."

Yes! it is *life* which is here, which is here unnalled. We all remember that poem of Whittier's on "Forgiveness," in which the poet describes himself as having been once very greatly wronged and was able to forgive, as wandering one day in the village burial-place he pondered

'. . . how all human love and hate
Find one sad level, and how soon or late
Wronged and wrong-doer . . .
Pass the green threshold of our common grave;
Our common sorrow, like a mighty wave,
Swept all my pride away and trembling I *forgave*."

The humor of the burying-grounds in Berkshire may also be had for the seeking. One or two instances must suffice; and first of all as I was threading my way through the Lanesborough Cemetery one day my eye caught in large letters on a sarcophagus up the slope a name familiar to every American household: "JOSH BILLINGS." On another side of the stone was the real name of the quaint humorist, "Henry Wheeler Shaw, b. 1818, d. 1885."

Here is an epitaph taken from one of the stones in eastern Berkshire:

> "He hath gone to the upper blue,
>   Where he is free from care and pain,
>   For he was to our Saviour true,
>   And never was profane."

Tradition says that he "swore like a pirate," but to the loving descendant who erected the stone his vices were only foibles.

Perhaps the richest "finds" in a humorous way are to be obtained in one of the cemeteries where the monument-maker supplied poetry as a part of his stock in trade, as the sign which hung over his shop-door indicates:

> "Sculptured marble done here
>   Of every kind
>   To suit the fancy
>   Of the most refined"

He was proud of his stones and with an artist's privilege affixed his name to all in the lower right-hand corner. Moreover he doubtless caused a panic among his rival craftsmen by his ability to pictorially represent on the marble the scene of death; a death on the railroad, by a man and an engine, a death from drowning, by a man in a boat fishing, and so on. His poetry is—but let us have a few specimens.

Here is one of this artist's *chefs-d'œuvres*, with accompanying entablature :

> "I died a fishing as this picture shows,
> And left this world with all its woes,
> To another region I took my flight
> In Co.ʸ with angels adoreing Chiist."

Above the poetry (?) is a baptism, below a man sitting in a boat with pole and line.

One more from this cemetery in the sculptor-poet's best vein :

> "Here lies Mag
> No brag,
> Both fair
> And wise."

It is unfair to judge this versatile stone-cutter by our poetical standards, but by those of the time, and he was only a little, if at all, inferior in this respect to his contemporaries. Many, many are the atrocious poetizings in all the Berkshire churchyards; the only conception of poetry being rhyme, not rhythm :

> "Farewell, all sublunary things,
> I go to see the King of Kings."

or this :

> "They have gone to where—Ah! pause and see.
> Gone to a longe [*sic*] eternety [*sic*]."

The doctrines of the Church stand out conspicuously on these ancient slabs, as might be expected.

Here is one on the eternal damnation of those who die impenitent, a dogma the Church is sloughing off with its advancing knowledge of God:

> "Where vicious lives all hope deny,
> A falling tear is nature's due."

Here is one in scriptural form to illustrate the prevailing belief of old days in the divine hatred and loathing of the creature, man:

> "Blessed in the sight of the Lord is the death of his saints. But God is angry with the wicked every day."

Here is another to show the faith of the Church in a bodily resurrection:

> "Though worms my poor body may claim
> As their prey,
> 'T will outshine when rising the sun
> At noonday."

One of the most interesting features of these ancient cemeteries is the interment within them of very many of the old pastors, who, beloved of their flock, ministered in these parishes for thirty, forty, fifty, and in one case almost sixty years, and then found a resting-place amid the scenes of their life-work. Those were the days of long pastorates and installa-

The Church-on-the-Hill.

Lenox Congregational Church, dedicated January 1, 1806. Monument with urn at the left marks Dr. Shepard's grave.

Berkshire Epitaphs 353

tion was the marriage of pastor and people for life. Reviewing his ministry on the fiftieth anniversary of his settlement over the church in Lenox, Dr. Shepard said:

"Fifty years ago this day, and at this very hour of the day (April 30, 1795), a scene was witnessed upon this hill, of deep moral interest. A youth was solemnly consecrated to the Gospel ministry, but who would recognize in the time-worn pilgrim who now stands before you the same man who was then stationed upon these heights of Zion. Since my ordination here I have received into the church 815 persons, baptized 969, attended the funerals of 953, and have probably preached on an average four sermons a week. Your fathers did not despise my youth on account of its weaknesses and imperfections; and I am encouraged by past experience to rely on your patience, forbearance, and sympathy when all the reward you can hope for will consist in the satisfaction of having aided an old man down the steep of age and through the last stages of his weary pilgrimage."

Dr. Shepard's grave is just outside the door of the village church on the hilltop, with the appropriate inscription on the stone:

"Remember the words that I spake unto you while I was yet with you."

I cannot close this chapter on Berkshire epitaphs without saying that laudatory inscriptions in these ancient churchyards are extremely rare. One of the best is this:

> "Reader, expect the day that shall reveal
> to an assembled world the piety and virtues
> of Deacon James Wadsworth."

But as a rule it was a modest age, for the modesty of true worth says sincerely and becomingly, "When saw we thee an hungered and fed thee? or sick and in prison and ministered unto thee?" The story of the epitaphs is mostly a lesson in mortality, yet here is another laudatory one which shows that our fathers recognized in what true religion consisted. It is to the memory of Timothy Woodbridge, who died in Stockbridge, 1774:

> "Beneath the sacred honors of the tomb,
> In awful and majestic gloom,
> The man of mercy here conceals his head
> Amidst the awful mansions of the dead.
> No more his liberal hand shall keep the poor,
> Relieve distress, nor scatter joy no more."

There are other cemeteries in Berkshire besides those which were common to the people of the village; and here and there in out-of-the-way places one runs across family burying-grounds, which, however, yield nothing of

nterest to the epitaph-seeker, who with rev-
rent hand removes the moss from the "un-
outh rhymes, the short and simple annals"
in these hoary slabs.

INDEX

.cademy, Lenox, 2, 19–21; distinguished graduates 20, 179, 190
.dams, John Coleman, 105
.dams, Thatcher M., 199
.dams, town of, 210, 223, 225, 302, 306
gassiz, Louis, 159
lden, Rev. E. K., 40, 313
lford, 48, 303
llen, Ethan, 266
llen, Rev. Thos., 226, 227, 229, 300, 337, 339
llen, William, 312
merican Notes, 151
ppleton, Misses, 44
rnold, Matthew, 87–90
spinwall Hotel, 180, 186
spinwall, W. H., 170, 172
thenæum at Pittsfield, 228, 230
uchmuty, R. T., 167, 175, 183
uchmuty, Mrs. R. T., 50, 165
ugusta, Princess, 87
very, Rev. Stephen, 302

acon, Mrs. E. G., 187
ald Head, 97, 100, 172, 181
allantine, Rev. John, 303
arclay, Henry, 191
arlow, Gen. F., 175
arlow, Mrs. Francis C., 199
arnard, Pres. F. P., 219, 267
arnes, James, 84
arnes, John S., 200

Barrington, Great, 23, 48, 62, 219, 228, 249, 253, 297; picture of, century ago, 66
Bartlett, Gen. W. F., 230
Bash-Bish Falls, 221, 251
Bear Mountain, 84
Becket, 49, 299
Beecher, Henry Ward, 36, 37, 84, 103, 104, 171
Beecher Hill, 36
Belknap, Rev. Jeremy, 227
Berkshire Agricultural Society, 228
Berkshire Association, minutes of, 314–316
Berkshire Chronicle, The, 9
Berkshire Coffee-House, 69
Berkshire deserted villages, 268–274
Berkshire Medical Institution, 228
Berkshire, separated from Hampshire, 3, 52; first railroads in, 11, 12; schools in, 63; history of, by Field, 92, 177
Biddle, Mrs. J. W., 186
Bidwell, Rev. Adonijah, 299
Billings, Josh, grave of, at Lanesborough, 62, 349
Bishop, D. W., 182, 192
Bishop, Henry, 189
Bishop, Judge H. W., 189
Blithedale Romance, 152
Boston & Albany R. R., 222

357

358   Index

Bötta, Amelie, 153
Boundary line between Massachusetts and New York, 4, 52
Bradford, Rev. James, 312
Bradford, Wm. H., 183
Braem, Henry W., 175, 185
Brainerd, David, 243
Bremer, Frederika, 79, 80, 127
Briggs, Gen. H. S., 230
Briggs, Gov. Geo. N., 229
Bristed, Chas. Astor, 191
Browning, Elizabeth Barrett, 157
Bryant, Wm. Cullen, 23, 62, 89, 97–99, 127, 129, 218, 219, 253
Buckham, Pres. Matthew, 21
Bullard, Chas., 193
Bullard, Wm. S., 169, 170, 191
Burden, J. W., 184
Burgoyne's march to Boston, 266
Burr, Aaron, 247

Carey, Miss Mary De P., 175, 187
Catlin, Jacob, Rev., 93, 311, 319, 321–333, 337
Catskill Mountains, 172, 218
Channing, Ellery, 96, 141
Channing, Wm. Ellery, 9, 28, 102, 117, 127, 128
Chapel, St. Helena, New Lenox, 166
Chapin, Robert W., 200
Choate, Hon. Joseph, 216
Chisholm, Lord Provost, 87
Church, the Lenox Congregational, 38, 180, 299; Trinity Episcopal, 165, 198; Roman Catholic, 179; Methodist Episcopal, 197
Clarence, 121
Climate, Berkshire, 153, 154
Coleridge, Lord Chief Justice, 87
Collins, Rev. D., 301, 337
Cook, H. H., 181, 192
Cooper, Fenimore, 23, 110, 111
Country newspapers in early times, 10, 11

County conventions in Lenox, 41
County Court-house, second, 46, 68, 178
Crane, Gov. W. Murray, 215
Crane, Zenas, 230
Curtis Hotel, 43, 68, 102, 203, 215
Curtisville, 305
Cushman, Charlotte, 36, 83, 175, 188

Dalton, 215, 223, 225, 229, 303
Dana, R. S., 175
Davis, the Hon. David, 20
Davis, Wm. Stearns, 63, 230
Dawes, Miss Anna, 229
Dawes, Senator Henry L., 229
Dewey, Mary, 79, 80
Dewey, the Rev. Orville, 28, 219, 267
Dickens, Chas., 143
Division line, between Massachusetts and New York, 221
Dome, Taghconic, 65, 74, 89, 100, 172, 194, 207, 219, 221, 249, 262
Duke of Stockbridge, Bellamy, 105
Dwight, Pres. T., 25, 37, 65

Edwards, Rev. Jonathan, 50, 51, 86, 93, 234, 239, 246–248, 258, 264, 271, 308, 309
Egleston, David, 165
Egleston, Prof. Thomas, 7, 164, 174
Egremont, 48, 301
Egremont, South, 220, 251
Eighteenth-century fiction, 109
Eliot, Geo., 143
Ellis, Rev. Dr., 156
Emerson, R. W., 141, 156, 159
English travellers in Berkshire, 85, 87
Epitaphs, Berkshire, 340–345
Evans, Marian, 143
Everett, Mt., 36, 58, 219, 221; by whom named, 61; as seen by Dr. Dwight, 65

Index

Face to Face, Grant, 106
Field, Cyrus W., 85, 340
Field, Hon. David Dudley, 340
Field, Rev. David Dudley, 101, 237, 244, 313, 340
Field, Rev. Henry M., 20, 102, 216, 340
Field, Judge Stephen, 340
Fields, Jas. T., 34
Fiske, John, 42
Florida, town of, 305
Folsom, Geo. F., 175, 187
Foster, Giraud, 200, 201
Freedom of the Will, 51
Frelinghuysen, T., 152, 202
"Friendly Union," Sheffield, 267
French and Indian War, 5
French officers at Stockbridge, 118
Frothingham, S., 193
Fuller, Margaret, 142
Furniss, Miss C., 175, 187

Gilder, R. W., 84, 101, 171
Gilmore, Alfred, 174
Gilmore, Mrs. Alfred, 196
Glass Works Grant, Lenox, 205
Glendale, 238
Glezen, Levi, 21
Goelet, Robert, 200
Goldsmith's *Deserted Village*, quotations from, 270, 271
Goodale sisters, 36, 63
Goodman, R., Sr., 167, 174, 195
Goodrich, Mrs. J. Z., 288
Grant, Ministers', 50
Grant, the Quincy, 50
Green River, 99
Greenleaf, Dr. R. C., 175, 184
Greylock, Mt., 36, 58, 68, 76, 183, 194, 207, 221, 231; view from, 210, 211
Griswold, D. F., 188

Haggerty, Ogden, 170
Hale, E. E., 152
Halleck, Fitz-Greene, 23
Hancock, town of, 225

Harris, Rev. Samuel, 229
Harrison, Mrs. Burton, 37, 83, 105
Haven, George G., 201
Hawthorne, Julian, 75, 147, 155
Hawthorne, Mrs., 137, 139, 140, 150, 154
Hawthorne, Nathaniel, 32-34, 75, 86, 100, 136-160; *American Note-books*, 96, 169
Hawthorne Street, 156
Haystack Monument, 213
Headley, J. T., 96
Herrick, Zebulon, 10
Higginson, Geo., 174, 191
Hinsdale, town of, 305
Holland, J. G., 277, 281
Holmes, O. W., 34, 61, 70, 96, 144, 159, 169, 215, 224, 229, 346
Home, 124
Home of Catherine Sedgwick, Lenox, 202
Hoosac Tunnel, 209
Hope Leslie, 121
Hopkins Memorial Manse at Great Barrington, 252
Hopkins, Pres. Mark, 20, 91
Hopkins, Rev. Samuel, 64, 66, 93, 236, 241, 252, 253-262, 271, 298, 308, 319, 321-333
Hosmer, Harriet, 23, 79
Hotchkin, Rev. John, 21, 189
Housatonic, town of, 218, 223, 250, 305
Housatonic River, 48, 59
"House of Mercy," Pittsfield, 224
House of the Seven Gables, 146, 149-151, 156, 192
Howe, Dr. Samuel, 169
Hubbard, Rev. Jonathan, 297
Humphrey, Rev. Heman, 226, 229, 312
Hyde, Rev. Alvan, 304, 338

"Ice Glen," Stockbridge, 66, 100
Indian chiefs, 94

Indian monument at Stockbridge, 86, 234, 238
Indian names, 58-60
Indian trail across the Hoosacs, 264
Indians, in Berkshire, 3, 48, 49, 51, 57-60, 205, 234, 240-249
Indians, Memoirs of Housatunnuk, by Samuel Hopkins (Springfield), 94
Interlaken (Curtisville), 238
Iron Works, Lenox, 205
Irving, Washington, 23, 110, 111

James, G. P. R., 34
Jameson, Mrs. Anna, 28, 69, 72, 79, 90, 113, 127, 128, 237
Jaques, Dr. Henry P., 185
Jesup, Morris K., 164, 184
Judson, Rev. Ephraim, 265, 311, 312, 339

Kelvin, Lord, 87
Kemble, Mrs. Fanny, 8, 17, 21, 28-31, 35, 44, 69-76, 80-82, 84, 90, 127, 128, 141, 164, 168, 169, 171
Kemble Street, 17
Kingsland, Mrs. A. C., 186
Kingsley, Chas., 85
Kinne, Rev. Aaron, 303
Kinnicutt, Dr. F. P., 87, 187
Kneeland, Miss Adele, 189
Kneeland, Chas., 165, 174
Kuhn, Mrs. H., 175, 186

Lanesborough, 214, 299
Lanier, Chas., 165, 170, 181, 196
Lathrop, Mrs. Rose Hawthorne, 35, 81, 140
Laurel Hill, 239
Laurel Hill Association, Stockbridge, 275-293
Laurel Lake, 84, 171, 193, 201
Lecky's *History of England*, 54
Lee, 48, 225, 303
Lee, Mrs., 189
Lenox, settlement and incorporation, 1, 4, 5, 53; old buildings, 2, 16; original name of settlement, 5; early ecclesiastical questions, 6; contributions to American Revolution, 7; non-importation agreement, 7; town minutes, 7; cemetery at, 8; Channing's address at, 9; becomes county seat, 9; weekly newspaper, 11; first Berkshire County railroad convention, 12; early stage-routes, 13, 14; Berkshire Coffee-House, 14; in court week, 15; fight to retain courts at, 16; removal of courts, 18; summer visitors at, 18; site of jail and "Gallows Hill," 18; early references to, 25-27, 30; literary society in, 35, 48, 122, 141; Beecher in, 36, 37; county conventions in, 41; temperance revival, 41; early industries in, 43, 205; beginnings of change to resort, 44; Library Association, 46; spelling of name of town, 56; no poor in, 71; social, 105; view from Hawthorne's house, 144; modern, 161-206; villas in, 172-176, 216; streets in, 177; valuation of, 204; population of, 204; business of, 205, 206; creation of post-office at, 228
Library, Town, 42, 46, 166
Linwoods, 121
Liquor, use of, in old times, 317, 318
Literary women in Berkshire, 79, 82, 83
"Little red house," 96, 100, 101, 143, 146, 154-156, 170, 171, 192
Live and Let Live, 123
Livingston, E. McA., 187
Longfellow, H. W., 141, 157, 159
Lothrop, Mrs. T. K., 188
Lowell, J. R., 34, 96, 141, 142, 150, 151, 159

Index 361

Lowell and His Friends, 152
Lydig, David, 199

McKim, Chas. F., 187
Mann, Horace, 132, 137
Maplewood Young Ladies' Institute, 228
Marble Faun, 158
Married or Single, 126
Martineau, Harriet, 23, 28, 76–79, 125, 237
Mason, Lowell, 42
Melville, Herman, 35, 62, 96, 142, 229
Mill River, 305
Ministers' Grant, 50
Mitchell, D. G., 121, 125, 202, 231
Mitford, Miss, 111, 130
Monson, Rev. Samuel, 6, 300
Monterey, 299
Monument Mt., 58, 95, 97, 172, 216–218, 221, 232, 249; why so called, 66
Monument Mountain, 99, 233
Morgan, Geo. H., 165, 170, 185, 199
Mosses from an Old Manse, 139, 143, 147
Motley, John L., 157
Mountainous region, Hawthorne's view of, 146
Movements of religious thought in New England, 260
Music, sacred, 42

Nature Studies in Berkshire, 105
New Ashford, 213
New England Tale, 100, 112, 113, 119, 131, 133, 258
New Marlborough, 49, 251; academy at, 272
Non-importation agreement, 7
North Adams, 209, 223, 305
"Northampton woods," 51

October Mt., 183, 194
Oliver, Gen., 175

Onota Lake, 231
Otis, 225, 302

Parish, Miss Helen, 189
Parkhurst, Rev. C. H., 40, 64
Parsons, John E., 87, 165, 166, 175, 185
Paterson, Major-General John, 7, 92, 164, 196; life of, by Egleston, 92
Paterson Monument, 177
Patterson, R. W., 174, 200
Pease, H. H., 191
Perry's Peak, 221
Peru, town of, 301
Pierce, Franklin, 158, 159
Pierpont, Judge, 162, 174, 175
Pitt, Wm., Earl of Chatham, 56, 225
Pittsfield, 10, 16, 57, 59, 62, 214, 222–231, 299
Planchette, amusing story about, 80
Pontoosuc Lake, 57, 230

Queechy Lake, 63
Quincy, Judge Edmund, 49, 50
Quincy Grant, 50

Rathbone, Gen. John F., 170, 174
Rattlesnake Mt., 58, 101, 172, 194, 221
Redwood, 121
Revolution, the American, 7
Richmond, Lennox, Duke of, 6, 53–57
Richmond, town of, 5, 53, 299
Robeson, W. R., 173, 188
Rockwell, Judge Julius, 202
Root, Geo. F., 219, 267

St. Helen's Home, Interlaken, 238
Salisbury, Conn., 74, 221
Salisbury, Prof., 173, 188
Sandisfield, 49, 299; ministers in, 271

Index

Sands, Philip, 193
Sargent, John O., 84
Sargent, Miss Georgiana, 200
Savoy, 305
Scarlet Letter, 137, 142, 144
Schermerhorn, Mrs. Adeline E., 46, 164, 171
Schermerhorn, F. Aug., 165, 170, 185, 199
Schermerhorn, J. Egmont, 189
Schermerhorn, W. C., 179
Sedgwick, Miss Catherine, 12-14, 22, 23, 27, 45, 61, 66, 70, 72, 77-79, 98, 102, 104, 108-135, 140, 163, 202, 231, 236, 237, 288, 335
Sedgwick, Charles, 122
Sedgwick, Mrs. Charles, 82, 102; school for girls, 22-24, 82, 202
Sedgwick, Ellery, 173, 188
Sedgwick, Hon. Theodore, 115, 231
Sergeant, John, 49, 94, 234, 241, 297, 334
Shaw, Miss Anna, 189
Shaw, S. Parkman, 174, 196
Shays' rebellion, 266
Sheffield, 48, 219, 250, 251, 262-268, 297
Shepard, Rev. Samuel, 19, 38-40, 313, 338, 353
Sigourney, Mrs., 82, 100
Silliman, Prof. B., 25, 66, 67, 270
Sismondi, 23, 127
Skinner's *Myths and Legends*, 60
"Sky Farm," 37
Sloane, John, 87, 170, 183, 200
Sloane, William D., 182, 193, 195
Snow Image and Other Tales, 151
Southfield, 305
Springfield, Mass., 228
Stanley, Dean, 85, 86
Star Papers, 36, 103, 104
Stebbins, Emma, 164, 188
Steele, Rev. E., 302

Stephens, Hon. Alexander H., 20
Stevens, B. K., 189
Stockbridge, 32, 48, 49, 51, 59, 77, 87, 89, 228, 231-248, 275-293
Stockbridge Bowl, 32, 61, 97, 100, 169-172, 181, 216
Stokes, Anson Phelps, 174, 181, 187
Stowe, Harriet Beecher, 79, 80, 111, 255, 260, 262
Strong, Rev. Cyprian, 39
Strong, Rev. Thos., 298
Struthers, Mrs. John, 199, 200
Sturgis, F. K., 174, 201
Sumner, Charles, 70, 74, 169
Surrender of Louisbourg, news of, 266
Swift, Rev. J., 300

Taghconic Mountains, 36, 48, 49
Tales and Sketches, 121, 131
Tanglewood Tales, 145
Tappan, William, 170, 191
Taylor, Zachary, 136
Temperance minute by Berkshire physicians, 41
Temperance revival, 41
Theology of the fathers, 319-332
Thompson, Mrs. William, 170
Thoreau, H. D., 142
Tiffany, Mrs., 164
Todd, Rev. John, 226, 229, 312
"Tom Ball" Mt., 221
Travellers, 121
Twice Told Tales, 139
Tyringham, 49, 84, 299

Unitarianism, rise of, 118

Village Improvement, 275-293

Wahconah Falls, 231
Walker, Judge Wm., 174, 195
Walpole, Horace, letters of, references to Duke of Richmond, 54
Ward, S. G., 70, 168, 174, 191
Warner, Charles Dudley, 106

Index 363

Warner, Susan, and *Wide Wide World*, 63
Washington, Mount, 48
Washington, town of, 225, 301
Watson, Elkanah, 229
Watson, John (Ian Maclaren), 87
Weather in England, 90
Welch, Rev. Whitman, 300
Wendell, Jacob, 61, 225
West, Stephen, 93, 236, 244, 309, 310, 336
West Stockbridge, 49, 305
West Stockbridge Centre, 303
Westinghouse, George, 87, 182, 193
Western Massachusetts, History of, by Holland, 177
Wharton, Mrs. Edith, 83
Wharton, Edward R., 200
Wharton, Mrs. Wm. C., 199
Wheeler, Miss, 154

Whipple, E. P., 34, 96, 141, 159
Whistler, Joseph S., 196
White, Mrs. Joseph, 174, 196
Whittier, reference to Hopkins, 255, 259, 261
Williams College, 36, 40, 61, 91, 213
Williamstown, 36, 212, 228, 299
Williamstown, South, 213, 305
Windsor, 301
Winthrop, Mrs. R., 185
Wolfe and Montcalm, 5
Wonder Book for Children, 100, 105, 149, 150, 152
Woolsey, E. J., 170–172
Writers, notable female, 110

Yale College, 38
Yancy, Hon. Wm. L., 20
"Yokun's Seat," 184

www.ingramcontent.com/pod-product-compliance
Lightning Source LLC
Chambersburg PA
CBHW052138300426
44115CB00011B/1428